# Black Matters

*Black Matters* presents an anthology of stories of African American and African undergraduate and graduate students' experiences at college, offering lifespan perspectives on their formative relationships and influences, life-changing events, and the role their heritage has played in shaping their personal identities, values, and choices.

Andrew Garrod and Robert Kilkenny bring together contributors who share personal memoirs reflecting on their experience of navigating life on campus as students of Dartmouth College, New Hampshire. The ten brave authors, six Black men and four Black women, present thoughtful, often emotional, accounts of moments that transformed their academic, professional, and racial identities. Supplemented by follow-up accounts of four of the graduates, the text underlines developmental perspectives whilst examining what has remained the same about their lives and values, and what has changed over time. The collection explores the notion of hard work and "grit" in overcoming discrimination, racism, and adversity, and how in reality college students who are not part of the racial/cultural majority must contend with the normative identity challenges of late adolescence while carrying the extra burden of "two-ness". Featuring an introduction by Chanté Mouton Kinyon, this anthology examines crucial topics including classroom experience; intellectual stimulation and learning environment; interactions with African American and African students; friendships that crossed the lines of race, ethnicity, class, gender, and sexual orientation, and how collegiate life affects issues related to personal and racial identities.

The rich narratives in *Black Matters* provide vital insight into the relationship between collegiate experiences and racial identities. It will be essential reading for students and scholars of psychology, education, cultural anthropology, sociology and creative writing, as well as for those responsible for campus climate and student experience.

**Andrew Garrod** is a professor emeritus at Dartmouth College, where he previously chaired the Department of Education, directed the Teacher Education Program, taught courses in adolescence, moral development, and contemporary issues in U.S. education. He has published widely on adolescence and race and ethnicity.

**Robert Kilkenny** is the founder and executive director of the Alliance for Inclusion and Prevention (AIP) in Boston, MA, a non-profit children's mental health agency working to promote childhood behavioral health and academic achievement by increasing the use of evidence-based mental health services in schools. He is also on the faculty of Simmons University in Boston, MA.

**Chanté Mouton Kinyon** is currently a Moreau Postdoctoral Fellow at the University of Notre Dame. Kinyon's primary research explores transnational African American literature, with a particular interest in the way in which that literature intersects with Irish literature.

# Black Matters

## African American and African College Students and Graduates Tell Their Life Stories

**Edited by**
**Andrew Garrod and Robert Kilkenny**

**Introduction by Chanté Mouton Kinyon**

Routledge
Taylor & Francis Group
LONDON AND NEW YORK

Designed cover image: Jacob Lawrence, "The Library", Photo Smithsonian American Art Museum/Art Resource/Scala, Florence

First published 2023
by Routledge
4 Park Square, Milton Park, Abingdon, Oxon OX14 4RN

and by Routledge
605 Third Avenue, New York, NY 10158

*Routledge is an imprint of the Taylor & Francis Group, an informa business*



*British Library Cataloguing-in-Publication Data*
A catalogue record for this book is available from the British Library

*Library of Congress Cataloging-in-Publication Data*
A catalog record has been requested for this book

ISBN: 978-1-032-39636-1 (hbk)
ISBN: 978-1-032-45278-4 (pbk)
ISBN: 978-1-003-37625-5 (ebk)

DOI: 10.4324/9781003376255

Typeset in Bembo
by Taylor & Francis Books

This book is dedicated to our eloquent and courageous contributors willing to share their pains and wisdom with the world.

It is also dedicated to the memory of Marzuq Muhammad

And, finally, it is dedicated to former African and African-American students, friends, and teachers at Dartmouth College, and in the Marshall Islands and Rwanda:

Kevin Ever
Zac Panton
Ken Gordon
Tobias Hohl
Jamal Brown
Richard Addo
Monica Miller
Ray Rochester
Kevin Nyayiha
Ping Ann Addo
Sereena Knight
Jasmine Panton
Jason Alphonse
Stephen Gumbs
Michael Markin
Kashay Sanders
Amiri Barksdale
Adedipo Adegunle
Hamadi Henderuson
Matthew Norwood
Pierre Nambajimana
Muhamadi Nshimiyamana
Muhammed Abdul-Shakoor
Erica Jones
Jeff Garrett
Lamar Moss
Theo Wilson
Keith Willacy
Marc Sepama
Kenny Muigai
Kaya Thomas
Cynthia Madu
Summer Cody
Kyle Roderick
Jarrett Matthis
Antonio Brown
Andrew Rayner
Brandon Gunter
Dallas Alexander
Courtney Reddix
Cassandra Tanner
Jonathan Marable
Linford Zarangwa
Christian Kwisanga
Patrick Iradukunda
Taylor Enoch-Stevens
Jude Chiy
Ed Atanda
Aisha Tyus
David Jiles
Eric Shema
Tete Loeper
Docia Atanda
David Knight
Greg Johnson
Clovis Shyaka
Leah Threatte
Julian Thomas
Shanée Brown
Jovilisi Fotofili
Dwayne Alexis
Damaris Walker
Eric Iradukunda
Timothy Johnson
Torrese Ouellette
Victor Lekweuwa
Demetrius Brunson
Olivier Nsanzabega
Augustus Karangwa
Emmanuel Blankson
Daudeline Meme

# Contents

# Preface

*Black Matters* is an anthology that presents 10 stories by African American and African students who were undergraduates at Dartmouth College in Hanover, New Hampshire, at the time of writing and four follow-up stories by Dartmouth graduates. These personal stories are essentially memoirs in which the authors reflect on their formative relationships and influences, life-changing events, and the role their heritage has played in shaping their personal identities, values, and choices. The stories are replete with accounts of survival, dignity, and resilience in the face of great challenges.

Each student's narrative explains how they navigated life on campus during their college years. These ten brave authors, six Black men and four Black women, offer thoughtful and sometimes emotional accounts of moments that transformed their academic, professional, and racial identities. Some of these young men and women offer personal details that illustrate their racial development at Dartmouth. One striking feature of this anthology is that it includes four follow-up narratives written by contributors who published earlier essays in similar anthologies. The two women published their earlier essays 23 years ago in *Souls Looking Back: Life Stories of Growing Up Black* (Garrod et al. 1999), and the two male writers contributed six years ago to the collection titled *Mixed: Multiracial College Students Tell Their Life Stories* (Garrod et al. 2013). These four writers were invited to bring their life stories up to date and to reflect on the continuities and discontinuities. Each addressed two particular questions: what has remained the same about you and your values? What has changed over time? These developmental perspectives add richness and heft to the stories in this current collection.

Because most of these memoirs were written by Dartmouth College undergraduates, it is worth noting the low percentage of Black students on that campus. According to the Dartmouth Office of Institutional Research, the undergraduate community at Dartmouth in 2019 comprised 4,459 students, 254 of whom identify as African American or Black, a total of merely 6 percent. The Black international student population at Dartmouth has remained steady since 2002, also at 6 percent. These numbers go a long way to explain the ensuing feelings of otherness, isolation, and lack of belonging many of the authors in this book describe. It makes all the more remarkable their ability to, as most of them did over time, carve out a social and psychological niche where they could succeed, even if they did not always feel fully part of the college ethos.

The assumption could be made that the authors of these memoirs have achieved the American Dream by dint of their hard work and "grit" in overcoming discrimination, racism, and all manner of adversity. However, that would be a simplistic and self-congratulatory interpretation premised on the belief that making it into an elite college represents a sort of personal end of history. In reality, college students who are not part of the racial/cultural majority must contend with all the normative identity challenges of late adolescence while carrying the extra burden of "two-ness," or double consciousness, as described by W.E.B. Du Bois:

> It is a peculiar sensation, this double-consciousness, this sense of always looking at one's self through the eyes of others, of measuring one's soul by the tape of a world that looks on in amused contempt and pity. One ever feels his two-ness, an American, a Negro; two souls, two thoughts, two unreconciled strivings; two warring ideals in one dark body, whose dogged strength alone keeps it from being torn asunder. The history of the American Negro is the history of this strife—this longing to attain self-conscious manhood, to merge his double self into a better and truer self. In this merging he wishes neither of the older selves to be lost.
>
> (Du Bois 1903: 2)

A version of double consciousness permeates these chapters, as our authors describe the achingly complex task of maintaining the identity of high-achieving young Black men and women they brought with them to college, most of them from radically less privileged circumstances than the majority of their Dartmouth peers. The societal assumption was that, for those who made it into Dartmouth, the barriers of historical racism had now been redressed and their lives could progress in tandem with their more advantaged classmates.

As if that were not pressure enough, in many of these stories we also encounter the poisonous assumption by those same white majority peers that their Black classmates' success should perhaps be discounted due to an alleged preference shown to them by affirmative action.

While the two-ness of success reflected in these stories is a window onto the lives of many Black students at selective colleges across the United States, it is important that the reader does not assume that these memoirs capture the full experience of growing up Black in America. They should be read as the unique and exquisitely intimate experiences of a select group of Black students within a predominantly white elite institution in the United States. The themes will be familiar to most college students of color but should not be generalized to the experience of a broader group of young Black Americans. Indeed, as Imani Perry writes about Black memoirs:

> the varieties of our racial experience are one thing, and the sense we make of them is yet another narrowing distinction. Yet the sense one individual Black writer makes of his or her life, from the perch of our wounds, our aspirations, our bourgeois frames of reference, are often read as saying much more than they actually can about the broader experiences and thoughts of Black people. That is dangerous.
>
> (Imani 2016)

Perry reminds us that Black identity is not a monolith; it is refracted by all the facets of identity common to all human beings, including social class, life history, intergenerational experience, culture, geography, and political contexts. There is no singular Black experience at an elite institution, nor at any other college or, for that matter, any other place in society. The authors of each memoir in this book do an admirable job of preparing the reader to understand their life story in terms of both their family, culture, class, and racial origins before coming to Dartmouth College. Our authors are both African American and African, come from both advantaged and profoundly disadvantaged backgrounds, and some are mixed race. Each author's origin story at once presages and defies easy assumptions about how they will cope with the tasks of late adolescent and early adulthood identity formation in the face of a "majority" institutional culture as uncertain of them as they are of it. But in every case, it is their story as they have chosen to tell it in the hope it will have meaning and purpose for others.

For many of these Black authors, the process of putting their experiences into words has been a catalyst for further reflection on their identities and life histories. In 31 years of encouraging this type of work, the editors have consistently observed that the process of autobiographical writing can have a profoundly transformative effect on the spiritual, moral, and emotional domains of a writer's life and that life is often enhanced by such deep introspection. We have found would-be contributors overwhelmingly open to making sense of their childhood and adolescent experiences, and of their young adulthood, which had thus far been inchoate and unintegrated. The opportunity to reflect can often reconcile a writer to trauma they have experienced and bring emotional resolution and understanding to their primary relationships and the vicissitudes in their lives. We have felt greatly privileged to guide our writers through deeper levels of self-understanding and to help them gain purchase on their personal worlds through self-analysis and articulation.

The editors encouraged the contributors to this volume to conduct the frankest possible examination of their lives and relationships, and of the role that the intersections of their various identities played in shaping their attitudes and behaviors. We encouraged the authors to follow broad guidelines as they began to reflect on how the formative aspects of their home culture, values, race, and personal identities had affected their transition to college and their experiences on campus. We asked them to think about their classroom experiences at Dartmouth in terms of the intellectual stimulation offered by the college learning environment; about their interactions with African American and African students, at Cutter-Shabazz (Dartmouth's African American house), and with fellow students of other racial backgrounds; and about their friendships that crossed the lines of race, ethnicity, class, gender, and sexual orientation. We asked how their engagement in college life affected issues related to their personal and racial identities.

To help our writers develop their stories, we offered the following guiding questions. They were meant only to suggest lines of thought and were not intended as a blueprint to be followed rigorously. Many of our writers chose to engage with some of the questions, while others found their own inspiration:

- What gets you up in the morning? What is most important in your life? What do you live for? What is of transcendent value to you?
- Have there been critical incidents in your life (i.e., religious conversion, divorce, death in the family, first love) after which nothing has been quite the same—for good or ill, or for some mixture of these two?
- Explore the most important relationships in your life—within the family and outside it.
- What sort of a child were you? Did you have a particular role within your family?
- What were you like in your early years at school? Were you popular? If so, with whom? Were you a lonely child? Did any teacher pick you out as promising?
- Were you an early or late developer as you moved into adolescence? Or did you move at about the normal pace? If you were an early developer, how do you think it affected the way people saw you?
- In high school, did you develop any particular skill or interest that made you stand out? Were your best friends of the same race and ethnicity as you? Discuss one or two of the most significant friendships you had in your later high school years.
- When you were a child, was race/ethnicity discussed at home? If so, in what way? When were you aware that yours was a "minority heritage"? Have you been the victim of racism? If so, describe the first time: how did you feel? How did you react? How did you come to terms, if you did, with this racism?
- Why did you come to Dartmouth? What were you looking for? Was this environment much more or much less diverse than your home or school environment?
- Has this been a supportive community for you? What are some of the biggest obstacles you have had to overcome? Have you been active in organizations that are concerned with issues of race and ethnicity? If so, how and why? If not, why not?
- As you think of moving on from Dartmouth, how do you see yourself moving into the outside world? Do you think your sense of racial identity has been strengthened in the last few years? What is the role of ethnic/

racial identity within your total identity (for some students, other aspects of identity may be more significant than race)?
- Does being Black help you understand racial dynamics in this culture in a more profound way than you believe many white individuals can?
- If you have a mixed heritage, do you identify with one component of your racial background more than another? If so, which one? Why? What are the perspectives or insights on life that this identity provides?
- What are some of the issues or tensions that are discussed among the Black population at Dartmouth? How do some of these issues relate to you and your life?
- What has been most rewarding/most challenging about your academic engagement at Dartmouth?

While the editors worked on a weekly basis with the undergraduate writers, we made an effort to keep our assumptions about where the individual stories might go in our view but out of the way of the participants. Because the emphasis was on process—urging and helping the writers undertake that most complex of writerly tasks, the location of voice—we made no editorial interventions during the generative stage. Although the parameters were necessarily established by the editors, we encouraged writers to develop their own themes and to make sense of their own experience in ways that gave them significant meaning in their own lives. All we asked was that they keep their thinking, feeling, and writing as honest as they possibly could. There was no assumption on either part that the story was "in there" just waiting to come out, readily formed, as if from the head of Zeus. Rather, we shared the belief that the story had to be found, uncovered piece by piece as patterns and themes emerged. A student usually would submit six or seven pages to Andrew Garrod before each meeting, which we would discuss when we met. Editor and writer also discussed how to proceed with the next portion of the narrative. The writer was frequently halfway through the process before he or she came to understand the essay's central concerns or themes.

The first drafts of these essays usually ranged from 30 to 50 pages, although one or two were considerably longer (one essay in this anthology initially ran well over 100 pages) and some were much shorter. After careful consideration and discussion over many months (or even years), cutting and editing reduced and sharpened each text to a manageable 13 to 25 pages. Variations in the tone, degree of self-analysis, and style of expression reflect our commitment to respect each author's story and life, thus the editors' changes to the text were usually minimal. In light of this, we offered each writer the option of anonymity, and each writer was asked to give a final stamp of approval to their chapter.

First drafts were always the hardest part. Where to start? Why would anyone be interested in my story? How can I possibly fill up a whole book chapter? As Lorene Cary, author of *Black Ice,* says:

> the first draft is always for myself. The first draft, I think, needs to be for one's self. The first draft is about mapping the landscape, your own internal landscape, intellectually, emotionally, spiritually, physically. It's therapy. It's getting honest. It's getting the tone. Typically, I have to write 200 pages until I write my way to the door of the book. So a lot of it is throwaway. It's getting good enough. It's running laps.
>
> (Cary 2012)

While the two editors discussed the shape of the book and its contents in detail, each of us played a different role. After a draft was reduced approximately 25 pages with the guidance of Andrew Garrod, it was sent to Robert Kilkenny, who had not yet worked with the author and could therefore offer a more objective reaction to their essay. This was done to bring the essays to another level of psychological cohesion—for example, if a theme seemed undeveloped or surprisingly unaddressed in a story, Kilkenny brought it to the writer's attention. He tried to push the writers to the edge of their ability to self-reflect and would suggest how and why a story would be better understood if particular lacunae were explored more thoroughly. It was not unusual for a writer to balk or to claim that they were unable to reflect any further about an experience that was still raw and unresolved. We always respected that boundary.

Memoirs written at a young age have an open ending, so readers are naturally curious to know how it all turned out. One advantage of gathering these stories for our memoir series over the past several decades is that we were able to ask contributors from long ago to write a reflection on the memoir they wrote when they were much younger. A memoir written at a young age is more a prospectus for life ahead than a wise and soulful look-back from the mature perspective of a traditional memoir. In this collection, we have included four of those lookbacks. We hope that these authors' thoughtful reflections on their earlier selves will give the reader a new way to understand both the early and later memoirs. Despite a decade or more of life experience, we think the reader will find that the authors have the same voice and core selves but with a more nuanced understanding. In 2004, when reflecting on his 1995 memoir, *Dreams from My Father*, Barack Obama described finding an authentic and lasting voice:

> For the first time in many years, I've pulled out a copy and read a few chapters to see how much my voice may have changed over time. I confess to wincing every so often at a poorly chosen word, a mangled sentence, an expression of emotion that seems indulgent or overly practiced. I have the urge to cut the book by fifty pages or so, possessed as I am with a keener appreciation for brevity. I cannot honestly say, however, that the voice in this book is not mine—that I would tell the story much differently today than I did ten years ago.
>
> (Obama 1995)

The editors are deeply grateful to many student researchers and assistants, friends, and associates for the realization of this book. Dody Riggs, a great friend and a colleague on our anthology projects over many iterations, offered essential editorial suggestions as the manuscripts achieved their final forms. Her unerring eye for how things might be said more simply and more gracefully was always appreciated. Given that this project has been eight or nine years in the making, there is little surprise that we have many Dartmouth students and graduates to thank for their organizational, administrative, and computer assistance. We particularly thank Laura Rosenthal, Raphie Orleck-Jetter, Antony Guzman, Andrew Weckstein, Kotaro Horiuchi, and Ruba Iqbal for their research and clerical skills. We owe very special thanks to Dayle Wang, who has been our research assistant throughout her four years at Dartmouth and has contributed immeasurably to the quality of this book; and to Zachary Panton, who has researched the background for this book and made himself available at all times of the day and evening, even while he was a medical student at Dartmouth's Geisel School of Medicine. Pulling the text together in preparation for the publisher had been the responsibility of Gustavo de Almeida, Angelo Pedro, Nathan Syvash, and Sumreet Sandhu; all of whom have completed this task admirably. Finally, we are most grateful to the two anonymous reviewers for Routledge.

It is not easy to open your life and your reflections on that life to public inspection. We wish to recognize all the contributors who have written with such courage and commitment in bringing their stories into the public domain. While most of the contributors have written in their own name, a few have not. The choice was theirs to make.

# About the Editors, the Introduction Writer

**Andrew Garrod** is a professor emeritus at Dartmouth College, where he previously chaired the Department of Education, directed the Teacher Education Program, and taught courses in adolescence, moral development, and contemporary issues in U.S. education. For a number of years, he conducted a research project in Bosnia and Herzegovina on forgiveness, faith development, and moral reasoning. He also directed six bilingual Shakespearean productions in Bosnia and Herzegovina that have played in Mostar and elsewhere in the Balkans. He has also directed a trilingual production of Romeo and Juliet in Kigali, Rwanda and directed numerous bilingual Shakespearean plays and Broadway musicals in the Marshall Islands. From 2000–2014, he directed a volunteer teaching program in the Marshall Islands in the Central Pacific. His recent publications include the coedited books *Growing Up Muslim: Muslim College Students In American Tell Their Life Stories* (Garrod et al. 2014); *I Am Where I Come From: Native American College Students and Graduates Tell Their Life Stories* (Garrod et al. 2017); and the chapter "Bridging the Divide with Shakespeare: Theatre as Moral Education in Bosnia and Herzegovina" in *The Reflexive Teaching Artist* (Garrod 2014). In 1991 and 2009, he was awarded Dartmouth College's Distinguished Teaching Award. He holds an Honorary Doctorate in Humane Letters from the University of New Brunswick, Canada. In 2019, he was made an Honorary Citizen of the Marshall Islands.

**Robert Kilkenny** is the founder and executive director of the Alliance for Inclusion and Prevention (AIP) in Boston, MA. AIP is a non-profit children's mental health agency working to promote childhood behavioral health and academic achievement by increasing the use of evidence-based mental health services in schools. He is the principal investigator for AIP's federally-funded Center for Trauma Care in Schools which promotes trauma-informed schooling, and also serves unaccompanied and refugee youth. He is also the Boston site Principal Investigator for the National Center for Safe and Supportive Schools at the University of Maryland School of Medicine, as well as the site PI for the Institute for Trauma Treatment in Schools at Simmons University where he is on the faculty. He is coeditor with Andrew Garrod and others of a series of books exploring the identity development of multiple ethnic, racial, and religious subgroups of college age Americans.

**Chanté Mouton Kinyon** is currently a Moreau Postdoctoral Fellow at the University of Notre Dame. Kinyon's primary research explores transnational African American literature, with a particular interest in the way in which that literature intersects with Irish literature. Her book project focuses on the transatlantic gestures between Ireland and Afro-America; concentrating on the particular way Irish and African American artists reference each other in their work while theorizing the ways in which these artists signify and conceptualize race and marginality. The 2018–2019 NEH Fellow at the Keogh-Naughton Institute for Irish Studies, Kinyon was previously a four-year recipient of the Galway Research Fellowship. In 2013, Kinyon came to Dartmouth College as a visiting scholar/predoctoral fellow and worked as a lecturer there from 2015–2018. Originally from San Francisco, CA, Kinyon worked in publishing after college for two of San Francisco's most iconic publishers: City Lights Books and Chronicle Books.

# Introduction

*Chanté Mouton Kinyon*

The eight-minute, 46-second video showing the vicious killing of George Floyd by four Minneapolis police officers on May 25, 2020 was the last straw and set off a chain of turbulent events in an already fraught world. Protesters in the United States and abroad flooded the streets to make a statement — not only about Mr. Floyd's murder but about the systemic racial structure his murder stems from. George Floyd's name joins a long grim list of other Black Americans who have been over-policed and murdered unjustly throughout United States history. His murder, along with the police and vigilante killings of Breonna Taylor in Kentucky and Ahmaud Arbery in Georgia, and numerous other unarmed Blacks are reminders that Black Americans are often perceived as a threat by both law enforcement and the larger American public, and too often are not given the benefit of the doubt or even due process. This has caused an awakening among a significant portion of the world's population who collectively scream, "Black Lives Matter."

As a Black female who grew up in California in the 80s and 90s, I remember the 1992 LA Riots after Rodney King's brutal beating at the hands of Los Angeles police officers. I recall watching the video and having his criminality debated on television and at my primarily white, all girls parochial school. I remember the explosive anger when the four cops charged with his assault were acquitted. The despair and rage expressed in rioting was mostly limited to my home state, and to Los Angeles in particular. The four police officers were not only exonerated, there were no substantial systemic changes to the treatment of Black people by law enforcement in Los Angeles or elsewhere. Only history will reveal whether the outrage heard across the world at George Floyd's murder, along with the Black Lives Matter protest marches and various promises of systemic change, will amount to anything that makes a difference in Black people's lives. The cumulative impact of racism can also be found not only in large public injustices like these, but also in the day to day inequalities and racial insensitivities experienced by Black people everywhere, every day.

The memoirs presented in this book were written by undergraduates and recent graduates of Dartmouth College. Understanding the demographic context of the Black community and other minority communities at Dartmouth, which is located in predominantly white Hanover, New Hampshire, is helpful in understanding these essays. Dartmouth's Black community is very small. The 2019 racial enrollment statistics for students are as follows: African American, 6 percent; Hispanic or Latino, 9 percent; Asian American 14 percent; Native American, 1 percent; and Mixed Race, 4 percent; of the remaining 66 percent, 50 percent are white and 16 percent are non-resident Asians. While African Americans comprise 6 percent of Dartmouth students and 13 percent of the US population, only 2 percent of the Dartmouth faculty are Black. Reading through the chapters in this collection, one is led to consider how much more positive these Black students' experiences, and those of all Dartmouth students for that matter, would have been if the college were more effective in meeting its stated goal of creating an ethnically and racially diverse faculty from whom students can learn and grow. Despite the lack of diversity, Dartmouth is a respected institution known for its commitment to outstanding research and teaching. As the Black students describe in the fourteen chapters included in this collection, the opportunity to matriculate at Dartmouth was initially a joyful experience. Yet, at some point from the day they received their acceptance letters to when they wrote their chapters, the joy of attending Dartmouth College was diminished by a cultural milieu that questioned their earned right to be there. As a consequence, these students began to question their own worth.

I recently taught classes at Dartmouth over a five-year period. When race and the privileges associated with having white skin were discussed in my courses, I received pushback from white students who had trouble understanding white privilege generally. This is understandable because understanding the complexity of white privilege is more difficult to understand than conceptualizing what it means to have economic, social class, or gender privilege. In America, the privilege of having white skin includes seeing the proliferation of images of people who look like you on television and in the media. It means going to the corner convenience store and finding pantyhose and makeup that match your white skin tone. For many, the privilege of having white skin in America means having a large network of multi-generational support at the college you attend.

While most students at Dartmouth and similarly elite colleges come from families that represent the wealthiest members of our society, many students at these schools receive full-ride financial aid packages. However, despite the persistent alignment between minority students and poverty, not all the students who receive full financial aid packages are non-white. Many of the white students who receive full financial aid at Dartmouth are the first in their family to attend college, but because they feel distinctly unprivileged in the context of so many privileged peers, it can be challenging for them to see themselves as a beneficiary of white privilege, as disadvantage and discrimination are unquestionably effects of social class as well as race. The difference for white students from poor families is that a solid education enables them to slip invisibly into the middle classes and assume all the privileges that pertain. Black students who receive the same education might also be able to join the middle classes, but they will always carry the racial burdens that pertain.

The experiences of the Black memoir writers in this book illuminate important aspects of what it means to be a Black student at a primarily white institution. One of the Black students in his chapter calls his blackness a burden. Another articulates having to confront his blackness daily, reminding himself constantly that he is worthy and that his successes are because of his efforts, and not because of the color of his skin. Understood in the context of the Black Lives Matter movement, we are reminded that each day these writers, like the vast majority of Black people in the United States, must look over their shoulder whenever they see a police officer and think twice about each action they take in the officer's presence. The Black students who authored these chapters—who are African American as well as African, Afro-European, Afro-Asian, Afro-Hispanic, and biracial—engage with their surroundings in complex ways, and their narratives will help readers to understand some of the unique challenges related to being Black in America.

## From Interloper to Independence

"Things fall apart; the centre cannot hold" is a frequently repeated line from William Butler Yeats's poem, "The Second Coming" (1919), which he wrote during the 1918 flu pandemic—a turbulent time in his native Ireland and the world. Yeats's line feels appropriately recalled when reading the chapters in Part I, Lost and Found: Coming Into Independence, each of which grapples with student's feelings of placelessness as they describe a time when their personal center collapsed and things fell apart. Each chapter focuses on the author's formative life experiences and explores moments when the student felt as if he or she did not belong in their various communities—from familial settings to enclaves of white privilege.

In describing incidents of racial marginalization, cultural dissonance, chaos, and dysfunction that occurred in their lives, the writers reveal feelings of isolation and otherness. At times these traumatic and often racialized incidents were compounded by further trauma, including absent parents, violent sexual assaults, and mental health issues. By the time they wrote these memoirs while they were in or recently graduated from college, each author had achieved a degree of agency in his or her life. Their willingness to share their stories suggests that these authors have found enough personal autonomy that they no longer feel like interlopers in spaces where they feel out of place. Their narratives show that they are more firmly on their own unique path toward independence.

"Multihued," Anthony R. Luckett's chapter, describes how he was placed in various foster care situations by a mother who felt she was unable to properly provide for him, and how in his first foster home he was repeatedly molested by the family grandfather. He writes:

> Of all the bad things I remember, the most difficult to deal with was the fact that something bad was happening to me, and my foster parents *knew*. They knew, and they knew that I knew they knew, and still nothing. No protection, no nothing—except for more walks with Grandpa.

The feeling of being unprotected, unwanted, and not belonging continued throughout Anthony's life and his persistent feeling of not belonging led to a profound loneliness that only made him ever more aware of how different he was. He writes:

> I wanted attention and to belong. The difficulty of dealing with my loneliness was more than feeling I didn't belong in my various foster homes—it was complicated by my developing racial identity. I had lived with a white family, a single Korean woman, and two very different Korean families. But I am Korean and Black. No one I lived with could fully understand what it was to be a mix of two separate minority worlds, and until later in my life, neither could I.

Anthony writes at the end of his chapter that the "search for a complete me is undying. The motivation it generates is eternal."

Many of the writers in this collection articulate a desire for college to be a space where they are accepted for their specific accomplishments, knowledge, and intelligence. The trauma of seeing oneself as an interloper in an educational setting—especially knowing that some of one's white peers might harbor feelings toward Black people that reflect a stereotyped understanding of blackness—creates a specific type of isolation in a Black person's life.

Even though Tyler Malbreaux saw himself as exceptional, he writes in his chapter, "Learning in Black and White," that his experiences with his white peers and with white police officers always made him feel as if he was unwelcome. Tyler writes that at the elite Christian private schools he attended in Louisiana, he was derided with racist verbal assaults disguised as "jokes and off-hand comments," for no other reason than that he is Black. This interloper status was accentuated by the fact that Tyler was very often the only or one of very few Black students at his schools. That simultaneous visibility and invisibility of his blackness affected the way in which Tyler saw himself. Tyler's peers told him in a multitude of ways that he should embody his Black identity in a manner to confirm their own racist stereotypes and caricatures. This ruptured how he saw himself as a Black person, and caused him to lose his sense of identity just when he was trying to understand who he was. Tyler begins his chapter by describing how his understanding of his own blackness changed after the election of Barack Obama. He rhetorically asks, "How could my best friend be a boy who wants to move to Argentina because a man who looks like me was elected president?" Tyler was inundated by his peers with racist tropes that drastically contrasted with how he experienced what it meant to be Black at home. And while he hoped for inclusion and acceptance at Dartmouth, he writes that, "I found instead that my upbringing still adversely affected how I related to others." Instead of becoming a member of the Dartmouth community, he continued to see himself as an interloper. He states that, "at Dartmouth I felt ignored and replaceable—anyone could do what I did. Most of the time they could do it better than I could." Yet, at the end of Tyler's chapter he asserts that he is ready to take ownership of his life and his identity.

In her chapter, "Finding My Lost Voice," Sabyne Free Pierre describes growing up in the "bad area" of Newark. As a young Black woman who struggled with the realities of gang culture and violence, she faced many challenges, including her mother's death, but her identity as a Black person was not one of them. However, when she made the transition to Dartmouth, she found that she was now part of a sub-group of Black students who came from impoverished backgrounds. She felt judged by many of the moneyed class of Blacks at Dartmouth, who ostracized her for fear of being conflated not only with racist stereotypes about Black people, but with those Black people who in many ways personified those stereotypes.

At Dartmouth, Sabyne experienced a hierarchy of Black students from different social classes, where those from a more advantaged background felt free to critique her self-presentation when it does not meet their own inchoate standards for how one should express their Black identity. She captures this dynamic by describing a party she attended on campus where she wore her hair in a straight style. A Black male student told her that her hair indicated she was seeking to engage in "respectability politics." She writes:

> That night I left the party angry. How could someone accuse me of catering to the majority community because I put on a straight wig? I simply wanted to change my hair style for a while, and I felt this guy was telling me I was not allowed to. I did not want anybody else to tell me what hair style was valid, let alone a Black man, or to write me off as trying to conform to norms of "respectability." I still used the slang I learned on the streets of Newark and rocked hoop earrings bigger than this man's head—a man who had never faced the struggles I had as a poor Black girl in the 'hood—and yet he felt entitled to tell me I was "not Black enough." Some days I feel I do not belong at Dartmouth, due to either my identity or my ability. Incidents like this highlight why I am insecure about my place at Dartmouth.

In "Quest for Peace," Deirdre Harris details her life after the traumatic death of her stepfather at the hands of police. Returning home from third grade one day, Deirdre learns that her stepfather (whom she thought of as her father) had been shot and killed by Houston police officers. The story she details connects to multiple experiences far too many Black Americans can relate to. Deirdre reports that doctors had refused to believe her mother's pleas that her stepfather's medication dosage needed altering; that after months of a downward-spiraling mental state her father had a mental breakdown; that the cops were called on her father after he barricaded himself inside his mother's house and then refused to comply with the police officer's orders to vacate; and when he finally did exit the house, "police shot dozens of bullets into my father, an unarmed, mentally ill, Black man." When the police officers involved were exempted from responsibility for his death, Deirdre decided that her country had betrayed her. As an act of resistance, long before Colin Kaepernick decided to take a knee, Deirdre decided that she could no longer "say the Pledge of Allegiance at the beginning of each school day." Deirdre would stand silently, with her hand over her heart, and say nothing.

Deirdre also was a student at Dartmouth during the 1992 LA Riots. The viral dissemination of the video of Rodney King's beating, the subsequent acquittal of the four officers, and the resulting riots all exacerbated Deirdre's anxiety. The injustice in the jury finding the LAPD officers not guilty for Rodney King's beating triggered her long-suppressed trauma over her father's murder. Deirdre feared that someone else in her family would be killed. She writes, "I didn't feel safe anywhere." Yet Deirdre did not share these feelings with anyone, including her mother. As is often the case with trauma survivors, Deirdre believed that her feelings of anxiety were unwarranted and that it was important to maintain an exterior that showed everything was all right, but this deception tended to isolate her from others. Her isolation while at college, combined with the Rodney King incident, led to an emotional breakdown that made college "a debilitating experience to endure rather than an empowering experience to embrace." She relates that she finally got the counseling she needed at college which, combined with the catharsis of writing her chapter here, helped heal the fracture of self that resulted from multiple childhood traumas and a stressful college experience.

"Things fall apart; the centre cannot hold." For Black Americans who primarily exist on the periphery of American life, the center rarely holds. Or if it holds, it is by their staying on the periphery. Whatever stability there is for Black families in America, it did not hold for the four students whose essays appear in this section. At one point or another throughout these young peoples' lives, things fell apart. Yet each of them was able to regain their footing and found peace to begin on a path toward independence. Things might fall apart, but the writers whose chapters appear here suggest that individuals do not necessarily fall with them.

## Both Inside and Outside of Blackness

There is a perception in America, and perhaps in much of the rest of the world, that light-skinned people are more valued and worthy. This perception means that light-skinned people are often conferred better treatment and experience less discrimination. Yet that desirability does not always enable light-skinned Blacks in America to feel accepted in either Black or non-Black communities. The writers in Part II, Both Inside and Outside of Blackness, describe the double-bind of their light skin color. They write of lives in which they struggle with a lack of acceptance in both white and nonwhite communities. These authors describe the feeling of living on the outside of one racial group or another and relate that they often feel as if they cannot comfortably belong anywhere. They may experience this feeling of otherness even in their families if they happen to look different from a parent or their siblings. Their biracial appearance often makes them stand out among their peers in school as well. They write that they are regularly questioning their existence and negotiating the ways in which they belong. Though each of these writers identifies as Black, what Black means to each one appears to shift depending on how they are perceived by others.

For Zane Williams, who is Black but visually reads as biracial, his struggle to affirm his blackness is challenged daily. In his chapter titled, "Outside and Between," Zane begins by writing that he "always wanted to make sure nobody could ever say I was given a leg up on account of my blackness." In his estimation, the majority of his white peers see blackness as a debilitating factor in one's life—an attribute that one must overcome rather than embrace or celebrate. Yet Zane's chapter demonstrates his determination that no one will ever second guess his abilities based on his blackness. He writes:

> "No, I am not an affirmative action case. No, I was not chosen to fulfill any quota. I deserve my place." This is what I told myself every day, along with a litany of other pep talk: Your hair *is* cool, not straight and blonde, but just as sweet; You *are* good-looking, not thin-lipped or pointy-nosed, but handsome nonetheless (after all, you were picked as a Hollister model, right?); and on it went. Over time I began to realize that there's not much I could do about how I look; I can't change my physiognomy to make me more "legitimate" in the eyes of American social constructs.

Being from a more economically privileged background than the majority of Black Americans, Zane details his internal struggle with the perception that he did not belong among his white peers of the same social class because of his race. This outside/inside identity struggle is a frequent theme among many of the writers in this collection.

For upper-class white Americans, white privilege means not having to constantly question your worth or your place in society because you know that you belong. For Zane, proving he belonged meant joining a historically white fraternity at Dartmouth because he felt he had to make a choice between the two groups he is both inside and outside of. He writes that, if he had joined the Black community in a more exclusive way, it would have meant "only" fraternizing with Black students at the school. For Zane, such an existence would have been "detrimental" to his emotional health and his social success while at college, and in his life thereafter. Zane's rational calculation carried profound identity and friendship implications. As Lawrence Blum writes in, *"I'm Not a Racist, but . . .": The Moral Quandary of Race*, nonwhite students might find fellowship among members of the same race, and in an environment where they are able to freely "discuss race-based experiences," yet the choice to interact only with members of the same race can have severe consequences, "since being comfortable with whites, or making whites comfortable with oneself, is generally a requirement of professional success" (Blum 2002).

Each writer in this section labored over the choice of the race and other identity aspects of the friend group they will join at college—a choice that other students, and especially non-multiracial students, might not agonize over so acutely. Samiir Bolston writes in "Finding Blackness," that it was not until he moved to the United States that the option of associating with Black or white peers was a consideration for him. Born in Denmark, Samiir grew up in an almost entirely white community where, even though he was a Danish citizen with a Danish mother and Moroccan father and spoke only Danish, "my skin color caused other [Danes] to classify me as an immigrant, or at the very least to associate me with the resentment they had toward immigrants." Upon moving to the U.S., Samiir found that how he was perceived by others had shifted. In Denmark, the primarily white population saw him as dark, visibly Black; upon moving to the U.S., where he associated with a predominately Black population, he was perceived as light-skinned or, as he describes it, as "'other' rather than Black." In the U.S., Samiir once again found himself an outsider among people who had a similar physiognomy. Though he "found blackness" at Dartmouth, Samiir continued to find himself on the outside of both Black and white groups. Yet it was Samiir's peripheral racial status that gave him the chance to understand more deeply how he views himself as Black. He writes:

> So while I consider myself Black (well, half Black), I will never again allow this label to dictate the way I interact with others or present myself to the outside world. At times it will change how I am perceived and treated, but as a man who has endured this label my entire life, I shall not let myself be affected. Through the same actions, thoughts, and expressions that make me so hard to define, I will continue to prove to those around me that it is best to define me by my character and not my complexion.

Samiir's life inside and outside racial boundaries emphasizes many of the other struggles the writers in this section of the book describe. The struggle to assert who we are is a particularly unique challenge for Black people in America. While the identity development process is difficult enough, defining one's identity when race is a factor, or when one is constantly challenged by racial stereotypes, or when one's scholastic achievements are denigrated as being unearned can be mentally debilitating. The expectations Black people in America are meant to meet and the ways in which Black people are judged based on their appearance are exacerbated for those Blacks with light-skin. The writers in this section poignantly negotiate life both inside and outside racial identity boundaries, yet not without everlasting psychic pain.

## Growing into Blackness

While most students who matriculate at college are legal adults, they are still teenagers tasked with deciding what they will major in, what courses to take, and how they will present themselves in their new environment. The process of leaving home, immersing oneself in new situations, and being introduced to texts on a range of new subjects supports their development in multiple ways. The choices that these young adults make as they grow into their identities is a constant of their development throughout the college years. The experiences detailed in the chapters in Part III Becoming: Growing Into Adulthood, exemplify how students are continuously becoming and growing into their adult identities. For these students, and countless others like them around the world, growing into adulthood also means understanding what it means to be a Black adult.

Andrew Nalani left his home in Uganda to attend an elite U.S. boarding school intended exclusively for outstanding students from around the world. Experiencing life in a new culture and being far away from the familiar comforts of home, Andrew was also thrust into a world in which how others perceived him differed profoundly from the way he perceived himself. In "Metamorphosis," Andrew reflects on the evolution of his identity as a Black person from age 16 to 22. A Ugandan, prior to moving to the U.S. Andrew would not have ever described himself as Black. He writes:

> I never was Black until I stepped off KLM flight DL9319 in Amsterdam, en route to the UWC [United World College] site in New Mexico. This was the first time in my life I'd been off the African continent or even outside Uganda. Up to now I had been surrounded by people who looked like me, who spoke with the same accent, and whose beliefs did not differ drastically from mine. But when I got off my flight, I saw more white skin than dark skin, and for the first time I was acutely conscious of myself as a Black person in this muzungu (white) land.

Andrew's chapter is a poignant example of how growing into a Black identity is not limited to a racial awakening. He describes how his understanding of gender and sexual identities were also challenged when he moved to the U.S. In Uganda, heteronormative gender was a definitive aspect of Andrew's rearing, but his understanding of gender expanded after he interacted with men who defied these norms; he eventually majored in gender studies. Andrew writes that "for the first time in my life I became aware of my blackness, my prejudice, my overly sensitive nature, and the impact family violence had on shaping who I am. I have changed since leaving home."

Britt Coomb's chapter, "The Big Chop" is another story in this section that grapples with an expanded understanding of gender identity and how one fits into the world. Britt writes that her understanding of who she is as a double minority—a woman and a Black person—grew during college where she learned that she could be sexually attracted to white men, something she had thought impossible. This awakening was initially liberating, and for the first time she discovered that "not all white people are bad!" After college, when Britt actively attempted to date a variety of men she was confronted with white standards of beauty she could not live up to. The lack of connections in Britt's online dating left her feeling despondent about her desirability. She writes that "the white standard of beauty and the white superiority complex are so deeply engrained in Western culture that" of course she was seen as undesirable by the majority of men on online dating platforms who vociferously proclaimed that they were interested in dating any race, "except African American" women. She writes that:

> race is both internal and external, a product of our acceptance of elements that are given weight by other people. I am a self-identified Black person: one who may seem blackish to some, non-Black but for my hair to others, and unequivocally Black to countless more.

Candice Jimerson is yet another writer in this collection who has had to overcome multiple challenges. In her chapter, "Gotta Keep Climbin' All De Time," she writes of some of those challenges, including the death of her mother at the age of thirteen, an event that changed the course of her life and forced her to accelerate her growth into adulthood. She writes:

> My mother's death has changed my entire outlook on life. I feel I skipped my adolescence, a time, in my eyes, of careless abandon, silly mistakes, and independence. Instead, I found myself overwhelmed with sorrow, depression, and responsibility. My brother, who was six at the time of my mother's death, and my father, who was psychologically devastated by it, both depended on me. I resented having this responsibility during my teen years; I felt that it wasn't fair that I had to clean up "all the time," that I had to worry about my brother's clothes, homework, and discipline while the majority of my friends did not have to deal with these issues.

This overwhelming desire to exceed expectations carried over into Candice's academic life as well. Motivated and determined to live up to what she believed her mother envisioned for her, Candice excelled at school and refused to let any obstacle deter her in pursuit of her dreams, despite those in her life who believed that her career goal of becoming a teacher was unworthy of her skills and abilities. Faced with this overwhelming pressure to live up to the other's expectations, Candice's ultimate act of growing into adulthood was her steadfast determination to be herself.

Anise Vance's story, "A Work in Progress," captures well what all the chapters in this section articulate. Anise also has benefited from privileges that many of the other writers in this collection did not have. His story is a reminder that there is beauty in growing up Black and in a multi-cultural world. Anise was raised outside of the United States in an upper-class environment, and he had the benefit of attending elite schools around the world. These privileges protected him from some of the trauma that his fellow Black Dartmouth alums have been subjected to. Nevertheless, a privileged upbringing did not stop Anise from experiencing racism, and his story is an example of how the social construction of whiteness and systematic racism in the United States is also a global reality. Anise's description of blackness articulates that it is not a monolithic characteristic. He acknowledges that there are shared experiences and shared understandings of what it means to be Black in the world, and he notes the pervasiveness of American culture and American blackness he observed in his travels around the world, but the greatest reminder in Anise's story is that each person who identifies as Black, is Black in their own way.

Anise refers to himself jokingly as "America's worst nightmare." Both African American and Middle Eastern, Anise writes that there "is a sad truth in the joke—Blacks and Middle Easterners are certainly stereotyped and often portrayed as elements to be feared by much of American society." The lightness and warmth of Anise's writing clearly illustrates what the author himself suggests, that he recognizes how he is perceived in the world and that he delights in using the visibility and invisibility of his racial otherness to provoke those around him who hold racial prejudices. The last sentence of his essay reiterates the title, "I am a work in progress," and that phrase also expresses the theme of this section of chapters. One's identity, especially one that is comprised of multiple racial features, is a work in progress. Growing into Blackness also means growing into an understanding that race is not a stable category, but instead must be navigated and renegotiated continually throughout one's life.

## Finding Liberty: Renewal, Reflection, and Regeneration

The four chapters included in Part IV are retrospectives written years after the author's first chapters were published in a previous collection by the editors of this book. Their original chapters can be found in other sections of this book: "Quest for Peace," by Deidre Harris; "Finding Blackness," by Samiir Bolsten; "Gotta Keep Climbin' All De Time," by Candace Jimerson; and "Forever Home," by Anise Vance. Read in conjunction with their first chapters, these inspirational follow-up stories provide hope that the identity struggles and self-doubt that many Black students face in college are not insurmountable. There is often a feeling by those who have "made it" that they are leaving others behind. This can be especially true for Black Americans who have achieved status or position and fulfillment in their lives, while the persistent racial divide denies other Black people the simplicity of a peaceful life.

Twenty years after writing, "Quest for Peace," Deirdre Harris is still haunted by the death of her stepfather, but she has found peace and acceptance in her life. For Deirdre, finding liberty meant abandoning the ethos that her southern Christian community insisted life should be like for women. While in her initial chapter Deirdre wrote about her struggle with sexual attraction to women, she wrote in her follow-up chapter that she is happily married to a woman. She was also able to bring her mother to understand that hell is not a place one journeys to after a misled life—that hell is the place that she, Deirdre, was living in when masquerading as a "normal" person. Deirdre, who suffered from a mental breakdown during her fourth year of college that was related to multiple childhood traumas, has come to the mature understanding that her experience was not so much a "breakdown but my breakthrough—the catalyst that helped me face my childhood trauma."

Samiir Bolsten is still negotiating the trauma he experienced early in life while also navigating what it means to be Black in America. A Danish-born, self-identified Black man who now resides primarily in the United States, Samiir still finds his interactions with white Americans disorienting. He uses his interactions with white police officers as an example of how he has settled into his blackness and is able to disarm white people by projecting his European heritage and his elite education. While others still question whether Samiir is truly Black, he knows that his biracial appearance and European birth do not stop the world from seeing a Black man when they look at him. Samiir no longer bases his "self-worth" based on other's perceptions, writing that "I've become much better at understanding the nuances and differences in race and class." He has found peace and confidence in his identity, but he now faces other challenges that arose with reaching adulthood, which he describes eloquently in his retrospective here.

After college, Candice Jimerson found purpose as an educator working with students of color at college preparatory schools. In that role, Candice had often to explain the difference between equality and equity to her white colleagues. She emphasizes that blanket color blindness gives teachers permission to treat everyone the same without accounting for their dissimilar experiences. She writes that:

> many baby-boomer teachers have taken Martin Luther King Jr.'s statement about people being judged not by the color of their skin but by the content of their character to the extreme… "If you say you don't see me as Black when you see me, then you don't really see me! Blackness is who I am. Don't ignore who I am!"

The challenge of explaining the nuances of racism to her liberal-minded colleagues was accentuated when Candice moved to New England with her husband and her four stepsons. There, she was introduced to an aspect of life she had been shielded from at Dartmouth: the absence of a Black community. As a parent and employee at a primarily white college preparatory school, Candice quickly learns what it is like to be Black in a community that, although it professes liberal ideologies, her Black family found uncomfortable and disorienting.

One persistent theme of nearly all of these stories is the over-policing of Black bodies in the United States. Anise's first chapter, "A Work in Progress," is a beautifully written memoir that suggests a hopeful future for the writer. And while his follow-up chapter confirms that Anise is living a peaceful life, it is not a life without tribulation caused by the implicit bias behind over-policing. Anise writes:

> I get stopped by the police at least once every six months. My wife and I moved to North Carolina almost three years ago, and geography has made no difference in the frequency with which I am pulled over. Boston, D.C., Chapel Hill—it doesn't matter. About a year ago, I was driving with a couple of 14-year-old Black boys whom my wife and I mentor. As we passed their middle school, I noticed police lights flashing behind me and heard a siren. I pulled over and glanced at the two youth. They were frozen in self-consciously relaxed poses. In my side mirror, I watched the officer approach. It was 10 on a Saturday morning, and I was driving no faster than the person in front of me. Except for the occasional passing car, there was nobody else around.

Throughout the history of the United States, Black bodies have been over-policed. As the chapters in this book illustrate, being Black includes people who are African, of African descent, and people with mixed a heritage where only some fraction is connected to African peoples. This wide framing of blackness in the United States, which has determined in some places by statute that those of mixed parentage with even a "drop" of Black blood shall be considered socially and legally as Black. While no longer law, it is a de facto assumption in policing. Antebellum United States policed Black bodies by branding slaves, posting runaway slave notices throughout the country, allowing runaway slaves to be recaptured in the "free" North, and passing "lantern laws"—eighteenth-century laws that required even free Black people in northern U.S. cities to carry lanterns at night so as to be identified and challenged for their right to be out. During the Jim Crow era, policing Black bodies meant redlining housing and schools, and laws that segregated public spaces. Today, while virtually all the laws that legally marginalized Blacks to specific spaces in our country have been abolished, systematic racism in law enforcement and de facto segregation in housing and education persists. The belief that a Black person in a primarily white area is there for nefarious reasons is ingrained into American thinking. In a country that is resolute in its belief that the second amendment to the U.S. Constitution guarantees independent gun ownership as a means of self-defense—that indeed allows the open carrying of guns in many states—an armed Black person is seen as a threat rather than as a citizen exercising that same right, and is therefore at extreme risk of being killed by police in routine interactions such as traffic stops. As Anise Vance writes, "Boston, D.C., Chapel Hill—it doesn't matter." If we Black people are seen in places that are deemed nonblack spaces, we are suspected of criminality and questioned. So, while Anise's story is one of optimism and assurance, it is also a reminder that the struggle continues.

Black Lives Matter. The assertion within that statement has caused controversy since a group of Black women first started promoting the idea in 2013 in response to a string of Black murders by the police and white vigilantes. "White fragility" responds to Black Lives Matter with angry mantras that Blue Lives Matter or All Lives Matter, as if those lives are exclusive of Black lives being cared about equally—and at long last. The assertion that Black Lives Matter confronts the clear evidence that Black life has not mattered equally—throughout the history of the United States but globally as well—and that the lives of Black people need to be valued equally to those of our fellow white citizens.

The description of U.S. police violence that echo through many of these chapters—which are written by Black students rich and poor, including Americans, Africans, and Europeans—are further evidence that there are few safe spaces for Black people. The seeming expendability of Black people as demonstrated by so many examples of police violence constrains how Black people function and move through the world. This can have a devastating psychological impact on one's sense of safety, happiness, and belonging. Yes, the Black Lives Matter movement is certainly about preventing the unnecessary death of Black people, but it is also about the *lives* of Back people. Living in a state of fear and uncertainty; living with the knowledge that many of your fellow citizens deny your first-hand experience with the fact of systemic racism and institutional discrimination; living knowing that you can be arrested or even killed for doing almost anything while Black, takes a deep toll on one's spirit. Life is hard enough for everyone without having to carry such an added burden.

Each chapter in this collection illustrates a different way of being Black, yet the common theme running through all of the stories is the courage each of these young authors shows in telling tell their most intimate and painful secrets to the world in the hope of creating better understanding about what it means to be Black in a white-dominant culture. They might also serve to illuminate the way for Black college students who follow. The stories here are also united by their young authors' optimism and determination to make something out of their lives—despite the extra hurdles. These are themes common to Black experience and are part of what defines blackness. They reflect Black identity as a constantly changing and creative adaptation.

Black life is a celebration of survival and confluence, a merging of the hardships of the past with the promise of the future. Each of the essays in this collection provides evidence of this dynamism. These young authors' ability to live and grow and succeed matters. Their lives matter.

## References

Blum, Lawrence. *"I'm Not a Racist, But…": The Moral Quandary of Race*. Ithaca: Cornell University Press, 2002.

Du Bois, W. E. B. *The Souls of Black Folk*. New York: Dover Publications, 1903, p. 2.

Cary, Lorene. "A Memoir Should Be More Than a History Lesson." Interview on NPR's *Tell Me More*, February 1, 2012.

Garrod, A.. "Bridging the divide with Shakespeare: Theatre as moral education in Bosnia and Herzegovina." In *The Reflexive Teaching Artist: Collected Wisdom from The Drama/Theatre Field*, edited by Daniel A. Kelin II and Kathryn Dawson, 145–150. Chicago: Intellect, The University of Chicago Press, 2014.

Garrod, A., and Kilkenny, R. (Eds.). *Balancing Two Worlds: Asian American College Students Tell Their Life Stories*. Ithaca: Cornell University Press, 2007.

Garrod, A., Kilkenny, R., & Gomez, C. (Eds.). *Mi Voz, Mi Vida: Latino College Students Tell Their Life Stories*. Ithaca: Cornell University Press, 2007.

Garrod, A., Ward, J. V., Robinson, T. L., & Kilkenny, R. (Eds.). *Souls Looking Back. Life Stories of Growing up Black*. New York: Routledge, 1999.

Garrod, A., Kilkenny, R., & Gomez, C. *Mixed: Multiracial College Students Tell Their Life Stories* (1st ed.). Ithaca: Cornell University Press, 2013.

Garrod, A., Kilkenny, R., & Patel, E. *Growing Up Muslim: Muslim College Students in America Tell Their Life Stories* (1st ed.). Ithaca: Cornell University Press, 2014.

Garrod, A., Kilkenny, R., Taylor, M. B., & Lomawaima, T. K. *I Am Where I Come From: Native American College Students and Graduates Tell Their Life Stories* (1st ed.). Ithaca: Cornell University Press, 2017.

Garrod, A., and Kilkenny, R. (Eds.). *Adolescent Portraits: Identity and Challenges* (8th ed.). New York: Routledge, 2022.

Obama, Barack. *Dreams from My Father*. New York: Times Books, 1995.

Perry, Imani. *The Year of Black Memoir*. New York: Columbia University Press, Public Books Series, 2016. Retrieved from https://www.publicbooks.org/the-year-of-black-memoir/

Yeats, William Butler. The Collected Poems of W. B. Yeats. London: Wordsworth Editions Ltd, 1994.

# Part I

# Lost and Found: Coming Into Independence

# 1 Learning in Black and White

*Tyler Malbreaux*

I was in fifth grade and living in Louisiana when America elected its first Black president. I remember sitting on the floor in the living room as my parents switched between channels. Despite the historic occasion, my mom was intent on watching her Tuesday-night dramas, but she allowed my dad to tune in to CNN during commercial breaks. Wolf Blitzer's roundtable of experts was rattling off the path to electoral votes as polling data trickled in. Correspondents stood dutifully by a digital electoral map, highlighting states as they went either red or blue. "The white people are gonna be mad as hell at work tomorrow," I heard my mom say.

And mad they were, as were the young white fifth graders at Westminster, the predominately white Christian academy I attended. Before the daily prayer the morning after election night, my teacher instructed the class not to talk about the election results. My so-called friends already had made disparaging comments about a possible Obama victory; one said his parents would move to Argentina, another said Louisiana would have to secede, and I overheard more on the playground: "My dad says Obama will make us into slaves." "He'll start another Civil War." Or, my favorite, "He'll take away the guns so we won't be able to duck hunt anymore."

I'd like to have been happy Obama won, but his victory confused how I felt about my friendships. How could my best friend be a boy who wants to move to Argentina because a man who looks like me was elected president? I heard my parents say that white people took issue with Obama being Black, while white people claimed to abhor the notion that their objections to him had anything to do with race—whom was I to believe? When someone asked whom I had supported in the election, I'd reluctantly say, "I couldn't vote, so it doesn't matter." If that didn't work, I tried, "They were all bad. Obama was too young and McCain was too old."

I partly blame my teachers for my confusion. While none of them ever said anything directly about the election or whom they supported, they had this sly way of implying that there was only one clear choice. They said there was one truth, Jesus Christ, that the leader of our nation had to be ordained by God, His Father, and that voting was not merely a civic choice but a religious one, a private display of love for your country and of your love for God. And if that

DOI: 10.4324/9781003376255-2

doesn't make it obvious enough, remember that 40 percent of registered Republicans believed Obama was a Kenyan-born Muslim. In effect, my parents and my private school were teaching me ideals that were at odds with each other. For instance, I could not reconcile learning "We the people" at school with hearing "We as Black people" at home. My teachers said America was exceptional for its commitment to justice for everyone, but my parents said that was not true. And why did the color of my skin matter? I did everything the white kids did. I went to white birthday parties and ate their white food—I had fun with white people. And, of course, I was taught that God saw all of us the same.

My parents never took issue with my dueling educations. I'd say that this was the product of ignorance rather than indifference, as I don't think they knew any more than I about how growing up in a racially charged, radically Christian environment would hinder my own racial identity formation.

In sixth grade, I transferred from Westminster to Ascension Episcopal School. You would think that being governed by the Episcopal church would have made Ascension a more stringent Christian environment, but that wasn't the case. There were no mandatory Bible classes that required students to memorize passages and parables and recite them on demand. And if you didn't know an answer on a science test, you couldn't get a half-credit by writing, "because Jesus made it so." However, Ascension had a significantly more hostile racial environment than Westminster, which made it increasingly difficult for an already confused Black boy to understand his role in the world. I was the only Black boy in my class. There were two or three Black girls, but for some reason they never seemed to encounter the overt racism I did. Maybe boys are generally more likely than girls to be the brunt of crude taunts and jokes, which sometimes involve skin color. Many of these boys' first interactions with a Black kid were with me.

At Ascension, I was taught not only to disown my blackness but to be disgusted by it. My white friends—a laughably loose definition of "friend"—would discuss the most "ghetto" thing they had seen on the good—that is, white—side of town. There was nothing that could not be racialized. Luxury cars with extended wheelbases were a white person thing, while bouncy "hoop 'd's" sporting 30-inch rims and flashy paint jobs were crass and tasteless. And Black. George, a short blonde kid with a freckled face, asked me during lunch one day, "Does anyone in your family drive one of those?" Another boy at the table added, "Yeah, I mean, his dad is Black," grinning at his ingenious remark. They likely knew that the pudgy nerdy Black kid lacked the gusto to assert himself. Mustering up a fake laugh, I responded to George, "No, no hoop 'd's in my family."

I can see how some might think I am hypersensitive. How could mere boyish jokes confuse my self-understanding so much? For all I knew, the jokesters had no ill intent—after all, they called me their friend. And shouldn't any African American boy think himself lucky to attend a school that, despite its faults, gave him a formidable education that put him well ahead of his peers and prepared him to attend an Ivy League college? That may be, but I am willing to be accused of melodrama because the origins of my racial identity, the point at which I could look in the mirror and say, "I am Tyler and I am African American"—began with my interactions with racism. I experienced it at Westminster and Ascension through jokes and off-hand comments. Regardless of how jokey or off-handed the white boys' intentions were, they forced me to reckon with the fact that I was different from them in ways I could not fully comprehend at that age, though I could superficially grasp it by sight, by our different skin color.

How could I, a Black boy, ever have grasped his condition in society without the help of others who also identified as Black? For me to come to terms with that difference, to fully recognize that I'm Black, I would have needed more interaction with other Black peers. Unfortunately, even though we lived on the Black side of town and had Black neighbors and Black family friends, I was never exposed much to other Black children. In the racially charged schools where I spent my childhood days, I was exposed primarily to white people. The conflicting educations I received at home and at school left me with an ill-formed racial identity that makes it difficult to relate to others and understand my place within society. This confusion manifested in my struggle with how to begin and maintain friendships in high school and college, and continues in my efforts to understand my identity in the world beyond school.

One March night in my senior year, I got pulled over by the police for the first time. "Turn off the engine and step out of the car with your hands up!" I looked in my rear view mirror and was blinded by a blazing white light. "Get out!" the voice repeated from the cruiser's speakers. I knew I had taken an illegal right turn at a red light, so I stepped out of my truck slowly and planted my feet on the ground, careful not to make any sudden movements. "Walk slowly, then turn around!" I walked to the back wheel of my truck, then turned as ordered and stopped. "Don't move." There were two cops. The one who yelled the orders grabbed me with his meaty hands, feeling upwards toward my chest. He put on a production that made me feel like a criminal. "Do you have anything on you that I should know about? Drugs, weapons, anything like that?" "No." "Are you sure?" he asked incredulously. "No," I responded. "Then what's this?" He reached for the white lining dangling from my pocket, from which I had removed the car keys a few minutes earlier. "What did you take out of your pocket, son?" "*Son,*" I thought to myself, "Why *son*?"

He continued to ask me about the crimes he thought I might be guilty of—drug possession, illegal possession of a firearm, even that the truck might be stolen. For a moment I thought the other cop, the calmer of the two, might vouch for me to his rather aggressive partner. "If this makes it any better, I'm going to Dartmouth." This was desperation, a Hail Mary pass. The Ivy League name would make me respectable, I thought, put me in the aura of whiteness. But to this the cop replied, "Then this makes your mistake even more stupid."

I arrived home sometime after 9 p.m. My dad sat relaxing in his usual position on the living room sofa, scrolling through news stories on his brightly lit iPad as CNN pundits rambled on on the television screen in front of him. Not too much bothers my dad. My concerns as a child were met with some version of, "It's gonna be alright, son." "Umm, I have something to tell you," I said, unsure what his reaction would be. He still hadn't looked up but he nodded, which told me to continue. "The light was still red when I turned, and there was a cop who saw me. He pulled me over." He stopped reading. I was expecting to hear something encouraging about how everyone makes mistakes, or maybe he would use this as a teaching moment about being more mindful of what I do. I thought he would ask what the officer did or how he treated me.

Instead, he asked, "Did he give you a ticket?"

> "Yes."
> "How much?"
> "$150."
> "Oh. That's all?"

That's all? No, of course it wasn't all. I proceeded to tell him how my hands trembled as the blue lights danced in my rear view mirror. I told him how the cop used a loudspeaker when it was unnecessary. I told him that he called me "son" as he thrust my hands above my head and interrogated me. I wanted him to see what I saw, to feel the embarrassment I felt—a straight-A Dartmouth student profiled as a thug…that's what I expected my father to understand. But all I got was, "Well, that's what happens when you're Black in a bad neighborhood, driving a nice car too late at night." Though correct, his words upset me. I wanted him to be furious, to threaten to call his lawyer and demand that I not have to pay the ticket, but he didn't even get angry. I should have known that he wouldn't but I just couldn't help feeling let down.

Looking back, I realize that this incident highlights my theory of exceptionality, that I somehow saw myself as the exception to Black stereotypes and expected to be treated accordingly by white people—even cops. I can understand that my outraged reaction to the cop's treatment and the banal outcome of receiving a ticket reflects my rather charmed and privileged life being shattered by a real-world experience. It also illustrates the conflict between what I learned about being Black at the southern, mostly white Christian academies I attended and what I learned at home. These messages were so conflicting that my view of reality was utterly confused.

In the midst of my confusion I thought that, although my white school environment could never help me fully recognize myself as a Black man, it could give me the means to achieve success in a white man's world. After all, the one common belief I learned from my schools and my diligent parents was that America rewards those who work hard and educate themselves, which is why my parents sent me to private school and had high expectations for me from a young age. But where I was perhaps and most confused—and where my confusion was most consequential—was being convinced that I was an exception to the racial stereotypes that surrounded me. This was reinforced by frequent affirmation of my worth through the awards and leadership positions I won. My high school teachers told me I was the most eloquent and gifted speaker in the class, and my fellow students elected me president of the debate team and head of the student government. I also earned good grades. My achievements were highly visible, in no small part because I am Black. I thought, naively, that earning such accolades would prevent me from having to *feel* Black—that is, unprivileged, having to fear racist police. I thought I could inhabit a protective bubble created by getting good grades in a good school and having good standing in society. However, I had a rude awakening to the fact that "being Black" only means what white people decide it means.

I have come to learn that my theory of exceptionality was false. The incident with the cops dispelled everything I had grown up believing about privilege and education and freedom and what those things could do for you in the real world. The reality was that my exceptionality did not extend beyond the schoolyard fence. I had a full taste of this not long after matriculating to Dartmouth. I nearly flunked my first freshman computer science exam and would have failed the course had I not withdrawn. All I did was take classes. I was rejected from some clubs and was too intimidated to join others. For example, although I had excelled at mock trial in high school, I did not pass the first round of auditions for the Dartmouth Mock Trial Team, while the members of the Model UN Club, the closest equivalent to my high school debate team, were fast-talking pros from some of the best high school teams in the country—far too good for me.

My goals when starting college were loosely based on what my parents envisioned for me and my own ill-formed ideas about creating a life of meaning. My parents were models of the American dream. Both were from rural working-class backgrounds and had worked themselves into a comfortable life. They could enjoy an annual vacation and afford to send me to private school to prepare me for college, advantages they had not had while growing up. I was the privileged beneficiary of all their hard work, and they didn't have to tell me that money and a comfortable life were goals I should aim for, as they had themselves. Thus, I initially wanted to be a lawyer, which my parents said was a respectable profession that could earn me a lot of money.

I began college with the hope of building new friendships, as I desperately longed for human connection. But I found instead that my upbringing still adversely affected how I related to others. Pedro, another first-generation college student, was the first close friend I made at Dartmouth. Unlike any male friend I had in high school, he took great care not to offend me in our conversations. Pedro had a sort of vulnerability I had never seen in a guy. He was emotionally present and would initiate a hug if we were leaving to go on break—in fact, his gentle presence reminded me of my female high school friends. He was always concerned about how I was doing and at times quite clingy, to the point of being obsequious. But I didn't mind and we were inseparable. We had most meals together and attended the same parties. If I was out on campus alone for too long, someone would jokingly ask me, "Where's your boyfriend at?"

Then, one night of sophomore year, Pedro came out to me as bisexual. "I've known this about myself for a long time," he told me. I told Pedro that I loved him and that while others may not be as accepting—primarily his own family—I would support him. He thanked me, we hugged, and we went to sleep.

I ought to mention that my high school was not any less hostile to different sexual identities than it was to race. I look back regretfully at the many times I heard someone use the word "faggot" or "gay" to attack someone and I didn't say anything. But the truth is, I had not been taught to be totally accepting either. I knew all people should be treated respectfully, but I don't recall being told that being gay was acceptable—definitely not by anyone at my white Christian academies or in my white Southern community.

But, after Pedro came out to me, something changed. When he started talking to a guy who eventually became his boyfriend, he stopped talking to me. He frequently cancelled our lunch plans and, although we shared a dorm room, we usually only had contact in the morning when we woke up. One day in late spring we stopped being friends. He invited me to lunch, our first meal together in months, and proceeded to tell me that he had decided it was best for him to end our friendship. He was carefully evasive and did not give me any concrete reasons for the break or tell me what I had done, if anything. I was devastated.

From then on, my only friend was my girlfriend, Stéphanie, a first-generation Haitian American woman I met in freshman year. We had started dating in my sophomore year. Unfortunately, she received the full brunt of my anger and hurt from the loss of Pedro. I came to depend too much on Stéphanie because, without Pedro, she was all I had. After I lost him, I fell into a depressive state. I stopped caring about my coursework and was barely able to finish school that summer. I frequently missed classes and didn't complete assignments on time. In fact, I never would have completed the final essay for my classics course without Stéphanie's help. She sat by me in my room for hours and refused to let me step away from my keyboard until the paper was done.

For the next few months, I struggled with deciding how much I could admit to Stéphanie. How could I admit that I was slowly going mad, that I thought I might need anti-depressants? I wanted to be strong, and I thought that being strong meant not showing vulnerability. I did not want to depend on a women for emotional support, but the truth is that I desperately needed Stéphanie and all of her tears, her hugs, her text messages asking if I was alright. I needed her to urge me to seek counseling—without her urging I probably would not have.

I remember reading a poem Stéphanie wrote while we were still together. I can't recall if it was before or after I became such a mess. It's called "Black Girl, Black Boy," and a few lines stayed with me:

> And Black girl will have seen it all
> And she will carry his body home
> after the world has destroyed everything Black boy is made out of
> After everyone else has no more use for him

Black girl will tear out the nails from his wrists
and carry the weight of Black boy on her shoulders like it's scripture

The truth is that without Stéphanie I might have not made it to my junior year. I could see the toll my uncontrollable emotions were taking on her—she was becoming physically weaker and sluggish, and her countenance changed significantly after months of futilely trying to care for me. I didn't want any of this to happen to her and, in part out of shame for failing to fulfill my role as a man, I broke up with her less than a year later.

In the winter term of my junior year, I spent three months working for a nonprofit in the Marshall Islands, a tiny island nation in the South Pacific that, only months before I boarded the plane to go there, I didn't know existed. I was working for an organization that puts on theatrical productions with high school students in distressed parts of the world. I was an assistant producer responsible for things like casting, set construction, ticket sales, etc.

In a nation whose population is just over 50,000, you start to recognize names and faces quickly. After a week, you may still feel like a tourist but a welcome one. After two weeks, you become part of the community. And you are not only a part of the community, you're expected to participate in it. If I saw the parent of a kid who was in our play or the bartender from the restaurant I frequented, I was expected to say hi or wave. These small acts of hospitality made me feel like a valued member of the community. By contrast, Dartmouth is a much smaller community than the Marshalls, with only four thousand undergraduates, and although I've come to recognize so many faces there over the past three years, I have never once said hi to them. There is no expectation of community at Dartmouth, which I think is part of the reason I had such a hard time there. In the Marshalls, I felt valued, unique, and purposeful—what I did had meaning! At Dartmouth I felt ignored and replaceable—anyone could do what I did. Most of the time they could do it better than I could.

My negative feelings disappeared whenever I was with Stéphanie. She adored me. But after being in the Marshall Islands, I realized that Stéphanie's love was the only way I could find meaning for myself. I couldn't find it in anything else—not classwork, not extracurriculars, not books, nothing. I was hopelessly dependent on Stéphanie while at Dartmouth, but in the Marshalls I was forced to be independent because I couldn't talk to her regularly. By the end of my time there, having had a taste of independence, I vowed to myself that I could be independent at home too. I was going to be as independent as a man should be.

I still do not know what will come of my former friendships with Pedro and Stéphanie. Both of them refuse to speak to me to this day. I am still trying to figure out and understand what went so wrong—or, perhaps I should be asking where I went wrong? I can at least understand that my educational upbringing plays some part in my lack of understanding, that my upbringing in the racially charged, racially hostile environments of Westminster and Ascension strongly affected my now ill-formed racial identity. I think this has made it hard for me to maintain relationships, made me wary of any deep commitment, which leaves me feeling isolated and incomplete. I do not say this to excuse my shortcomings or to shift blame onto my parents for the choices they made about my education. I say it to help me understand my past and inform my future.

I remember the last night I spent in my hometown of Lafayette, Louisiana, before leaving to begin my freshman year at Dartmouth. My mom hosted a dinner of about twenty close family and friends at a favorite restaurant, a spectacle I had specifically asked her not to put on. But this dinner was more for her than for me. As the dinner came to a close, my mom stood up to say some kind words about me—"Tyler is a very promising young man" and so forth—and then asked everyone sitting around me to do the same. That meant, of course, that I would have to say something about myself once everyone else had finished. In a regrettably sanctimonious moment (granted, I had to improvise this shit), I rose and said something like, "Getting into Dartmouth and starting a new chapter is not just for me. It's for all of you. You all in some way have helped me to get to this point. And I will not let you down. This one is for you."

But here's the thing: it was not for them, at least not entirely. For I control the terms I will live by, which is the reason I am writing this chapter—to assert control over my own life narrative and, with newly found understanding, contentment, and resolve, my new life trajectory.

# 2 Multihued

*Anthony Luckett*

## On Being Asian

They asked me to write about why choosing
or choosing not to choose sides is relevant
in my life.
I told them that before my thoughts could travel from mind to mouth
I heard the universe whisper life into my mother's womb.
Lucky me.
I might have survived the sound of fate mumbling destiny
while reading a novel on a love unfilled.
He book marked where love had been emptied
and now I'm pessimistic.
I'd give up but which way is up to me?
Where is down to earth when I can't stop thinking about having left heaven.
I've danced with angels and solved multiracial differential equations
in three dimensions. I stand in the fourth now speaking
about the three axial frames of reference and not one of them
described what it was to be Asian.
Sometimes, when I'm not being Korean,
I speak Konglish with my mother and eat Kimchee
alone in my dorm so my roommates can't smell it …
I hum Ah-Ri-Rhang to my dreams so they and sleep can be lovers.
Under the covers in the dark I imagine myself with straight hair
and a grandmother that cooks for me every night despite her own desires.
But when I close my double eyes in private I remember my birthright
birthplace and inner fires.
If I had a log for every time I've been asked
whose side I would have taken in the Riots,
the earth would be a ball of flame and we'd wander lost in our lust to label everything
we see because for every sort of people you think I might be,
they all know they're not in me
and all I hear are voices in my head still asking questions that don't move me any more.
I'm Black and Korean, devoid of sympathy for culture vultures that
circle over my head, a fateful halo reminds me that it's time to be free

DOI: 10.4324/9781003376255-3

of the 38 parallels I've seen folks draw on me …
They asked me to write about why choosing
or choosing not to choose sides is relevant in my life.
I told them that before my mouth was informed by mind that
I piggy backed the universe's spine and tapped into my Chi …
Lucky Me.
I might not have survived nearly four years of fate's interpretation of destiny.
But.
Here I am.

## On Being Black

I feel as if I am an interloper in a land where the packed snow smells of watermelon.
And I traverse the hills picking snowflakes and spitting seeds that plant themselves in my journey.
Walking in circles.
My racial profile eludes my facial style.
I don't look the part.
and I am Black by association.
Misappropriate usage of my visage has been the ground on which I walk alone treading the Mason-Dixon poverty line.
Perforated like my spinal cordless phonetic Nile tones.
I'm light skinneded.
Where do I fit in next to "I've seen you before's" and "my cousin look just like you's"? And, because I've got Seoul in the windows of my soul, I've also heard "He ain't just Black I told you so's." So.
Sometimes when I'm not being Black, I speak in Ebonics and quote Ca$h Money's Greatest Hits.
I purposely fail tests just to see … just to see if I'm keepin' it real. I walk slowly and strut, nod to say "what's up dogg, peace, ah-ight, that's tight, smoke? Nah, shit shorty and hey. My. Nigga."
I've got my finger on figuring it out but when I'm out of my mind what is in sane?
My father gave me the greatest lesson on what a Black man should be by not being around for me to follow his bad example.
Now Jazz is my mother and Hip Hop my sample of what daddies be like.
I feel as if I've intruded into a land where the snow smells of watermelons and I'm no longer picking cotton snowflakes but bad decisions.
Ones that spit the seeds of a freer future plantation.
Walking in circles encircled by miracle manacles I be dazzled and unfocused.
Black by association.
And, I don't look the part that's played me.
only.
time isn't planted with watermelon seeds.

I felt the beat of my mother's chest against the side of my face. Drowsily I looked up and out of the taxicab window. I fell back to sleep against my mother's chest. I was snug and clinging to Mom as best I could. Finally, we stopped. Mom nudged me awake and brought me out of the car. There was a large wood house in front of me. There were two shadows in the doorway of this house. I walked into the house and sat down at a table and put my head down. My eyes were cracked open, and I caught sight of Mom talking with one of the shadows. They spoke and spoke. Then without warning, Mom started walking out the door and I ran after her. As I descended the steps in front of the house I saw Mom get back into the cab. The tailpipe exhaust made the red lights eerie at night as the cab drove off and I screamed, "Mommy! Where are you going? Mommy!" I couldn't say anything else. I was so shocked that she would just leave me. All I saw were the red taillights getting smaller and smaller and more and more blurry as my tears fell.

The lady escorted me back into the house. As I sat down at the table, the man and woman looked at me. She began to peel a tangerine and asked me if I wanted any. No, I didn't want any! I wanted my Mom. I wanted my Mom. The impact of my mother leaving left me speechless for a long, long time. I remember sitting at that table for what felt like hours—long enough for there to be veins of salt down my cheeks where the tears had tumbled. There were things running through my body and soul that I didn't have the words to fit to. All through my childhood, that image of the dwindling taillights haunted me because I still hadn't come to terms with being left in the care of strangers. The household that I was born into had fallen apart by the time I was four years old. This is how my story begins.

I was born in Suwon, Korea, to a Korean mother and African American father. In less than a year, my mother, father, and I moved to London, England, where my mother had a job as a model and teacher, and my father was still in the service of the United States Air Force. We somehow ended up in San Francisco, California, where we lived near an air force base. I don't remember moving, just being in different places and different feelings that come with it. I don't remember having friends, and I wasn't allowed to be in the same room as my father when he and his friends watched adult movies and smoked. He flickered in my mind until his presence disappeared.

When I was left with the tangerine family, each day was like awaking from one bad dream into another. They were a white family. Looking back, I cannot remember a time when I felt like I was a part of that family, perhaps because my recollection of the negative outweighs the occasional happy moments that I can only vaguely remember. My memory serves me tidbits of history salvaged after a tumultuous beginning to life. One of the most enduring memories I have of my time there was the way I spent a number of my weekend mornings on nice days. The funnies were handed to me by one of my foster parents, Jim and Marcy. A hand on my shoulder turned me toward the side door, and I was asked to go outside and read. Jim gave me a hasty nod and told me it was OK to go outside in my underwear. I was uncomfortable but didn't know what to say. I walked slowly out of the door and sat down on the picnic bench with the funnies. Before I started reading I carefully screened the surroundings for onlookers. I opened the pages slowly, hesitantly, and read at an even slower pace. Systematically, I scanned the premises for onlookers as I read the funnies. When I was done with the funnies, I thought it would be all right to go back inside the house; I felt as if my reading the comics was a punishment. I stood up and walked up to the screen door, and it was locked. When I finally got back inside it wasn't long before I was outside again; at least I was clothed on my return excursions. The words were usually, "It's nice out, so why don't you go outside?" Those innocuous words never really sparked any real thought until I heard them repeated over and over again. Nobody ever wanted me in the house. It wasn't as if I truly wanted to be inside so much as I wanted to belong. I just wanted to feel accepted, but nobody wanted to know what I wanted. I missed my Mom, and I didn't like living with this tangerine family.

My unstable disposition was kept aflame by my anger and aggression. In school I was your typical problem child—the kid who doesn't keep quiet, who is always running around and won't listen. My rage would cause me to get into fistfights, and I can even recall throwing a chair across the classroom at another student and hitting the teacher by mistake. My tangerine family foster father, Jim, was called and that night he spanked contempt and embarrassment into my backside at the dinner table. It didn't hurt anything but my pride.

In retrospect, I suppose I should be grateful that a family would take me in and care for me for as long as they did. I suppose that I should thank them for providing a roof over my head and food for me to eat. I suppose that I would indeed be grateful if it were not for memories riddled with nightmares and a feeling of emptiness that fills my gut. Each day I was made to feel as if I wasn't wanted. The house was a large beautifully crafted wood house with a basement, two floors, and an attic. They kept bees on the side of their house to collect honey to sell. The garage was a bottomless pit of baubles, toys, auto parts, and other things that families accumulate over years. The pond behind the house was connected to a creek that was filled with tadpoles. The woods were deep and magnificent. Unfortunately, there was no home for me in that picturesque niche down a quarter of a mile driveway off of Whitney Road. When I think back, the darkness overshadows the light. There were things that happened in that niche that my mother does not know about to this day. The worst part about that tale is that Jim and Marcy knew—and did nothing to protect me.

Jim's father must have been in his sixties when I met him. He was a large heavyset man with gray stubble, a dirty T-shirt, and a dirty odor. I didn't care much for him so I never understood why they ever left me alone with him. They knew what he did on those walks out in the woods at night. He would lead me around behind the pond, and we'd sit on the bench. In a gruff voice he'd ask me if I liked him. I was frozen because even the first time it happened didn't seem like the first time it happened. His coarse hands would find their way on to my back and the friction would rattle my tiny six-year-old frame. His large body overwhelmed me as his large hands found their way off of my back and into my pants. I felt his stubble on my face and in my mouth. I wanted to scream but couldn't. Who would come? Jim and Marcy knew already, I was certain, and Mommy was not there. He touched me where I hadn't even discovered myself and asked again if I liked him. No, I did not like him! I wanted him to go away but I couldn't tell him that. I sat quiet and wished that it would end sooner and sooner each time. I hated walking with Jim's father.

Jim and Marcy were aware because one night after I had "taken a walk," they asked me what happened on the walk with Grandpa. "He touched me here," I said pointing to my groin. "And kissed me. Then he touched me here ..." There was a pause as the two stood there. The sad truth is I don't remember that being the last night that he sapped, rubbed away, and swore to secrecy my childhood with his sixty-plus-year-old mouth, disturbing hands, and five o'clock shadow.

Of all the bad things I remember, the most difficult to deal with was the fact that something bad was happening to me, and my foster parents knew. They knew, and they knew that I knew they knew, and still nothing. No protection, no nothing—except for more walks with Grandpa. I didn't feel as if it was my fault, but for some perverted reason I thought that I might have deserved treatment like that. If everybody knew, maybe it was normal, but part of me knew it couldn't have been. I don't remember too much else about the tangerine family; their faces are murky images of exaggerated features. Fortunately, life is very different for me now. But family secrets have to start somewhere. I had come to terms with what had happened during the summer after my senior year of high school, but I was twenty years old when I finally came around to writing about this incident.

> The night that cried for those
> Hands to stop
> That! Stop That! ... Stops that Rock my brain,
> My pains to sleep in that
> Cradle made for one ... I would still Kill the night that cried for
> Me.

There is a part of me that would commit murder to regain the innocence, security, and trust I had taken from me on those walks. Mother- fuckers! I will never forget what I lost there. I often wonder what life would have been like had I not lived with that tangerine family: Jim, Marcy, and their children. It is difficult to think outside of the past because my history is documented in who I am as a person. Scholars say that a child's personality is shaped by the time he is five years of age. I'm beginning to think there is some truth to that. I was dealt a pair of incompatible, strong-willed parents and confusion, chaos, and abandonment before the age of five. I sometimes wonder how I got through four years with Jim and Marcy's family—misbehaving in school, missing my mother, and all the while feeling I didn't belong.

When my mom finally came to get me out of that tiny niche on Whitney Road when I was eight years old, I didn't know then that I would move twice more before the fifth grade. I moved next to Astoria, Queens, in New York, where I lived with my mom's friend, Kyoung. I attended parochial school for the third grade and just as the school year ended, I moved back to Ohio.

This time Ohio was different. I stayed with a Korean woman named Young. She lived with a Tae Kwon Do instructor and her two sons, Tony, age sixteen, and Andy, age fourteen. The few months that I was with this family, a number of things came to light. I found out that my mother was paying for me to live there when Young became increasingly angry with me for no reason that I could see. Tony pulled me aside one day after I had been yelled at and told me that his mother wasn't angry with me but was angry with my mother because she hadn't paid. Hadn't paid? Why hadn't she paid? I wondered. I understood that raising someone costs money, but why hadn't she paid? Young once told me that she was raising me because my mom didn't know how to take care of me. She said that if my mom left me I would have nothing to worry about because she would take care of me. As hard as I found that to believe since the lady was always angry with me, I wanted to believe that I had nothing to worry about. Her offer, though strange and twisted to me, sounded somewhat inviting since I hated moving and I didn't know what to believe.

Young's words seared my ears, and the thought of mom not returning haunted me. As it turned out, mom also had paid Jim, Marcy, and Kyoung. This new information forced the connection in my mind between my mom's missed payments and the treatment I was receiving. I resented both my foster families and my mother. It was difficult enough to comprehend these families being paid for my care, but I really resented the thought that my mother would dare miss a payment. My resentment was twofold. First, the untainted perception I had of my mother began to soil. Then, when I began questioning my mother, I began losing faith in my own judgment and trusted no one. In a matter of months, Mom came back and moved me once again.

It was in the middle of the fourth grade that I arrived in New York City for the second time. This time it was the Woodside section of Queens where I stayed with the Kims until I went away to college. At this house were the head of the family, "Uncle," his wife, and their two sons, James and John. The Kims had six other foster children in addition to me. All of the kids in Uncle's care attended Public School 11 only five blocks away. Most of the class dismissed me as the new kid dressed in hand-me-downs until people noticed that I was artistically inclined and athletically adept— which was at least a start and more than I had ever had before. School didn't mean much to me until I reached the sixth grade where I met Mr. Meadow. He was the first person to take a genuine interest in my abilities as a student, athlete, and scientist. His charisma would fill the room, and the amount of passion and energy he devoted to his students was peerless. Mr. Meadow motivated my curiosity, intelligence, and creativity. He changed my outlook on school and on myself.

Mr. Meadow was about five feet ten inches and had what I can only describe as a white Afro, only his hair isn't thick and he isn't Black. He looked a lot like pictures I had seen of Mark Twain. He let me sit in the back of class with the microscope. I would bring in samples of dirty water that I had retrieved from various sources in the neighborhood. When my face was in that microscope the world around me did not exist. I watched in awe the paramecia and other microorganisms swimming around in the water. The truth is that I was teacher's pet, and I liked it even if some other people didn't. Mr. Meadow's spirit was very apparent to me, and I basked in his presence. He used to tell me to train for the decathlon before I knew what one was. He always asked that I remain true to myself and taught me not to be influenced by others. One conversation we had shines above all others. We had been talking and then he looked into my eyes. "Tony, don't ever change. I'm serious. Don't ever change. OK?" I didn't know how to react to the solemnity behind his words, so all I could muster was a simple nod of affirmation. Don't change? I couldn't understand the full meaning of what he was trying to say or how to take it truly to heart. His investment in me was matched by my desire to learn from him and the genuine respect I had for this man who respected me and believed in me. He helped to erase a great deal of my self-doubt, and he built my confidence.

I wish my life at school were even remotely representative of my life in the Kim residence. Perhaps it would be asking too much of life to have things go well in both worlds. During my stay with the Kim family, I never once felt as if I was a part of the family. Aside from the mistrust they had of the world in general, the way in which they ran a family was not healthy. According to the Korean old school of thought, children were commodities and were to be seen and not heard.

I distanced myself from everything in the Kim's household except from Uncle's son James. He was the only member of that family with whom I felt I had any connection. The Kims owned two apartments on the same floor of the building. James and I stayed in apartment 4D with his grandmother while the rest of the family lived in apartment 4B. James and I would stay up late playing video games or watching television. Sometimes, we'd play basketball together and for about a year, he was one of my Tae Kwon Do instructors. James also tutored me in math. He was my older brother and I looked up to him. We never spoke about what I was truly feeling except for once.

> "You know bro, I've never really felt at home here," I said to James softly.
>
> "I know. I can understand that."
>
> "It's like ... well, it's not like I'm very upset that I wasn't a part of this family because, well ... you know "
>
> "Yeah," he said as he shook his head. "It's kind of sad, bro," I said.
>
> "It is. That it is," he said softly.

A moment of silence overtook the room and he gave me an understanding nod, as if to say he understood my discomfort of never feeling "at home" and my struggle to get away. I was sad that I had lived with a family for almost a decade and never felt truly welcome there. Beyond not feeling welcome, I was so uncomfortable I didn't like being in the physical presence or close vicinity of

Uncle or Auntie. So that I could spend the least amount of time at home with the Kims I would go out as much as I could and stay out late, and I was as active as I possibly could be in high school. Looking back I can see the irony that at age six I was always upset at being made to stay out of Jim and Marcy's house, twelve years later I was doing everything I could to stay out of the house. "Men don't run from their problems." Who could have taught me this? Jim? The Tae Kwon Do instructor? Tony or Andy? Uncle? James? I wouldn't know. Though I picked up pieces of manhood from each of them along my path of development, I am unclear how to apportion to what extent these male foster figures have affected me.

With loneliness as my companion and introspection my bedfellow, I brooded over the questions that challenged my understanding of my circumstances, my mother, and the world around me. The changes happening to my body only contributed to my confusion and lack of understanding. While undergoing these changes in my life, Mom was still a sporadic beacon of light, and while I took her for granted, I resented my predicament and wanted more from her than just an escape from my current environment. I wanted attention and to belong. The difficulty of dealing with my loneliness was more than feeling I didn't belong in my various foster homes—it was complicated by my developing racial identity. I had lived with one white family, a single Korean woman, and two very different Korean families. But I am Korean and Black. No one I lived with could fully understand what it was to be a mix of two separate minority worlds, and until later in my life, neither could I.

I always knew that I was different. With the tangerine family it was very obvious, especially when they picked me up from school. Everywhere I went, including New York City, I managed to warrant a second look. This made me so terribly self-conscious that I was embarrassed by my heritage. I remember once, Mom and I were on the subway. I sat next to Mom who was dressed in a white linen outfit and sat reading the latest volume of Korean Health Digest. As I sat there, I stared around me and secretly hoped that no one was staring back. I don't know whether it was the book she was reading or the clothes she was wearing, but I felt like everyone on the train was looking at us. My uneasiness at her presence was displayed on my face. I was so unused to being in my mother's presence that it was as if she were some strange foreigner reading her magazine right next to me. Then she turned to me and began speaking Korean in front of everyone. As her native language entered my ears, perfectly intelligible, I wanted her to stop. My brusque responses to her were in English, my native language. But she was happy speaking to me that way, showing her affection, and I should have been too, but instead I was overwhelmed by feelings of embarrassment. I was certain that everyone on the train could see that I was not fully Korean and so was wondering why this woman was speaking to me in that tongue. Not coincidentally, that is exactly what I was wondering, too.

I will never forget that painful train ride with Mom in which the most important thing to me was not wanting a subway car full of strangers to know that I spoke or understood my mother's native language. I felt as if she were determined to make me fully Korean. The language barrier that exists between us has really hindered our relationship. On the one hand, Mom is this loving person, her caring and warmth just flowing over me. On the other hand, my mother is a person whom I've had very little time to get to know. My mom has been absent nearly all my life, yet strangely enough she knows me a lot better than I have given her credit for. That day on the train she looked deep into my eyes as she was speaking to me and then stopped and went back to reading her magazine. It was as if she had sensed my innermost thoughts; the discomfort and conflict I sat with. So for the rest of the journey we rode in silence.

I have always prided myself on being different, but for a long time, I felt funny. The type of "funny" that I felt the first time I heard someone call me a "Chink," an experience only matched by the first time I was called a "nigger." As the hapless victim of the synergy in being the biracial new guy, I have always been conscious of my differences, externally and internally. To my Korean friends I always felt like the token Black guy. To those two Black men who passed me on 43rd Avenue one indelible night, I was a "Chink." The powerful feelings of contempt and racism are vivid and lasting. So permanent, that I revisit them every now and again. What is it that people see when they look at me, and why do their furtive stares make me uncomfortable? As I attempt to answer these questions, I find myself caught in life's gauntlet of self-discovery.

During my years in high school I had not fully come to terms with my racial identity, but at least my relationship with my mother was getting better. It was no consolation that we couldn't be together, but I began to realize that she had really wanted the best for me all along. The sacrifice my mother made transcends human emotion and reason, at least to any American or any non-Korean way of thinking. My mother gave up her life so that I might have a better chance at success than she. In my selfish adolescence, I was unable to recognize her strength, humility, and sacrifice. After my freshman year at college, however, I was blessed with the opportunity to fully appreciate my mother's gift of life and my responsibility for it.

By the time I had finished my first year at college I had not seen my mother since my high school graduation. I spent the summer working to raise enough money to visit my mother in Houston, Texas. I had changed since I last saw her. My first year of college had filled my life with new academic and extra-curricular experiences, and I had braided my hair in cornrows and put on fifteen pounds. What would she think? As I disembarked the plane my mother stood at the gate anticipating my arrival. I saw her radiant five foot five inch frame tiptoeing, almost hovering. Her caring eyes scanned each passenger with X-ray precision and surprisingly looked right through me. I nearly passed her before she recognized who I was. In an instant, her eyes lit up and her smile increased tenfold and her arms reached out for me. "Oh my goodness! I almost didn't recognize my Tony—so handsome and tall. Oh my goodness!" she exclaimed. It certainly had been a long time.

When we arrived at the apartment my mother had been living in for some time, I couldn't help but notice it looked like she had just moved in, because of the lack of any furnishings. In the living room there was a table on which was a small pewter picture frame with a picture of us on my sixteenth birthday. The kitchen had not been touched. My thoughts echoed off of the bare walls as I helped to put away the groceries we had bought for dinner. I asked my mother why there wasn't anything in her house. I could almost hear her response before she answered: she spent so much of her time working that she had no need for an apartment to look and feel comfortable. Before I could even enjoy having spent twelve hours with Mom, she had to go to help out at the store where she worked.

When she came home she began cooking. I helped her for a short while, then relaxed and sat watching her in action from the living room. We finally sat down to a feast, and I gorged myself and we spoke. It wasn't the kind of hapless chatter that you might expect two people to have after a long separation. Every gesture and word was a conversation in its own right. The synergy of mother and child contributed to the regenerative air in that humble room. We finished our meal, and I remember her teasing me about my hair. She didn't want me to have long hair, and she also didn't like my cornrow braids. Seeing through my snappy excuses she said, "You don't always have to wear your culture out like that." I spent all night thinking about her insight.

My last day in Houston came quickly. I packed quietly and wore a smile of satisfaction on my face. I was happy that I had the opportunity to see my mother. She offered her motherly words of wisdom as the taxi pulled up to her door. I asked the driver if he would take pictures of my mother and me together. He took a step back and aimed the camera at us. I told Mom to get on my back and when she did, I carried her around the parking lot. Her laughter was so pure I almost collapsed. When I let her down, I hugged her as the driver snapped another picture. After giving my mom the biggest hug and kiss any son could muster, I called on the Lord's strength to prevent my tears from surfacing. It wasn't that I was afraid of being unmanly, I just chose not to cry all the tears behind the ones on the surface. If I started, she would too, and I don't think the taxi driver was prepared to deal with a bawling mother and equally torn son, so I stared out of the taxi window and smiled. She stood there waving back with the same painful grin on her face. As the car pulled away I felt as if my brain was saturated from holding back all of the contentment and tears. I made small talk with the driver during the ride to the airport.

I thought about her meager living conditions and how blessed I was to have a mother who cared about me so much. I have been asked why she didn't keep me by her side. Other people have questioned her motives for placing me in the foster care of other families. This visit answered my own questions. It is difficult to put into words what my mother's burden is. Like many traditional Korean parents she wanted for me all that she had missed in her own life. She dropped out of college to work to support me when I was six or seven. And although I moved many times to different foster families, I was uprooted less often than she was during that time. As the object of her love, I felt obligated to my Korean heritage and how important it is to her that I don't lose what little I know. I thought about her words of advice that I don't always have to "wear my culture out." I felt as if I did in order to remind myself of my own background. It was a constant struggle. The pride I had for my mother's heritage was countered by the overwhelming negative feeling I got when she would overemphasize my Koreanness. At one point, she asked if I would change my last name from that of my father to her own. I was torn up by the powerful nature of that request. It was as if she wanted me to discard my blackness or to destroy the traces I had of my father's heritage. On one hand, my father was absent from my life so why should I carry his name? On the other hand, my name has been my basic identity since I was born. In the end, I didn't change my name and my mother understood.

Race matters. And it doesn't. I cannot detach myself from the biracial aspects of my background. Though I state this obvious fact about my racial identity, I sometimes wonder how my life would have been different if I were just of a single race. I have been told that I have benefited by having received the best of both worlds. And while I have been exposed to both the ugliness and benefits of multiracial life, I have not felt the need to choose one side of my racial background over the other. I have reached a level of comfort where I am proud of all that I am. In some respects I would say that I am more of a New Yorker culturally than either Korean or Black. For me, the distinction is important. Race and culture are synonymous when people with a similar history or genetic make-up share common life experiences unique to their heritage. There is no singular Black experience in America that I can identify with. Neither is there any definitive Korean or multiracial experience. To say the very least, growing up multihued has never been dull. But my racial composition is deeply intertwined with all the important relationships in my life. My relationships with my mother, with friends, and with the opposite sex all reflect the intricate connections between different parts of my life.

An important illustration of this connectivity is how I have interacted with the opposite sex. I have not had much difficulty attracting women because of my physical appearance, which undoubtedly has to do with my multiracial look.

But physical attractiveness has not been the only source of my appeal. Because I have craved the attention of women from the day my mother left me with the tangerine family, over the years I have developed a personality and demeanor that commands attention. Merely attracting women, however, has not solved my loneliness or other interpersonal problems. The obstacle to my having more meaningful and satisfying intimate relationships is rooted in all of the baggage I bring to the table when I get involved in a relationship. Since everything is connected, many of the ways in which I interact with my mother have carried over into my intimate relationships. It therefore makes sense to me that I am an emotionally difficult person to get to know. It seems reasonable and rational to me that I can love someone and then leave her in a heartbeat.

These patterns are a reality in my life. I believe that the lack of family and maternal stability while I was growing up has fostered my pick-up-and-go mentality when it comes to intimacy. I have had to be somewhat callous emotionally to avoid breaking down. My perspective has undergone a number of changes with each new relationship. In the past year I have made conscious efforts to dim the glowing lack of faith I have in womanhood. I feel betrayed in many ways by girls I date. Perhaps I am holding them accountable for my subconscious disappointment with my nomadic lifestyle, and because everything is so short-lived.

It is easier for me to become physically involved with a woman than to invest any serious emotions or real love. The few times that I have really trusted and loved, the relationship failed to survive long distances and miscommunications. Emotional self-preservation outshines my desire for true companionship and so I have closed off parts of myself. In addition to repressing parts of my personality, at the start of a new relationship I determine just how much feeling I am willing to put into a particular relationship, and I seldom deviate from that plan. Some people say that a person should love like they've never loved before, but what about hurting like never before? A guiding truth is that I don't want to hurt like I have before. Every time I grow close to someone, thoughts of long distances and miscommunications remind me of past pains. Many of my friends, past girlfriends, and sexual partners have questioned my dead-end response to them:

> Why don't you just let go of your past? Why can't you just enjoy us right now?
> Can you stop dwelling on what went wrong before? Why don't you want to be with me?
> Why don't you just open up?

How could they not know that, of course, I have asked myself the same questions a thousand times over.

"My future wife is not enrolled at this college" is how I euphemistically put the lack of companionship in my college experience. My desire to transcend my personal history and emotional limitations has been nullified, and I am presently torn between sexual attraction to multiple females and meaningful co-existence with one woman. College life is not conducive to long-distance relationships. Consequently, I am ill prepared for what it is I am wishing for. I come to the relationship table with baggage. All of my unsolved and unanswered problems and questions stay packed up, and I expect these females to magically shed light on something they know nothing about—the deeper me.

With each encounter I either find out something new about myself, or I am reminded of some undesirable quality in my personality. In short, I am still searching for myself. I am afraid of being hurt again. My relationships with the opposite sex have left a stone in my heart. I have weathered self-induced loneliness because of my closed nature. And, through understanding, I have broken the stone in my heart. It's a healing process. I don't think that I will be able to have a meaningful and healthy relationship until I have rid myself of all of these smaller stones. Mistrust, fear, anger, and resentment must fade behind love for me to move on.

Even the longest journey begins with one step. Over the years the stride, pace, and frequency of these steps have all changed. Now, twenty-two years later, my journey continues. I feel as if I have revealed as much about the journey as I have about the traveler. The words and stories I have shared highlight the most powerful memories I have of people and experiences that helped determine my path in life. However, they are only fractions of my entire story. I have not mentioned my true friends who have been my surrogate family and support every step of the way. I am eternally grateful for having them in my life. Neither have I mentioned my involvement in student organizations, dance, my fraternity, or my academics. One can imagine the gamut of things I found to enhance my only-child existence. My search for a complete me is undying. The motivation it generates is eternal.

For my narrative to be complete, I need to know the full story for myself. So, I have begun to search for my father, who was my age when my mother conceived me. The thought that a man out there somewhere is the provider of half my genetic code, and that his presence in my life before the age of five has influenced my growth, sparks insurmountable curiosity. My search has begun with the help and support of my mother and my friends. I have no expectations, but whether I find him or not, the search itself can only further my journey of self-discovery.

# 3 On Finding My Mother's Voice In My Own

*Sabyne "free" Pierre*

These days, I keep quotes on my computer screen to remind myself that I am my top priority in life. I've been particularly enjoying a quote an anthropology professor somewhere once said, "You all have a little bit of 'I want to save the world' in you, that's why you're here, in college. I want you to know that it's okay if you only save one person, and it's okay if that person is you."

Newark, New Jersey, is the place I call home in my social media bios and whenever someone asks me where I'm from. I was born in Newark, but for most of my life I lived right outside the city in a town called Irvington. But Newark is where I went to school and where all my friends were. Most of my family, including my parents, were born in Haiti; my mother moved to the United States a little before she had us. Even though I was born and raised in the States, my household was in every way Haitian: Haitian rules, Haitian food, Haitian music, and, of course, Haitian church at least three times a week. Mom never wanted us to join the wrong group of friends, fall into a life of drugs, or get caught in the wrong place at the wrong time.

Mom was always busy taking care of a house full of children, balancing two or three jobs at a time, and cooking for all of us. I now understand how much she had to sacrifice to ensure that our bellies were full and clothes were clean, but back then I always longed for her to be home with us more. At Christmas she would get a day or two off, and those were the best times. We'd spend the whole day preparing a Christmas feast consisting of fried Haitian pork and colored rice, dancing to Christmas tunes, and celebrating with our cousins. After dinner, Mom would take us to church. At that point in my teenage life I didn't fully buy into the idea of a God above, but seeing her dance and praise a higher power was beautiful to me.

My family is a pyramid. There's Danielle, the oldest; Waliah and Rebecca, the twins; and lastly Fentie, Robert, and me, the triplets. My three sisters were all born in Haiti, like my mother. After their father passed away, my mother met my father while working at a clothing store in Haiti. He took her to America, where she had the triplets. My eldest sister, Danielle, is the strong one in the family. After Mom passed away during my sophomore year of high school, Danielle took us in. Her son and I spent a lot of time doing homework together when I was home, and his abundant energy gives me hope that the

DOI: 10.4324/9781003376255-4

world truly is a good place. Then there are my twin sisters, Rebecca and Waliah. Waliah is the sister who had an impact on my educational goals. Waliah was smart and studied hard, and she was the first person in our family to attend college. Waliah is powerful in more ways than one, and I think she'd say the same for me. Mom agreed to help pay for Waliah's schooling so long as she studied medicine. When she changed her major to journalism, Mom stopped paying, which forced Waliah to take out loans. That didn't stop her and she ran with her passion. She now works for the state parole board and is finishing her graduate degree, still trying to find her own way and still inspiring me to do the same.

The triplets consist of two boys and one girl—me. I spent most of my childhood with the two boys, Fentie and Robert. They were always closer, but they let me tag along on the fun. We joined the basketball team together, had the same friends, shared secrets, and looked out for each other. Mom was strict with us and never liked us to stay outside after the streetlights came on because we lived in a bad area. Newark was known for its gang violence, and there were kids from our school who stopped coming to class so they could join the gangs their brothers had been in. Their choices often resulted in a drug- or gang-related arrest, or even death. Hakeem, a boy who had gone to our school, was shot dead late one night, which greatly affected my brothers. Since my mother worked until late, we sometimes played in the streets with our friends, and we took turns being the lookout.

Robert and I went to the same high school, while Fentie went to a different school so he could be with his friends. We spent the next few years trying to find our own niches and create our own individual identities. Robert was the laid-back, cool kid everyone was good with. He got good enough grades and was spectacular at every sport he played. I was the nerdy one, the sister who was really into spoken word poetry. My family wanted me to focus on my education because complex ideas came easily to me. My mom would be disappointed if I came home with an A- on my report card, even though she'd praise the boys for having anything better than a failing grade. Eventually I heard about Questbridge, a scholarship program that bridges the financial gap between first-generation, low-income students and top-tier universities. I missed a lot of opportunities to socialize during my high school career because of my desire to do well in my studies, and during my freshman and sophomore year my mom wouldn't allow me to socialize. After Mom's passing, my sister Didi pushed me to keep my head in my books, but Mom's presence is still with me, pushing me to do better and to focus on my studies no matter what.

My mother had soft, almond-shaped brown eyes and a white smile. One of her teeth had a crown that you could see when she smiled wide enough. She was average height with a body that curved like a Pom bottle, and her walk was as confident as the words she spoke when she had something important to say. Her hair fell in blonde and brown ringlet curls, and the brown streaks complimented her coffee brown skin. My mother gave sermons at church on Sundays and would stomp all around the altar to praise God. When she cleaned the house on Saturday mornings, she sang along softly to Haitian gospel music.

She spent most of her adult life taking care of elderly people in their homes and caring for the sick.

My dad spent his days driving his cab around the city, cursing at customers who refused to pay the fare and getting into heated arguments with people attempting to rob his taxi; these incidents sometimes escalated and resulted in my dad being stabbed or shot. My dad was always rough around the edges, and when I rode with him around the city to pick up customers, he would raise his voice loudly as he spoke on the phone with his cousins in Haiti and France. Clearly my mother and father were very different, my mother being more graceful and quiet and my dad being a loud, angry presence, but they somehow made it work for the first 18 months of my life. After that, my dad left to chase other women. When I was in middle school, my dad re-entered the picture. It was great. My mother would drive us to Burger King to meet my dad, and we would all sit in the parking lot, eating burgers and fries and catching up on life. Early on, having this simple relationship with my dad seemed fine, but after a few months I found myself getting agitated as I sat in the front passenger seat of his taxi, with my brothers in the back. He'd ask the same few questions: "How's school? Are you doing good in school?" "No boys in your life, right? Don't focus on no boys." "Do you need money for school tomorrow?" I continued to accept the few dollars he'd give us for school, but over time the conversations got shorter. I no longer gave him detailed accounts of what had happened in my life. I kept my responses to just a few words and we'd sit there in silence.

My dad stopped coming around as often and would spend weeks at a time away visiting family, which meant he didn't answer my calls. It was disappointing—even though our relationship at that time consisted of eating fries and milkshakes in a burger joint parking lot every now and then, it was better than not having him around at all. When he did come back around, I pushed aside my frustrations about his absence and talked about my accomplishments instead. I was a teenager then, and I wanted him to be proud of me. His validation would have meant the world to me and I hoped my accomplishments would give him a reason to stay around. This hope proved fruitless, as he soon left town again, but that only made me work harder to make him proud. Coupled with my mother's strict household and high expectations for me to ace my classes, I was constantly working to impress them both.

*****

After my mother passed from cancer, my father became more involved in our lives. He bought me a cell phone so we could stay in contact and he visited more often. But after six months he stopped calling as often and his visits became less frequent, which left me disappointed once again. I finally realized that my dad still preferred his freedom over seeing me, and that's how our relationship has been to this day. I used to pick up Dad's calls no matter how long it had been since we last talked, but the frustration of attempting to find my sense of self while pleasing others led me to develop a new identity on the stage and eventually in my life.

*****

During my senior year of high school, poetry became my therapy, a way to battle with my thoughts on paper, to make sense of pent-up emotions. Slam poetry became a particular focus for me, and I would no longer write just to write. Anything I felt was not worth a slam event was not written down. I eventually was invited to compete in the College Union Poetry Slam Invitational, the biggest college poetry slam event in the country. Halfway through my second performance I froze, so I simply walked off the stage and left the building. I was so focused on the performance that I forgot my place in the poem. I had let my teammates down, but I had let myself down even more, as I had lost a part of me in slam poetry. After that, I stopped performing competitively. I spent the next year and a half writing once again about the things I enjoyed, like Obama and ice, and I now allow myself to write about how I am feeling, even if it is not worthy of a poetry slam. I am still trying to find a voice in my poetry by letting go of the old voice that wrote to please the crowd.

*****

During my transition to college, I had few mentors outside of my family who offered me support. One high school teacher, Mrs. Cameron, encouraged me to network, to try to get to know strangers. "You never know how you can help others and how they will help you" she would say. Mrs. Cameron was the social butterfly I wanted to be, and she pushed me to be just that. As a business teacher and former bank teller, she also taught me financial lessons that were beneficial throughout my college life. I also could count on Mrs. Murrain, a Black woman I'd met through an online college mentorship program. She pushed me to share my story and helped me be selected for the Beating the Odds program, which gave us both the opportunity to meet Michelle Obama at the White House. Despite my mentors and supporters, however, I still had moments during college that were more challenging than anything I could have prepared for.

*****

In the summer after my sophomore year, I became more aware of my identity while taking an African American government course on racial justice. I had been on a quest to find new friends after parting ways with my old friends, as I began to realize that I knew hardly any people of my skin color and background. I had gone to a predominantly Hispanic and Black high school, so I never felt the need to question my "blackness"—I just *was*. One day, while walking past a college lawn party on campus in front of the historically Black dorm, I pulled my phone out to pretend I was busy on a call, as I didn't want to appear alone. But, in truth, I was alone. I realized that simply being African American at a predominantly white institution did not mean that that community was a united front based on the color of our skin.

Earlier that summer, I had reached out to a few students considered part of Dartmouth's Black crowd to make a lunch date, but my messages went unanswered or were forgotten. Things had been different during freshman year, as cliques had not yet been formed and you could find something in common with people just by having a shared racial background. Black women would smile at one another in a kind of solidarity. As time has gone on, however, it appears to me that the Black community on campus had become fragmented. I felt isolated largely because I no longer felt comfortable in certain spaces. My high school friends had been Black, like me, and we were all low income. Now I was surrounded by students who shared my ethnicity but came from more affluent backgrounds. Things such as socioeconomic status and high school education began to separate students; for example, the private school Black students would rarely attend an African event or dinner.

All of this is to say that I felt removed from the campus Black crowd. Even my hair became a political statement. While I was growing up, my mother liked me to wear my hair natural. I sported an afro and rocked my cornrows. During my freshman year of college, I sometimes spent three or four hours a night getting my hair ready for the next day. I was really proud that my hair looked exactly how I wanted it: loud and curly and voluminous! During the spring term I discovered the magical world of wigs! I could switch from straight to wavy to curly in an instant, and this was exciting for me. It was the first time I rocked a sleek, bone straight look and I genuinely enjoyed the different style. At a party one night, when I was wearing the straight wig, a Black student (a friend of mine until this interaction occurred) complimented my hair. He sounded disingenuous, so I asked him to elaborate. He responded, "Well, it's obvious you're playing into respectability politics." I had never felt so patronized and marginalized by someone the same color as me. This guy was known to question the blackness of others and frequently quoted Malcolm X in our Black political theory class, but he also had attended a private school and lived in a predominantly white suburb. My assumption was that, once he got to Dartmouth, he began overcompensating so he would be accepted by the "in crowd."

That night I left the party angry. How could someone accuse me of catering to the majority community because I put on a straight wig? I simply wanted to change my hair style for a while, and I felt this guy was telling me I was not allowed to. I did not want anybody else to tell me what hair style was valid, let alone a Black *man,* or to write me off as trying to conform to norms of "respectability." I still used the slang I learned on the streets of Newark and rocked hoop earrings bigger than this man's head—a man who had never faced the struggles I had as a poor Black girl in the 'hood—and yet he felt entitled to tell me I was "not Black enough." Some days I feel I do not belong at Dartmouth, due to either my identity or my ability. Incidents like the one described highlight why I am insecure about my place at Dartmouth.

It was not intentional, and we have always been cordial towards one another, but I found that my friend groups consisted of students of low socioeconomic status with different racial backgrounds. I ended up joining a predominantly POC sorority after sophomore summer, where my new friend group consisted of lower income students from different parts of the world. Before joining, I struggled to find a space on campus that felt like home base. I began branching out, reaching out friends to grab lunch and inviting newer sorority members to trivia night in my dorm. Eventually, a few months passed and I was spending almost every single night, and sometimes overnight, in this new space. I hadn't even realized a home was in the making.

During high school, my mom didn't want me to be focused on guys. It didn't bother me, as I wasn't pining for a man's validation and no man was offering that to me. But then, before I had my first real relationship, I was sexually assaulted. I understand that I was not at fault and talking through the situation in counseling and writing this chapter have been very helpful, but I am not prepared to go more into detail about the incident. The assault did and does still have a huge impact on how I see men. I almost always feel a man will disappoint me in some way. Another effect of the incident is that I often feel my voice is lost, especially during moments of pressure, which has put me in a few uncomfortable and unfortunate situations.

My first real relationship was during the summer after my freshman year of college, while I was interning in California. Wove, a college student, was also Haitian and from Newark. I was excited! He had a soft aura and was soft-spoken. Wove enjoyed playing the guitar, and one night he played Haitian *kompa* songs for me until I fell asleep. We were on and off for a few weeks, but the relationship ended quickly. It had become toxic; Wove's soft-spoken compliments quickly turned into insults and we got into senseless screaming matches. Ultimately, neither of us was prepared to handle a relationship. I later learned healthier ways to express sadness and jealousy, and I hope he learned the same.

A little after Wove and I parted ways, I met Jake, who was like a rainbow after the storm. He was from New Jersey as well, and we started seeing each other when we both returned home. Jake was an engineer who had recently begun his career at a prestigious company. He had his own house and car and took me out to expensive restaurants. It was all very enticing. My sister was happy that I was with someone who could support me financially. Emotionally, though, not so much. Jake's condominium was decorated with portraits of mathematical equations and complex coding and we had few common interests, but I enjoyed being with him and watching Netflix movies I'd never seen. He treated me in a way I'd never been treated before. Soon I told him I had strong feelings for him, which made him distance himself from me and tell me I deserved better. This only made me want him more. I thought that if I appeared more mature he would want me more, so I wore dresses with matching blazers and started reading up on current events. When that didn't work, I even suggested that we have an open relationship, where we'd still be together but he could see other people. Jake turned this suggestion down, repeating what he always said: "You deserve better." What he didn't realize was that, compared to the men of my past, he was the "better" I felt I deserved. And what I didn't yet realize was that there could be someone truly better in my future, someone who would want me in their life and see me as someone worthy of committing to fully.

After these two relationships, I felt I had failed to make men desire me. The false presentations of myself that I adopted to mold myself to the needs of the two men had ultimately left me alone. Looking back, I understand the incompatibility between these two men and myself. I never would have felt comfortable sharing every part of myself with them. If I measured my happiness based on how genuine I was in those relationships, I was miserable. What's more, there is so much to my identity that they did not get a chance to see. Jake was right in saying I deserved better because I was, and am, better.

*****

After my relationship with Jake I took a break from men for a while. I filled my time by binge-watching shows, beginning meditation sessions, and processing my past relationships—still an ongoing task. It was only after I had ended the relationships that I could see that keeping the attention of the men in my life was a top priority. Even after Wove had hurt my feelings time and time again, I pushed for us to make up, never allowing Wove or myself any space to reconcile our differences. I was prepared to do whatever it took for us to be on good terms again—I once even took an Uber in the middle of the night to take Wove a fruit tart I had baked to make up for a fight! My desire for a man's approval manifested itself in many ways, something I was able to understand through counseling and to begin to deconstruct.

After Wove and Jake, I had a short relationship with a man named Freddy, whose attention became concerning over time. Less than a month after we started dating, he began using phrases like "life partner" and "wife." I initially found it sweet, but when he began to tell me about his past those phrases began to scare me. He had a history of pursuing an ex-girlfriend of his, which ultimately led to an incident involving the police. As time went on his attention began to suffocate me, and I did not know how to voice this. I started to feel like a parent, telling him what to do and when to do it, reminding him about paying cable bills and taking his medication. Finally I realized he had become dependent on me and that I was suffocating. I ended things soon after that, even blocking him on my phone to make sure he couldn't contact me again. He "spam" called me more than a dozen times a day and emailed me saying "we both know" we still belong together. I finally told him that his antics were scaring me and asked him to stop contacting me. I did not want to be with him and I made sure he knew it…I had finally found my voice.

I have yet to find a relationship in which I am not investing more emotional labor than my partner. For a long time, I believed that this was how it should be, given the traditional gender roles I was exposed to while growing up. My mother and the women in my life worked endlessly to make sure their partners were well fed, cleaned up after, taken care of, and more. I have found that this approach leaves the woman with nothing for herself. My counselor, Michelle, to whom I am extremely grateful, once told me life is like a jar of marbles and that it seemed my jar was completely empty when she first met me. I had spent my whole life filling up my jar with love from my mother, my brothers, my poetry, and everything else that brought me happiness. Then, I would begin a relationship, and my jar weighed less because I wanted to give some of that love to my partner, and usually too much. I left no room for love for myself, which made me an anxious mess who always had my partner's concerns on my mind. My time being single has given me the space and freedom to replenish my jar—to truly heal—with the love of friends and sorority memories and new poems that I enjoy performing. It has been quite a journey to really find my voice and to let it sing in all aspects of my life.

I first searched for my voice through poetry, my one true passion. Another way I found my voice was by serving on the student government during my freshman year of college. I knocked on the doors of almost every freshman and attempted to persuade them to vote for me. After being elected, I was able to voice my ideas about more inclusion and help to raise awareness of political issues on campus. But I understand now that that was not my authentic voice. As I continue to receive counseling, I'm learning that, while it's okay to want to help everyone, it's also okay to be selfish sometimes. I am learning to curb my habit of giving all of my energy to everyone else and leaving none for myself.

To tie this issue of gaining my voice into my relationship with my dad, I know now that his pattern of not picking up when I call him played a huge part in my growing up. When he finally called me after one of his recent disappearing spells, I found myself screaming at him. I took the opportunity to let him know how I really felt—that his constant abandonment was hurting me and that he could do better as a father by simply calling me more often. Even though I didn't say all that I wanted to say and I know he still might not call more frequently, at least I know that I used my voice to express how I was feeling. As I practice using my voice, I have to remind myself that, if the other person decides to ignore my feelings, it is completely out of my control—but at least I will have tried. I no longer speak to my father, and in this instance I feel that my silence is the most powerful message I can give the world that I am finally putting my own needs first.

*****

I never felt the need to see a counselor until I realized that my internalized issues and insecurities were negatively affecting my relationships. I originally went to counseling to help understand the root of my jealous tendencies, but five months into counseling I'd unpacked so much more. My counselor's approach to asking questions was nothing I'd ever experienced before. She gave me the space to answer truthfully and to reflect on what those answers meant about my feelings toward myself. We spoke about my relationship with my parents, my insecurities, fears, and hopes, and she always asked questions that helped me ponder the idea of improving the way I navigate life. In my family, counseling wasn't considered normal or beneficial. Though I have been in counseling now for over a year, I have yet to find the courage to tell my family. Nevertheless, I am extremely grateful to receive counseling from Michelle. I never dreamed I would see myself change so much in such a short period of time.

*****

At some point a long time ago I lost my voice, and with it my confidence as well. This happened gradually as I grew up and came to understand that I would have to sacrifice my own voice to please the people in my life. If a conversation at home did not have to do with education or academic goals, I felt no one would care what I had to say. I turned to poetry to find a voice, to create a persona separate from the Haitian girl who always had her head in the books. Now I stand up for myself more often. I have cut off toxic friendships and relationships and taken more opportunities to step outside of my comfort zone. I spend more time self-reflecting, looking at the decisions I make in my life and making sure I do what's best for me. I know it all sounds easy, but this has been a difficult road for me. All of my life I have put the needs of others before my own and, as a result, people have taken advantage of me. Counseling is teaching me to handle my insecurities and address my jealousy head on so that I can maintain healthy, honest relationships with partners and understand that my worth lies within myself—not within anyone else. I am learning every day to be more comfortable in my own skin, especially at a place like Dartmouth, where my identity is constantly being challenged by anything from a conversation about my hair to how I feel when I find myself the only Black woman in a room. I used to fill with anxiety at the thought of speaking in class, which made me avoid raising my hand so as not to bring attention to myself. Now I write out what I want to say and remind myself that I, too, belong at Dartmouth. My college mentor Jay Davis once said, "I know many of you wonder whether you belong here, whether you have 'what it takes.' I am here to tell you not only that do you indeed belong, but that Dartmouth is so, so much better BECAUSE you are here." Had I not reflected on and talked through my problems outside of academics, I would never have come to believe him.

*****

What struck my interest in the class I took on racial justice was the idea of a double burden placed on women. This idea has been wrestled with and redefined by many political theorists within the Black community. It explores violence against women from within their own communities and from other communities, taking the form of labor, controlling their bodies, etc. For so long I put the needs of others before my own and finally found I was not okay with those decisions. My classes on race and politics forced me to grapple with the idea that, for a good portion of my life, I was trying to live up to standards I didn't fully agree with. My time at college has taken me down a path toward choosing my identity. I have found strength in advocating for myself through spoken word poetry and my passion for community service.

I continue to construct and deconstruct the idea of self-advocacy in my counseling sessions, and the person I am now is completely different from the person I was. My sense of self-advocacy could not be found in the girl who grew up in Newark or even the woman I was when I began this essay. After coming to college, I found myself wanting more agency in how I defined myself. At first I searched for it in the men I dated, believing that I should be defined by how well I could provide for someone else. After years of failure and dissatisfaction in feeling I had not found my voice—the kind of voice I had so often seen my mother use to move a congregation to tears on Sunday nights—I searched for it first through my poetry and then through my passion for addressing community issues. I am still learning to define my voice. I am a work in progress.

Coda: I am writing this postface years after I started writing this chapter and so much as changed since. These days, my voice looks like using my queer and trans identity to demand institutional changes at my places of employment and my law school administration. In my personal life, my voice looks like learning from my partner what it looks like to express my needs and have them be heard. I am still learning a lot about what it means to belong in this world, but one thing that has changed over time, the one thread that continues, is that I am learning to show up more authentically.

# 4 Quest for Peace

*Deirdre Harris*

My father was murdered while I was at my Houston, Texas elementary school. I was sitting quietly at my desk working on a class assignment when my teacher informed me that I needed to go home immediately. As I walked the three short blocks to my house, I thought about how good it felt to be outside instead of in that 3rd-grade classroom. I was about halfway home when a weird feeling came over me. Why did I have to go home? Who had sent for me? What was so important that I had to miss school? My parents always said that unless we were dying, we had to go to school. Education was everything. So why was I sent home? Had something happened? I started to worry.

When I walked through the front door of my house, a wave of sickness coursed through my nine-year-old body. Something was not right. Something bad had happened. I could feel it in the air. Although I knew they were there, I didn't really see my brothers and sisters standing in the living room.

My eyes focused immediately on my mother, who was standing in the kitchen. She was the only person I could see. I watched as her skin drained of its natural color, and her beautiful face took on a look of utter despair and terror. Her body trembled as she doubled over, fell to her knees, and cried out, "He's dead, He's dead!" over and over again. I knew who she was talking about at once. I don't know how I knew, but I did. The "he" whom she was crying about, the "he" who was dead, was my father.

My mother lay on the kitchen floor for what seemed like ten minutes with tears streaming down her face and her voice trembling, now barely above a whisper, "They shot him, they shot him. He's dead, he's dead."

At that moment I could not grasp exactly what she meant. My whole body was overwhelmed with sadness, fear, and disbelief. There were so many questions. What happened to Daddy? Where was he? Who shot him? Why? I didn't cry. I didn't scream. I didn't say a word. I was in absolute shock. Nothing was real.

I went to my mother and put my arms around her. She wouldn't stop crying. She couldn't pick herself up from the kitchen floor. She had no strength, no power. What was going on? I was confused. I had never seen her like this before. What did it mean that daddy was dead? I had never known anyone who had died before. What did it mean?

DOI: 10.4324/9781003376255-5

> If you wanna get to heav'n lemme tell you how, juss keep yo' han' on de gospel plow. Keep yo' han' on de plow. Hold on, hold on.
>
> "Hold On," an African American Spiritual

A few months before my father was killed, his doctor told him that he no longer needed his medication or shock treatments. My father believed his doctor, whom he had been seeing for years. "Besides," he told my mother, "I have been taking this medication for half of my life to treat my schizophrenia. Now I am finally able to be normal." But soon after he stopped taking his mediation his behavior became strange. He was no longer the calm and gentle person I've been told he had once been. My sole memory of him is how strange he was acting. He paced back and forth and repeatedly checked all of the windows and doors of the house. Later, he talked to himself and heard voices. His behavior frightened me. What was happening to him? Why was he so fidgety and nervous?

My brothers and sisters and I didn't know that he was sick. We noticed that he was changing, but we couldn't understand why. We were not told that he had an illness. My mother pleaded with him for months to take his medicine again. He refused. She pleaded with the doctor to re-examine him and to make him take his medication again. The doctor refused. He thought that the shock treatments and the medication were no longer necessary. Why not? Didn't he believe that my mother was telling him the truth about the pacing, the nervousness, and the voices? Although she knew that it could have been prevented, she had no other choice but to begin seeking both a restraining order for our safety and the institutionalization of my father for his own safety.

My stepfather is the man whom I refer to as my "dad," as he is the only father I've ever known. (My biological father and mother divorced when I was a baby.) My stepdad was a self-employed watch repairman. He was a gentle man who used to bathe me and my siblings when we were young and volunteered for our little league teams, but he didn't talk much. As a child, I used to sit on his lap and play with him, and he'd ask me questions about how I was doing and how I was feeling. I can't remember the last time I ever saw my dad alive. In fact, I don't remember anything about him. My mother recently told me about how I interacted with him because I have blocked all but one memory. I have no recollection of his face, his voice, or his touch. I refused to remember all that I had shared with him—including his love.

On that morning, January 3, 1979, while people were still saying "Happy New Year" to anyone who would listen, my dad got his gun and drove to his mother's house. The newspapers wrote that neighbors called the police about a man shooting into the air and at parked cars. When the police arrived, no one was outside. My father, the man who had been shooting, was already inside the house. His mother was not home. My father was there alone. The first two officers on the scene tried to get him to open the front door or talk to them. He refused to respond. They called for backup. Carloads of police came and surrounded the house.

They tried coaxing him out using a bullhorn, but he wouldn't budge. They threw tear gas through a couple of windows, and the house caught on fire. My father came running out of the burning house and right into the hands of a great number of policemen. As he ran out, unarmed, they shot him repeatedly, even after he was lying on the ground, unmoving. Witnesses accounts in the newspaper described his limp body dancing on the ground from the impact of the bullets that ripped through him. Their accounts stated that it was "like watching an assassination." The police shot dozens of bullets into my father, an unarmed, mentally ill, Black man.

I was not directly told any of this in great detail. I caught snatches of it here and there, mainly through the TV news, newspapers, grown-ups' whispers, and the interviews my mother gave on our living room couch to hungry reporters night after night.

They would not leave us alone because two officers had been wounded; one died a few days later. There were conflicting accounts about what happened. The official police report stated that they had no choice but to open fire because my father was armed and shooting at them as he ran out of the house. Witnesses to the shooting declared that he was unarmed as he ran out of the burning house. This clear discrepancy was just cause for a year-long FBI investigation which revealed that the police report was a cover-up for the officers' mistake of getting trigger happy on a defenseless Black man. The firefighters' official report showed evidence that the gun that supposedly killed the officer was found charred, on the coffee table in the living room of the burned-down house. My father could not have shot anyone, much less killed someone. As it turned out, one officer had mistakenly shot and killed another officer while trying to shoot my father. The surviving officer injured himself when his gun backfired.

That was the year that I learned what "expendable" meant and to whom the term applied. I could no longer live in a world that saw me, and people who looked like me, as expendable. I could no longer say the Pledge of Allegiance at the beginning of each school day. How could I allow the words "liberty and justice for all" to cross my lips, knowing that they were untrue? Knowing that my dad did not get liberty or justice? Would the white police officers have paid more attention to what was or was not in his hands if my father had been white and not Black? I would simply stand there with my hand over my heart and say nothing. I performed my own silent protest. My country had betrayed me.

I felt very alone and frightened. Which one of us would be killed next? Who would protect the rest of us from doctors who did not care to give us an accurate diagnosis? Who would protect the rest of us from brutes with badges and guns? Who? No one could protect us. It was horrifying to think that no one would come to our rescue, no one would get punished, and no one would care. In fact, the first question would be, "What did you do this time to bring it on yourself?"

My mind searched for a way out of this reality. My self-defense mechanism must have kicked in at that point because somehow I began to distance myself from my emotions. I struggled daily to keep my thoughts and emotions under control. In my all-out effort to protect myself from painful emotions, I had to suppress *all* emotions. I paid a price, however, because this protective measure stripped me of my passions as well as my anguish.

Throughout my schooling, my teachers never noticed that I wasn't saying the pledge to the flag. This oversight, I believe, was because I always did what was expected of me. I never got out of line. I was a "teacher's pet," a class clown, and an athlete. On the first day of school each year, my teachers were usually pleased to know that I was a Johnson kid because we all did well. I strove to be accepted by my classmates and had a smile for everyone all of the time. My father's murder did not phase me. I simply blocked it out of my mind. I never thought about him.

It wasn't too difficult not to think about him or how he died because my family never talked about him. After his funeral, his murder was a taboo subject. In the midst of our denial, however, the police department would call to frighten my mother into not pressing charges against them. They knew that they were wrong and they did not want to be taken to court. The FBI investigation showed clear evidence of police brutality with malicious intent. My mother, a newly widowed Black woman with eight children and only a high school diploma, was scared to death for our safety. She did not want to risk losing anyone else. Her white lawyer convinced her that if she settled out of court she would get monetary retribution, but if she didn't settle, she would get nothing because "Blacks did not win cases against the city" in Texas. So, she settled out of court. A couple of officers were fired, and we received a few thousand dollars. The settlement was able to pay for most of the funeral expenses and all of the lawyer's fees. To me, no amount of money could replace a human life, especially the life of my father.

I didn't witness any anger in my mother, and because she didn't display any anger, I didn't either. I followed her lead because I didn't know how I was supposed to react to this whole thing, other than to try my best to forget that it had ever happened. She said, "Being who we are and where we are has its consequences. That's how things are right now. We have to accept that and go on." Our extended family was nearby, also in Houston. Furthermore, we didn't have the funds to move anywhere else and we needed the support of our friends and family.

We restructured our lives after my father's murder. It took two years to reach a settlement, during which time my mother was preoccupied with finding a way to feed us. She had eight mouths to feed, in addition to her own, and she didn't have a job that could support us all. Mom was a very religious young woman who believed that "God would make a way somehow" and that "if you lived right, talked right, and prayed right, then heaven belonged to you." For a while we had food and clothes, and most of our bills were being paid. The bank miraculously allowed a one-year grace period for the house notes, which kept a roof over our heads. But we had less and less food, and funds were always low or even non-existent. We could no longer afford to take piano lessons, or play on little league teams. We could no longer take ballet lessons or drama classes. All of these things stopped abruptly. We understood that we had no money, so we didn't complain.

However, we couldn't understand why we didn't have food to eat. At one time or another, we each complained to our frustrated and overwhelmed mother that we were hungry. I'm sure that she hated to see us go to bed hungry, to wake up hungry, and to send us to school hungry. How could we learn when our minds were drawn to our stomachs and our hunger pangs? We were also constantly growing, but we couldn't afford to buy clothes. My relatives and people from the church and community gave us their old clothes to wear. We had to take the public bus everywhere or walk because our car had burned along with our grandmother's house. My mother eventually had to go on public assistance until she could acquire enough skills to get a job that paid well enough to feed us and put clothes on our backs. I hated the stigma of food stamps and school lunch cards. Being poor is "sinful" in this society, and I learned to be ashamed of our poverty, although I knew that what had happened to us was not our fault. Our sense of humor sharpened; we had to laugh to keep from crying, because our existence was so dismal.

I started constantly misplacing things and forgetting what I was saying in the middle of sentences because I had difficulty dealing with the present. I lost the ability or the will to concentrate. I was always so spaced out that I acquired the new nickname "the absent-minded professor" at home. Upon my father's death, my books, my writing, and my mother became my world. It was difficult being Black and female and having a creative relationship with words while growing up in Houston. My verbal expression was indicative of my different way of thinking, and it set me apart from my siblings. I am the sixth child out of eight. I have four older brothers, one older sister, and a younger sister and brother. I felt misunderstood by them because of their teasing. My use of language caused me to stick out. Like most Texans I used words and phrases like "y'all" and "fixin' to," but I didn't have the drawl or the dialect of most Southern Black people. Being an avid reader gave me a different vocabulary, and it also sharpened my thought processes. The combined effect of people, culture, and the shaping of language fascinated me. I read books about how people in various cultures lived and I took notice of how language shaped their interaction, their environment, and each other. I became fascinated with the possibilities of what could be, which helped to ameliorate my pain.

Something spiritual stirred inside of me when I expressed myself on paper. I used writing to take me away from everything. This desire to write down what was on my mind was an inexplicable, yet exceedingly powerful force. In sports I could only express myself within the boundaries of the game. Usually that was enough, as I could release a lot of frustration in a non-self-destructive way. But writing was an experience without restrictions. I wrote poetry about race relations, the oppression of females, religion, violence, and longings. I felt free of these things when I wrote about them, lessening the power of their hold on me. I felt like a healer and a creator. I felt important without feeling judged or alienated. I felt complete, lacking nothing. I spent as much time writing and reading as I possibly could. Only on rare occasions did I share my poetry. I learned very early in my life to fear sharing such deep emotions and thoughts with anyone.

I never thought to assign value to my way of thinking because it came naturally to me. Other people, however, valued my thinking process. They never let me forget that I was different. "You don't talk like us," they would say. "You soun' like a white girl." I wanted to forget that I was different because it made other people uncomfortable, which made interactions between us difficult. This made me uncomfortable with myself.

Like most people, my siblings often mistook my different way of thinking for me wanting to be something or someone other than who and what I was. "Why she talk propa' like white people? She muss wanna be white," they agreed among themselves, unable to understand or make sense of my unique behavior. This was not a compliment. They believed, as did I, that white people were greedy and violent. Nevertheless, because I would not conceal my intelligence, they would exclaim, "You're an Oreo!" with great conviction.

Ever since I could speak, my brothers and sisters insulted me, and this continued throughout high school. I could not understand how the way I spoke indicated to them what I "muss wanna be." Still, my self-expression became unacceptable to me because it was unacceptable to others. I began to believe that I could not accept myself until other Black people accepted me. New doubts augmented the loss of self-worth I had experienced upon my father's murder.

In my effort to be accepted, I found myself making constant readjustments so that I would not stand out. I didn't want to be considered different. My siblings taught me that to be singled out intellectually among other Black people meant automatic rejection. If I were rejected by my Black sisters and brothers, then I had nowhere left to turn for comfort or protection. Their negative reactions taught me to be silent or to suffer consequences. By the time I reached adolescence, I had become silent, reactionary, defensive, and eager to be accepted. When I met other Black people I would wait for them to speak before I opened my mouth. This allowed me to judge the way that they expressed themselves so that I could have some idea of how they would regard me after hearing me speak.

The only person who constantly supported me through life and didn't think me a "freak" was my mother. A teacher's aide, she took an active interest in the education of all her children. Beaming, she would introduce me to people as "the smart one," which, although it saddened me somewhat, always made me feel that she was on my side. It seemed to make her happy to tell people that I was smart, so I dealt with the consequences. One consequence was that it made me very aware that I was different from my siblings. Throughout my childhood, strangers would exclaim, "This one here is going to college." I felt like a curiosity, somehow alienated, as if I were more desirable, yet less understood than my siblings. My mother's acknowledgment of my intellect seemed to give them permission to tease me, to dislike me, and to question my "blackness." They had bought into white stereotypes of Black people—that we must all be alike, and that we could not excel intellectually, only athletically. My siblings had other gifts such as visual artistry, athletics, and technical knowledge, but I was the first one to go to a four-year college. I felt all the pressure was on me to succeed on behalf of my family.

I had conflicts sharing a bed with my two sisters, and the only other place available was with my mother in her king-sized bed. So I shared a bed with my mother from grade school until I left for college. That shift in sleeping arrangements shaped the dynamics of my relationship with my two sisters until high school. Pam, who is two years younger than me, became very close to my older sister, Cynthia. They shared laughter, clothing, and secrets. They made fun of me while I looked on, feeling left out, lonely, and betrayed. They were friends. It was them against me. I escaped into my books and writing even more. It wasn't until Pam and I attended the same high school that we became friends.

The new sleeping arrangements also influenced my relationship with my mother. After mom became a widow, I tried, in my little kid kind of kid way, to make sure that she was ok. At night I'd occasionally hear her crying herself to sleep and I would ask her why she was crying. She really missed dad. I didn't have tears of my own to shed. I was not an orphan because I still had mom. She, on the other hand, had lost everything that our society said gave her worth—her husband. At that point I swore to never allow myself to become dependent on anyone or anything other than myself.

Though I continued to do well in school, I was struggling to hide my anxiety. I lived with the fear that someone else in my family was going to be killed. I didn't feel safe anywhere but I didn't show this fear. I put on smiles for everyone. Through the years, my mom and I became each other's confidante, but I couldn't share these thoughts with her. I knew better than to break the family taboo of talking about our father's murder.

Beginning in third grade, each year I was bussed to one school or another to be in special programs for "gifted" students where most kids were white, a handful were Mexican American, and only a few were African American or Asian American. I had become very conscious of race and of people noticing me. I spent a lot of time with Constance, whom I met when I first switched schools in fourth grade. She mostly kept to herself at school, but after school Constance hung out at the YWCA located directly across the street from her house. It didn't cost anything to attend, so I went with her. The two of us became inseparable. We shared secrets, and I slept over at her house sometimes. She loved to read as much as I did, so we exchanged library books. We remained best friends throughout junior high school, where we were placed in the same honors classes.

The summer before I started high school, when I was fourteen years old, I was molested by a stranger in my home. The house was being renovated that summer. One day the plumber and I were the only people in the house. He asked me to go back to the unfinished bathroom with him to show me what kind of pipe I needed to tell my mother to get. I had no reason not to believe him, yet as soon as we got to the bathroom I felt uneasy. The bathroom was very small, and he was standing much too close to me. Even more disturbing was the fact that he was standing between me and the door. He shut it behind him. When I turned around to ask what he was talking about, he pounced on me. He pushed me up against the wall and began groping me. I tried to fight him off but he was so big. His hands were all over me. My heart was beating fast. I had to get out of there. I tried talking him into letting me go. He wasn't listening. I tried to hit him, but he just grabbed my hands and pinned me hard against the wall and made me touch him. I panicked even more. Sweat was pouring down his white face and his hot breath was all over me, I almost got sick. Finally, after much struggling, groping, screaming, and fast talking, he let me go. I ran into my sisters' bedroom. There was no lock on the door, so I put furniture up against it. I curled up on the bed in a fetal position and tried to block out what had just happened.

The only thing that my mother had to say about sex was that it was to be saved for marriage, and I thought that it would upset my mom too much to tell her that I was molested. I didn't want to make her feel bad. I tried to protect her and I felt as if I were to blame. The reaction to my father's murder taught me that denial and silence were how to handle traumatic events in my life. I was becoming accustomed to suffering alone in silence. Constance was the only person that I felt I could tell. The next day I biked over to Constance's house and told her what had transpired. I was very upset and crying and I wanted to forget. But I could not forget. Instead, I stuck the memory in that section of my brain where I put things I couldn't handle. I was getting better at denying traumatic events. While my house was being completed, I spent time at Constance's; I didn't feel safe in my own home anymore.

Apparently, molestation was becoming an important issue in this country at that time. I read articles and books and watched a TV movie called *Something About Amelia* about a girl who was sexually abused by her father. I learned that it wasn't my fault. My body belonged to me. Still, I couldn't help but feel responsible in some way. I told myself I shouldn't have been there, but then reminded myself that I was in my own home and I had every right to be there. I was supposed to be safe at home. After the incident, I wanted to be invisible.

My grandmother died about a month later. I wasn't sure how much more I could take. I wanted to scream NO at the top of my lungs to let out the pain that I was feeling. I didn't want males looking at me. I started wearing really oversized t-shirts and baggy jeans and shorts. I kept to myself. I felt trapped in a body that no longer belonged to me. I felt trapped in a life that I didn't want.

When school started I dove into my schoolwork and tried to keep my chin up. It was difficult having guys close to me, and I became very suspicious of them. I didn't want to be touched by anyone, but at the same time I needed to be comforted. I couldn't bring myself to tell my mother about what had happened, but I needed her reassurance that everything was going to be okay. I would sit on her lap and hug her. She would call me her "big baby" and roll her eyes but I didn't care as long as she held me. I forced myself to smile and pretend that everything was okay. I tried to project outward the security I craved inside. I longed to feel calm, but my stomach was always in knots and I never felt the same as before I was molested. I always felt on edge but tried hard not to show it.

My days were filled with church activities, school, reading books that I borrowed from the library, and hanging out with Constance at the YWCA. I listened to my brothers' and sisters' conflicts with mom, but I told myself that I didn't have any. I denied the fact that I was sexually assaulted. I was the perfect daughter who never gave mom any trouble nor had any problems. I did what I thought she expected of me. I did well in school, did not show any interest in boys, and put God first. I convinced myself that I also wanted these things for myself. Constance, though, was getting out of control. Her grandparents, who had raised her and her younger sister, both died within six months of each other and a few months before we started high school. Her mother moved into the house with Constance and her sister. Constance and her mom fought a lot. She needed things that I was incapable of giving her because I, too, was struggling. On weekends spent with her cousin, she was introduced to drugs. Before long she was skipping school and shooting up. I kept asking her why she was doing this to herself, but she didn't know why. I stopped asking her why, but I warned her about HIV transmission through sharing needles. We grew apart.

> Sister, you've been on my mind. Oh sister, we're two of a kind
> So sister, I'm keepin' my eyes on you.
>
> "Miss Celie's Blues," *The Color Purple*

At the same time that Constance and I were growing apart, Trisha and I were growing closer. Trisha intimidated me, but she was so appealing that I could not resist trying to know her and spend time with her. She had a radiant energy about her that was captivating. She and I both ranked first in our class the first semester of our freshman year. We were recommended by our math and science teachers for a special program for minority students. She didn't want to go, but I did.

The program at a New England boarding school lasted for six weeks each summer in high school. It opened up a whole new world for me. For the first time in my life, I was interacting with Black students who were smart like me. It amazed me that they were not afraid to show their intelligence. For the first time in my life, I felt ok about being young, gifted, and Black. The classes were surprisingly challenging. In the public schools back home I was usually bored, but there I constantly learned new things. I didn't feel compelled to stifle my enthusiasm for learning. I was, however, disturbed by the great discrepancy between my public school education and my private school education which was so much better than what I got in public school. It upset me that I had to get a full scholarship to attend a school far away from home to get a challenging education. Most inner-city kids could not afford to wait on such "thoughtfulness" because most times it did not come.

Back in public school my sophomore year, I decided that I was wasting my time at the Medical Professions High School. I wanted to own a bookstore and sell books by and about Black people. I also couldn't stand to watch Constance slowly killing herself and not be able to do anything about it. I also knew I didn't want to be a doctor. After my father's misdiagnosis, I grew to mistrust doctors. So, I transferred to the Finance Professions High School, also known as FPHS. Before I left, I explained to Constance that I was not abandoning her. My mother asked why I wasn't spending as much time with Constance, so I told her she was doing drugs. There was nothing left to say. We were both familiar with how drugs were invading and devastating our own community and even our own home. Two of my older brothers' drug of choice was alcohol. In a drunken rage one night, one of them put his head through a wall, yelling that he wished he were dead. I thought to myself that he wasn't the only who wished to be dead.

The magnet program at the new school had dedicated teachers. My favorite teacher, Jim Trails, took time out of classes when he saw that something was bothering us. I felt comfortable talking to him. However, the atmosphere there was so depressing. The feeling of poverty and hopelessness hung in the air. Many teenage mothers attended the regular, nonmagnet high school because free child care was provided for the students' children. I felt other people's pain like it was my own.

I missed Trisha a lot also. We kept in touch by phone, but I wanted to see her. I called her two nights before Christmas when she said that she would be home, but strangely, no one answered. The next morning someone called very early, but I didn't answer the phone. A couple of minutes later Cynthia came in and woke me up with shocking news: Trisha had been killed in a car accident the night before. She was driving her parents' car home from her church's youth group meeting when she lost control. Her brother was seriously injured, but he had survived. I went numb.

That Christmas break, I felt ready to die. My heart felt so heavy. I marveled at the peace that I would surely have if I were dead. That's all I thought about for months. I didn't know how much more I could take without breaking down. Fortunately, Panu, who would become my good friend, transferred to FPH$ the next semester, so I didn't feel so alone. In fact, because I was a counselor's assistant, it was my duty to show her around the campus. When I walked into the counselor's office, our eyes met and smiles lit up our faces that whispered, "Where have you been?"

My attraction to females began to surface a little because of Panu, but I still wasn't ready to acknowledge my attraction. She shared her poetry with me. She was first-generation American, and her parents were strict. Half an hour on the phone in the evenings was her limit, so we wrote letters to each other almost daily and exchanged them at school the next day. Panu invited me to her home often for dinner and to spend the night. We slept together in her full-size bed, but we made sure not to touch each other at all. Her parents got to know me very well through our in-depth conversations about India's culture and languages. Her father and I had many debates about the value placed on male and female children in Pakistani culture. Occasionally Panu's parents would lend her the car to go to a movie or to the mall on the weekend, but only if I were going because they trusted me.

I think that there was a mutual attraction between us. She and another friend would praise my body parts when the three of us were alone. Panu would feel my behind as we walked down the hall or up the stairwell. I was definitely attracted to her, but I couldn't bring myself to return her touch. We never talked about what her "love pats" were about.

By the time I was sixteen or seventeen years old, I disagreed with church teachings which were prejudiced against people who were different. The minister, whom I looked up to, said that homosexuality was wrong and that women should submit to men. I wanted no part of that, but I went to church anyway because it was expected of me and I didn't want to disappoint my mom. I also had become dependent on gospel music as a source of strength. I learned to take what was good from the sermons and leave the rest at the church.

The summer before my senior year, I went to the last session of summer boarding school. It was great to return and see my old friends again. I had become good friends with a girl from New York City named Lisa, and that summer we were roommates. One day, I got surprising news from one of my public high school friends. She sent a newspaper clipping that said people with HIV shouldn't be allowed to teach, and there was a feature story on Jim Trails. My favorite teacher had died. Once again, I suppressed my feelings and threw myself into my work.

That summer, our class visited colleges in New England. Lisa and I both decided that we wanted to go to the same New England college. I liked the campus and the students and the administrators that I met on our visit, but mostly I liked the foreign study and language programs. I agonized over how I'd be received in this predominantly white college environment. I decided to apply because it was my right to go wherever I was accepted.

> They said I wouldn't make it. They said I wouldn't be here
> today. They said I'd never amount to anything. But I'm glad to
> say that I'm on my way, and I'm growing more and more each day.
> Though I've been talked about and I've been criticized
> I've had to wipe so many tears from my eyes. But I'm still
> holding on to His hand.
>
> "I'm Still Holding On," a gospel song,

Lisa and I were both accepted to the same New England college and we were roommates as freshmen. Our friendship didn't last the year. Lisa spent a lot of time in the room with her boyfriend. I studied best in my room and had problems concentrating because she and her boyfriend were so loud. She would try to be more considerate, but it never lasted. Her boyfriend, Chris, had moved in by the middle of fall term. Lisa got upset with me for locking our personal bathroom door while I showered. Between clenched teeth she said, "Deirdre, you need to keep the bathroom door unlocked. Chris had to go down four flights of stairs to use the public bathroom." I couldn't make her understand my need to feel safe. She didn't know about my molestation and my fear. By the end freshman year we weren't even speaking.

In addition to attending classes, I joined the school's gospel choir, worked and did some community service. Although I didn't attend church services regularly, gospel music and other African American music helped me to through many days. Music reminded me that my ancestors, who suffered through the Middle Passage and were enslaved, had paved the way for me to be where I was and to make the choices I made. In meditation, I drew upon their strength.

I also became close to Eddie, a guy from my home city. We clicked immediately. We felt incredibly comfortable with each other. We spent a lot of time together and became best friends. He was having a hard time at college. He was gay, Black, and, like me, had little or no financial support from home. When he confided in me about his sexuality, we became even closer. Part of me felt that I could open up to him even more because his gay identity made me feel safe with him. I didn't think that he would want to get close to me sexually. I grew up believing in society's assumption of heterosexuality; I naturally assumed that I was heterosexual although I hadn't even dated yet.

Freshman winter, Eddie decided that he had to leave college. I panicked. I felt as if I was going to die if he left me. After a while and after much analyzing, I told him that my dad had died when I was younger and that I never got to say good-bye. I told him about projecting my unresolved feelings for my dad onto him. He understood, but he had to leave anyway. After Eddie left, I had no support whatsoever. I tried to explain to my mom why I wasn't happy, but she couldn't understand. She pushed me into staying. "Oh, you're tough, you can stick it out," she said. So I stuck it out.

This particular college was not good for my self-esteem. I stopped writing poetry my freshman year. Most other African Americans acted as if they were from higher economic classes than me, and they mainly seemed to be concerned with which elite Black Greek house to join. Whites could not relate to what I felt at all. They couldn't seem to grasp that two or more drastically different realities could exist simultaneously. They were resistant to and doubtful of the validity of my thoughts, feelings, and reality. I believe their mistrust was due mainly to ignorance and fear, rather than hate.

College, for the most part, was a debilitating experience to endure rather than an empowering experience to embrace. Gradually, my spirit broke. I could not force myself to smile any longer. Many of my classmates' spirits seemed broken too. That is why Eddie left. What does this college do to us that breaks our spirit? For my part, I felt stifled, suffocated, and lacking a support system.

Although Eddie left, he and I remained close. I saw him during breaks from school. By sophomore year, I found myself falling in love with him, but I was confused because I thought that I was attracted to women. I just wasn't sure of anything. Eddie was sure, though, and he said that he must be bisexual because he had fallen in love with me. I told him that I liked him a lot but that I thought that I was attracted to women. He quickly yelled, "NO, you can't be!" He was the first person I told. It took me 2 years before I could voice that again. I dated only men throughout the rest of college. In fact, while I was on exchange at a university in California, I got engaged to Dan, a guy I loved dearly, but I was not "in love" with him.

> We who believe in freedom cannot rest.When will the killing of Black men, Black mothers' sons be as important as the killing of white men, white mothers' sons? We who believe in freedom cannot rest until it comes.
>
> "Ella's Song," Sweet Honey in the Rock

Up until the first week of May of my senior year in college, I never talked about my father to anyone except Eddie. It was much easier to push this loss out of my mind and to concentrate on achieving. I was pleasing my mother and preparing myself for independence. When the video of the Rodney King beating came out, I was not surprised. I was horrified, but not surprised. I wasn't that naive. Police brutality was nothing new to me. Still, I did not know how to react to it. Occasionally, I'd think that maybe this time would be different. Maybe, just maybe, our lives would be valued and something would be done. The video was proof to the rest of America what we've always known in the Black community—that Black people are second-class citizens, not protected under the law, nor by the law's enforcers. In my gut, I knew that the people responsible for King's beating would get around the law somehow. They always did, and I had to acknowledge that fact.

Although the television stations played the King videotape as if it were going out of style, it wasn't until the verdict was announced that I was able to feel any emotion and begin to mourn the loss of my father. My fiancé, Dan, called and told me the news. My heart sank. Although I expected the acquittal, I really didn't want to accept it. My mind groped for any hope at all I had for humanity. I hung up in total shock. I just went to bed and tried to think about something else.

I awoke the next morning, and the reality of the previous night's telephone conversation hit me. The acquittal of the LAPD officers represented yet another bullet through the heart of my father, to whom justice had also been denied. All hope for humanity left me. I tried to get out of bed, but my legs could not hold me up. I fell onto the floor next to my bed and tears came streaming out. I had no control over myself. My whole body was in convulsions. I think that I passed out at some point, but I don't recall. I remember raising my head from the floor and thinking that daddy was dead and that we were getting beaten and killed in the name of the law. Daddy was dead, and I didn't get to tell him that I loved him. I didn't get a chance to say good-bye. A knot formed in my throat, in my chest, and in my stomach. I was terrified. I felt like a helpless little kid who was confused and couldn't find her way. I didn't know what to do with my anger, but I knew that I had a right to it. I had a right to express that anger too.

I was afraid of my emotions, but most of all, I was afraid of my anger. Expression of anger is unacceptable even when it is legitimate. This perception is especially true for women. Our society has no acceptable way of expressing anger. Therefore, Black people's anger in this country has been left invalidated, which causes it to accumulate, to create a climate of hostility. I knew that most white people would not understand this concept. That would be acknowledging too much. They refuse to accept this concept because they continue to flourish financially from social conditions like the legacy of slavery and the "good ole boy" network.

My mother's comfort and happiness has always been a priority over my own. How could I express my anger without alienating myself from her and other people? I was determined not to be a part of the disappointment or chaos following the King verdict. This determination came at a great emotional and psychological price to me. It may have also had a physical price. My senior fall I found a hard lump in my right breast while performing my monthly breast self-examination. Upon discovering this intruder, I wondered where my rage had gone. If the rage didn't leave my body. then where did it go?

I went to class that morning, but I couldn't understand what people were saying. The professor mentioned the King verdict at the beginning of class, and afterward I went up to her and asked if she could make any sense of it. She could not. I found myself blurting out that my father had been unjustly murdered by police officers when I was nine years old. She and the other students who were standing nearby didn't know what to say. How is someone supposed to react to something like that? I felt so alone and confused as I went back to my room and tried to make sense of my existence. I couldn't think straight at all. I was in a daze.

All alone in my room, I cried for the loss of my father. All that I could do was cry. I cried for my inability to change the state of the world. I felt helpless and hopeless, and for the first time in my life I was able to admit those things to myself. I felt that whatever I could possibly do was never going to be enough. Why was I in college if I couldn't change things? I tried to get involved in the rallies and other things that were going on. but I was not really there. I had no strength.

On Monday morning, I called a counselor that I had been seeing over at the student infirmary about my sexuality and about why the time I spent with my fiancé was harder than the time we spent apart. I told her that I couldn't recall the last time that I had eaten or had a good night's rest. She strongly recommended that I stay in the infirmary so that I could rest and start eating again. I was there for a week and was medicated for my depression. I phoned my fiancé and told him where I was. After much debate, I phoned my mom and told her where I was and why I was there. I could hear her disappointment. She couldn't quite understand why I was allowing myself to think about my father. She wanted to protect me from this pain, but I told her that it was already too late. I finally found enough courage to allow myself to think about him and how he died. I asked her to send me some of the newspaper articles about his murder that she kept in the file cabinet in her bedroom closet. She refused.

I got angry at her, but I didn't tell her so. She answered a few questions that I had about the murder, but she urged me not to let my mind get caught up in that pain but to keep on going. I should be concerned with my studies and forget about this mess because "God will take care of it," she said. I told her that God has given us the ability to take care of it ourselves. She was trying to protect herself from her own doubt, fear, pain, and loss. I didn't tell any of my friends where I was. I felt that no one knew exactly what I was going through and so they couldn't possibly help me, other than by giving me time and space to get through this.

Upon the suggestion of my counselor, I began to write poetry again. I felt so much better while I wrote poetry. I allowed myself to connect with the pain and sorrow that comes with grief and mourning. I didn't fight it any more. I let it all out. I wrote a letter to my dad. I wrote a letter to the Houston Police Department. But mostly I wrote poetry. One poem in particular, entitled "Discomforting Thoughts," helped me to get all of my feelings out in a coherent way.

When daddy was murdered
my universe was no longer together.
I was no longer together.
There was only chaos, fear
and loneliness within me,
and in the world around me.

I constructed a high wall around me
to shield myself from everyone.
Everyone who had expectations of me
and from others who did not
yet know my name.
I could not let anyone know
that I knew that the world was not
perfect.
That I was not perfect.

"Everything's fine,"
said the nine-year-old smile
that I politely pasted onto my face
I had to put on an innocent smile for
everyone.

Only rarely could I smile for myself.
Others needed the reassurance
more than I.
Besides, what was there to smile
about?
How could I let them down
without letting myself down?
Either way I was dying.
A part of me is dying every day.
Who could I talk to about
my fears, my frustrations, my failures?
Oh, and I do fear, I get frustrated, and
I do fail.

Why does it seem as if I am not
allowed to fail? I am human, right?
Why do I have such different thoughts
from my peers?
We do not speak the same language.
Not inherently, for I always speak
in terms for others to understand.
In the process, I lost a part of me.
I lost the meaning of my words,
and what I really meant.

Why am I so different,
and feel things so differently?
I appreciate my differences
—my uniqueness makes me special.
But it also makes me lonely.
It places unfair burdens on me.
On the outside I put on a front that
I've learned to hide behind
It's called being polite, being a clown,
and being the intellect.
Doing the expected thing.
Always answering 'fine" and "okay"
when I am not fine, and when I am not
okay.

I hide the tears behind the laughter.
But how can I honestly cry
for having lost someone that I refuse
to remember ever having? Daddy.
The word seems so alien to me,

even coming from my own lips.
That's a word that the other kids used.
They were so certain that they'd get a
response from their calls to their
daddies.

What is it like to have a father, a
daddy?
Why don't I know what it's like to be
protected from hate and ignorance?

Why can't I let others know that I
hurt?
Why can't I admit to myself that I
have pain?
Why is everyone else's comfort
such a priority over my own?

I don't want to let momma down.
She works hard to make sure that I'm
okay.
She loves me and supports me,
so how can I tell her that there are
things
that I need that she can't possibly
offer?
Things that she does not understand?

Mom, I'm separate from you.
We are two different people.
You can't always speak for me.
I have to do that for myself now.
I know that I have to be strong.
That's one of the many things
that you've taught me.
But do I have to be strong all of the
time?
When do I get to be me?
A person with vulnerabilities and
dreams.
Maybe I'm not as strong or sure as I
let on.
I'm not yours or anyone else's Super-
woman.
In fact, I despise the term!
I am tired

Although writing poetry helped me to gather my thoughts, it was not enough. I still felt so much rage. Still, I was able to sleep and eat more and was released from the infirmary.

I happened to be taking a self-defense class for women at that time, and a couple of male volunteers came in to simulate physical attacks. They wore protective gear, so when it was my turn I went off on them. While I was fighting them off, I thought of them as police officers like the ones who killed my dad, the ones who beat my brothers, and the ones who beat Rodney King. I also thought of them as the plumber. I had so much rage inside that I vented onto them. While I was beating them, the other women in the class cheered me on and afterward they applauded me. I simply did everything that we were taught to do, but I felt bad getting praised for beating people up. I have felt so beaten down that I had trouble beating others, even defending my own life. Who had taught me that my life was less valuable than my attackers' lives were? Why did I believe that bullshit? After I finished with the men, they took off their face masks and sat out for a while. One of them had a bruised eye. I felt that I should apologize for hurting them, but I couldn't. I had to protect myself. They knew what they were getting into when they took on the job. I did ask them if they were okay. I told them that I felt bad, but they had these cheesy grins on their faces and said, "No, no, you were great!" If I was so great, then why did I feel so bad?

Reality was beginning to set in again. I was getting concerned about my classes. My professors knew that I would be in the infirmary for a few days, but I had to catch up on my work if I expected to graduate the next month as planned. I had three midterm exams to make up, in addition to papers. I had been doing very well in my classes until I went into the infirmary, but when I took my exams I couldn't concentrate. A week or two after I completed my exams, I finally felt like myself again. I resorted to blocking out my feelings and concentrated on my schoolwork. My key motivation was the fact that upon the completion of my course work, I could get out of there. I could leave this college and its discontents behind me and begin to nurture my broken spirit in a healthy environment of my choice. The sooner done, the better. I finished with grades ranging from B+ to A .

I am still struggling with my anger, but I've come to realize that emotions can be controlled. At least I know that I won't hurt anyone by allowing myself to be angry. I feel as if I can finally be myself and not have to live up to people's expectations. I'm living for me now, not for my mom or anyone else. I've learned that I cannot be held accountable for other people's feelings, especially my mother's. I am going to have a talk with her face-to-face and tell her how I feel. It's ok to be angry, even at those people we love the most. It's ok to remember someone who is dead. I feel as if I can finally say good-bye to my father.

(A follow-up life story by Deirdre appears in Part IV of this anthology.)

# Part II

# Both In and Outside of Blackness

# 5 Outside and Between

*Zane Williams*

I've always wanted to make sure nobody could ever say I was given a leg up on account of my blackness. I don't see my blackness as a crutch to lean on, so how dare anyone else? No, I am not an affirmative action case. No, I was not chosen to fulfill any quota. I deserve my place.

This is what I told myself every day, along with a litany of other pep talk: Your hair *is* cool, not straight and blonde, but just as sweet; you *are* good-looking, not thin-lipped or pointy-nosed, but handsome nonetheless (after all, you were picked as a Hollister model, right?); and on it went. Over time I began to realize that there's not much I could do about how I look; I can't change my physiognomy to make me more "legitimate" in the eyes of American social constructs. But what I can do is outperform everyone else and make sure everyone knows they're being outperformed—by the Black guy.

I push myself right up to the line of breaking down. I operate in the blurred space between what's possible and what's not, all the while being careful to uphold my personal values and priorities. I affect a façade of effortlessness while striving to perform to the highest expectations, and I constantly feel the need to remind people how smart I am—how much *smarter* I am. Some would say that truly gifted people don't have to talk about it; I say that truly gifted Black people do. This reminder may come across as arrogant to some who aren't privy to my internal dilemma, and perhaps even as self-serving. I would agree that it is, indeed, extremely self-serving, but not in the usual sense: it is self-serving in that it helps me alleviate my inferiority complex—a complex resulting from American society's perceptions of my skin color. When you grow up expected to get mediocre grades, to be accepted into a mediocre high school and a mediocre university, to get a mediocre middle-management job, and so on, despite being exposed to the same high-level privileges of your white peers, you can't help but do one of two things: accept what's been laid out for you, or rebuke it by proving your worth beyond any reasonable doubt.

The way I have dealt with my lifelong inferiority complex is by consciously transforming it into a superiority complex. I have a distinct sense of satisfaction when a peer exclaims, "Oh my god! You're a double major AND minor?!" "How many citations do you have?!" "You're co-director of that too?!" While they are surprised that anyone can pull it off, I believe they are particularly

DOI: 10.4324/9781003376255-7

astonished to see a Black person overachieving. And I love being the cause of that astonishment.

I recall introducing myself to a top executive while on the elevator at the luxury design firm in New York City where I was interning. Without even taking her eyes off the elevator door, she asked with polite annoyance where I went to school and what I studied. When I answered, "Dartmouth" and told her "I'm an English and studio art double major and a French minor," she turned around and looked me up and down. "Oh really! Well then, we'll talk later." I felt satisfaction at her astonishment, and I later was introduced to three vice presidents of the corporation. Was it because the executive was generally impressed by me, or was she impressed by my ambitious course load despite my blackness? I'll never know the reasons, but I do know the end result: I can control what I have to offer and how I present that offering.

So, my answer to the inevitable and often unspoken question about whether I have "earned" my place is to point out that it is a stupid question to begin with. In doing so, some in the Black community have accused me of being the worst kind of Black person—the kind who wants to present himself as better than the rest of the Black population, as a white appeaser who constantly reminds everyone that he is better than his fellow oppressed ones. To them I say that I think every Black person should be allowed to cope with low expectations however they see fit, so don't criticize my way. I just won't bother with underachievement. As James Baldwin so eloquently wrote,

> "There are, no doubt, as many ways of coping with the resulting complex of tensions as there are Black men in the world, but no Black man can hope ever to be entirely liberated from this internal warfare—rage, dissembling, and contempt having inevitably accompanied his first realization of the power of white men."
>
> (Baldwin 1955)

While attending my mostly white middle school, I began to reflect on the social nuances of my blackness. My thoughts went something like this:

Somewhere deep down I know that I'll never be able to be like you, Blake—effortlessly relevant, coolly confident, and openly ambivalent. I know I'll never have the surfer boy hair swoop the girls in our grade swoon over; and somewhere, deep down, I know that playing electric guitar and skateboarding won't look the same on me. It's clear to me that I can't be dumb and mean to girls and still have them write notes to each other about how cute I am. I know that I'll never be able to be like you, but I hoped I'd at least be accepted by you. When you invited me to your house today because I was standing nearby when you told Ricky and Josh they should come over after school to shoot hoops, I was so excited—finally, the chance to be one of them. You said you'd text me when it was chill to come over, and I played it off like I'd see if I had time … but now it's been five hours and the sun is down and every minute I lose hope that I'll have my chance to hang out with the guys … I don't know why I'm so bent out of shape that the dumbest kid in our sixth-grade class didn't text me to hang out. Why am I allowing myself to feel like this? I mean, I wasted my entire evening thinking about how badly I wanted to be a part of that group and go to Blake's house … Pathetic.

So what is that sense of wanting to feel a part of something that you're not truly interested in, of wanting something because it's being denied? As far back as I can remember, I've wanted to be part of the boys' club—or in the case of Pasadena Christian School, the white boys' club. For some reason I was an outsider to them. Their parents didn't invite me to play dates and sleepovers, and despite being a head taller than most of them I was always the last picked for playground games. Something was different. This continued through middle school—standing next to the table of "cool" white guys sitting down to eat lunch, leaning against the fence under the shade "with" them and pretending to laugh at vapid fart jokes. I wanted—*oh, how I wanted*—to be part of that group. What was this desire to be a part of a group I wanted nothing to do with?

## Outside and between, outside and between, sometimes I wish I could truly be seen

A feeling of belonging, always complicated and fleeting, is my constant search, but all too often my betweenness gets in the way. More than an issue of socialization, the feeling of betweenness epitomizes my position in my family, a position that first presented a challenge in my youth—especially during those forever-trying teenage years of endless questions and accusations. I used to wonder, Why can't I just have two parents like Grant and Blake? Why don't I have any real siblings? Can't I have my own room like all my friends? Why do I share a house with my grandparents? Why do I always have to "set the example" for the kids who aren't used to knowing a Black person?

During adolescence, I felt that so many fundamental things about my life were considered bizarre by most of my peers. Not only was my skin color not "normal" in our Pasadena private school (it went beyond not being white; I was, and continue to be, seen as biracial: "You're so smart, which one of your parents is white?"), it also was not normal to have five siblings who did not share my two parents, and it was not normal to have four parents living in three houses.

My parents split before I was born, and they were both married to my stepparents before I was old enough to know they had ever been together. My little sisters, one from each set of parents, were born within a year of each other. As a child you simply assume that your life is the norm, and even though I probably noticed that all of my friends had mommy-daddy-brother-sister families, I never really thought anything of it … until I *really* thought of it.

The concept of the nuclear family is still strange to me and bizarre in its simplicity: not having three houses in different Southern Californian suburbs; not dealing with feuding parents who stay in touch only because I exist; not navigating the complications of being a stepson; not doing Thanksgiving and Christmas at least three times a year; not feeling the support of culturally, socioeconomically, and ideologically distinct families—all of this seems unlivable. I owe much of my ability to acknowledge the reality of my life's complexity to my exposure to plurality in high school, and I owe much of this exposure to my mother.

My mother and I are very close. Although we interact as friends now, during my childhood she pushed me to achieve excellence, academic and otherwise, because she simply would accept no less. One day recently we drove down Pasadena's Colorado Boulevard into Old Town, one of our normal coffee date locales:

> *Mom*: "Remember that time in fifth grade you had the nerve to bring home a C-minus in Bible class—in Bible!" She laughed her "I'm not laughing because this is actually funny but because you had the audacity to pull that shit … which is funny to me" laugh. "Remember? You were on Mom and Poppie's kitchen floor crying because you'd 'tried your best!'"
>
> *Me*: "Hah, yeah."

I distinctly remember the scene: "*What is this?*" I could see her brown eyes turning a blazing shade of orange with every word she read on the pink report card. "Why"—her tone of voice could be described as one of genuine confusion—"are you getting a C-minus in Bible?" I didn't dare tell her that I couldn't care less about that subject, so I said, "I really don't know. I tried my best!" This was probably the worst thing I could have said because she became infuriated, and suddenly my daydream of her head spinning off didn't seem too far from reality. My mom rarely ever raises her voice at me, and her even, steady voice coming through clenched teeth is far more menacing. "Fine. You're saying this is your best—a C? You're saying you're a C-minus student? That's fine. I'm going to start treating you like a C-minus student." I can look back now and say she was brilliant. The idea of being treated like a C-minus student, as less-than, became unacceptable to me. From then on it wasn't the fear of my mother's fury that drove me but of being seen as a C-minus student. Mother doesn't remember posing that specific question, she's just amused that I tried to bullshit her into thinking I was trying my best in that Bible class.

Mother also encouraged—well, forced—me to take risks. If her parental success were assessed based on a single decision, it would be sending me to high school in downtown Los Angeles. Every morning her 13-year-old son, a naïve suburban boy, rode the train and the bus alone and unprotected into the real world, with only a cell phone as a defense from whatever he would encounter. Mother faced the criticism of my grandmother, the skepticism of my father, and the anger of others on both sides of my family, who at first thought she had to be kidding—even I thought she was kidding! But she was unmoving in her decision. Her son was going to the prestigious all-boys Catholic school curiously situated in a rough and underserved area of Los Angeles. And he was going alone. She later explained that she refused to let me grow up trapped in the "Pasadena Bubble"—a seemingly utopian world where "helicopter" parents and stay-at-home mothers drive their sheltered white children to private schools five minutes from home and pick them up no later than 3:00 PM. No, I instead went to the equally expensive private school in which 50 percent of each class consisted of the brightest minority students in Greater Los Angeles, regardless of their ability to pay. As a result, my friends ranged from bleached-blonde Hermosa Beach surfers to gay Dominican inner-city scholars, from Beverly Hills eccentrics to Silver Lake hipsters. My mother wanted me to see the diversity of the real world and to take full advantage of living in the City of Angels.

It didn't take long for my crash course in self-reliance, street smarts, empathy, and exposure to give me the maturity to understand exactly why my mother was putting me through so much. I am grateful I was not shielded from how people outside my suburban private school actually live. What I can say, however, is that Loyola High School dulled the blade of racial identity that had been sharpened by my middle school experience and handicapped my ability to attack the issue of race head on. Having been steeped for four years in a pluralistic community that made race an afterthought for me, I was lulled into a state of relative unconsciousness on the issue. For this I am thankful, because it allowed me to focus on the other formative aspects of my identity—my academic passions, my athletic goals, my Catholic morals, my brotherly obligations, and my political positions—everything else that makes Zane Zane. Soon enough, though, my college experience would teach me that everything I thought made me Zane was really just a consequence of my skin color. I was forced to acknowledge my blackness, to focus on its impact on my identity formation.

I am now aware that the white and Black communities have both always seen me as an outsider. For whites I was the Black boy in Mrs. Webster's fifth-grade class, the Black guy on the diving team. To the Black community I was that Black guy who won't associate with us, that light-skinned guy who wrote the article against us, that "bougie" Black guy who thinks he's too good for regular Black folk. Walking through life knowing that nothing I do will likely be interpreted as having originated from my person, independent of the connotations skin color lays on me, has made me thoughtful in ways that are hard to articulate. My sense is that many reflective Black people have the same experience, but the degree to which we're sensitive to this reality varies considerably.

At Dartmouth and during my time as a fraternity brother, I heard a few striking sentences from both within and outside the brotherhood that gave me pause. From within: "He doesn't understand that Black people would not have been allowed in the house back when we were an intellectual reading club"; "Wait guys, I have a joke: What did the chicken see when he crossed the road? A nigger"; "He told that Black professor who came to our house that we're just a 'glorified social club'"; "Is he really the direction we want to take this house? Is he who we want representing us?" And from outside: "I truly don't understand why you want to bring more Black males into the Greek system when you know how hard it is to navigate both worlds"; "I guess misery loves company with you affiliated Black people"; "Every HWCU [historically white college/university] needs its tokens who are sitting pretty atop a pillow of class, male, and light-skinned privilege, separating them from the issues tearing their race apart." This last quote, one of many just like it, was posted about me in a group forum for African American students at my college after I co-wrote an op-ed in the school newspaper explaining that fraternities can be safe places for Black students. We wrote that "the whole concept of brotherhood that we value so deeply is predicated on the very idea that, regardless of socioeconomic or racial status, everyone within the brotherhood is equal." As a relatively new member, I firmly believed that whatever tendency toward racism existed in the Greek system, it was at least partially overshadowed by bonds of brotherhood. I still believe that, and it's been proven to me time and again, but as a senior member of my organization I now hold a much more nuanced opinion.

I won't pretend for a moment that the Greek system, my house in particular, operates in a post-racial paradigm. If I were to do so I would lose every shred of legitimacy in this important conversation, even in my own eyes. In the same week that I was accused of encouraging Blacks to join my house so I could alleviate the pain of my so-called "regretful decision," an intoxicated brother betrayed, however subtly, a deep-seated prejudice against a Black professor. And the night before hosting an event celebrating the affiliated Black brothers and sisters, a member of my fraternity revealed his ignorance by inventing a "humorous" story that one of my brothers derogatorily said of a Black man, "He's just a nigger." Startled out of complacency, I knew that inaction in this case would have been tantamount to complicity. Shocked by the event, our chapter president asked me to help rewrite the bylaws of the entire organization to ensure that the arguments promoting the house in my article still held true. Willing to be an agent of change, I made sure the brotherhood addressed the use of such language and the sentiment from which it came, and we revised our bylaws to eradicate any facet that would ever allow such a comment to go unchecked.

Meanwhile I received no small amount of heat for my article, but I also received emails, texts, and calls from current Phi Delts and alums expressing their outrage that I, as the only current Black brother, would be made uncomfortable by such an ignorant statement. I appreciated their earnestness, despite being degraded by those who share my blackness but not my brotherhood, but the crux of the matter is that I was willing to be that agent of change—out of fidelity to my fraternal brotherhood and to my commitment to promote the celebration of blackness in my chosen communities.

## I'm now called their brother, considered a friend, but somewhere, deep down, does my presence offend?

Against this backdrop, I can only address those who question my Phi Delt affiliation, among whom I could at times include myself, by pointing to the individuals who have become my fraternity family—my true brothers within the brotherhood. I can only address my own doubt by reminding myself that, if not for my frat house, I would never have met Zac Moskow, a Jewish man a grade above me who will forever have my brotherly devotion. Zac and his abundantly generous family treat me like a member of the Moskow clan—putting me up in the family's Boston apartment; giving me sage advice after a strange sexual encounter with a girl; defending me when my brotherly allegiances are called into question; making himself available whenever I ask, "Hey, do you have a minute to talk?" Zac's commitment to me as a friend and as my older brother has profoundly ameliorated my Dartmouth experience by reminding me that I always have someone to lean on, someone who always cares. And the same is true for my other Phi Delt brothers, mentors, and friends who have made the trials of my fraternity experience exceedingly worth it. I probably would have made just as many important friends without the house, but I would never have met *these* friends, *these* mentors, *these* brothers, who made me feel unfailingly supported. I stand by my choice to rush and to remain affiliated and to tattoo our symbol on my body because, regardless of the bullshit that's been hurled my way from time to time, it's no worse than what I get from some of my "brothas" outside the house.

The fact is, I do not fully fit in anywhere, not because I can't decide but because, as a multifaceted, multilayered, multicultural individual, I cannot be neatly categorized, even by myself. Some people, white and Black, will always be upset by and uncomfortable with my choices, and I will always face stinging rebuke right along with the peace of belonging. Nevertheless, the mark my fraternity has made on me is indelible and exactly where I want it—impressed into my Black skin.

I know some will read this and draw a link between my preadolescent desire to be accepted by white males, gaining that acceptance in my adolescence, and grabbing, securing, prizing that (false) assurance of having made it in college. Some will believe that, although I hold my privileged white male friends dear to me, in the end they will not reciprocate; that my ability to understand and communicate with whiteness amounts to an irreproachable and illicit desire to identify with it. I can only say to those who think they've unmasked what's already been laid bare that I wholeheartedly disagree. I know who I am, and I no longer need to micro-analyze every friendship, every love interest to determine why I feel the way I do.

Despite my aversion to distinctions based solely on my race, I am beginning to believe that my blackness helps me understand many facets of the world better than my white counterparts. I understand more and more that, despite having grown up in an affluent, predominantly white environment, my condition as a Black male gives me a different and possibly more experienced worldview than the majority of the American population. Despite having almost everything in common with my peers at every stage of my life, there is always a certain knowledge, a profound insight that comes with knowing that everything I do is interpreted through a different, more critical lens than everyone else.

I wake up in the morning, take a shower, and look in the mirror. I see blackness. My best friend wakes up, takes a shower, and looks in the mirror. He sees a person. This is white privilege; and I tend to see it as simple reality. To harp on it or cry about it would burn me out, and I have no desire to add yet another mental stress to my daily existence. The dual lenses of scrutiny inherent in my betweenness are more than enough. It could be easier to remove one of these lenses by attempting to live a white-free existence, as some of my peers have decided to do. When you're not worried about what the other side thinks, you can move through life without the stress of forcing yourself into a mold you weren't cast for… but we all know that American society won't let us Black folks do that.

At Dartmouth, the idea of a black-only existence would be not only unrealistic but detrimental to the health of the entire community. I assume that if someone attends Dartmouth they aspire to some kind of success—financial or otherwise. Although the minority presence in the upper echelons of society is undoubtedly growing, it's foolish to think that these spaces are not dominated by white men. Therefore, I strongly believe that the ability to communicate, interact, and exist as a successful American, and as a successful Dartmouth student, means engaging with white America. How could it not? Why would the Black student not use their time at Dartmouth to prepare for the rest of their professional life?

I am grateful that engaging with white America wasn't a decision left up to me. The criticism leveled at me, however, is that my upbringing has so skewed my self-perception that I identify intensely with my white brothers and not at all with my Black brothers, that I've fooled myself into thinking that, if I pretend long enough, the color will drain from my skin, the curls will fall from my hair, and the flare of my nostrils will sharpen up. It's insulting. How could I forget my blackness, even if I did want to? It's outrageous for some Black person to insinuate that I've skipped through life and avoided the Black burden. Yes, it's a burden—regardless of how proudly I carry it. I often wish members of my community would listen and learn more than they assume.

The feeling of being accepted in the Black community has eluded me all my life. At college, the radical Black community was largely a negative force for me, as it called for division between groups I care for and belong to, and it advances positions I've had to firmly refute. Its "with us or against us" platform allows no room for gradations of opinion. It is accusatory toward Black students who, like me, actively thwart their movement for freedom by participating in the "white hegemony of Greekness." This generalization is in fact true of my experience with the Dartmouth African and African-American Society, and I've found real comfort and community among Black students cast out of the broader Black community—a real brother-/sisterhood, a minority of a minority. I know these brothers and sisters also feel the betweenness of our situation, and we do everything we can to support each other—thus we are never alienated, always loved, and often in opposition to the "activist" Black community. I'm grateful these people have been part of my college experience.

Never before have I felt such a strong connection with my Black peers. For the first time the people closest to me understand what it is to be the token, the representative of all thirteen million Black Americans; the kid in class expected to be the expert on MLK, Rosa Parks, slavery, and lynching; the arbiter of whether or not it's okay to say "ma nigga" to other Black people; what it's like to have the taxing sense that your every word and action is either too Black or not Black enough, uppity or patronizing. I thrive in my inner circle of Black male friends, where no topic is off limits or offensive, where an innately sympathetic perspective replaces judgment and accusation. We are eager, as Hilton Als describes, "to share our Black American maleness with another person who knew how flat and not descriptive those words were." My Black female circle reassures me that I am not alone in my distance from "the Black community" and that my feelings are valid; they echo the truth that I, that we, have never turned our backs on blackness and remind me that personhood is determined by more than the amount of melanin in our skin. They have saved me from giving up on my ability to relate to any Black community, and they are the foundation of *my* Black community.

The most unfortunate part of what I have described is that people who experience the double lens are either marginalized from the community in the same way I am, or their voices are overpowered by the "real" Black people. I've been compared to a house nigger during my time at college, as have many in my minority brother and sisterhood. The constant criticism that I do not want to associate with Black folks has caused me inner conflict and utter confusion. It also has filled me with the terrifying idea that maybe my critics knew what they were talking about all along.

But even such doubt can be defanged and manipulated into an opportunity for growth. Doubt can lead to self-reflection. My literary hero, James Baldwin, described his racial doubt as a looming fog in the back of his mind; I describe it as a serpent that has crept into my mind. It whispers to me of my inadequacies, real or imagined, and coils around my feet, preventing me from moving forward. It binds my arms and keeps me from reaching out to those I care for and those I want to care for. It leaves me paralyzed and static.

Doubt also raises questions: did I receive that fellowship because I'm Black, or did I earn it? Does that group of guys engage me because it looks good for them to have a Black friend or from genuine friendship? Am I the trendy new Black accessory? Is she not attracted to me because I'm Black? At times completely crazy, these are doubts I've had to dismiss in order to pursue my personal best. There are already enough real obstacles for me to overcome, race-related or otherwise, for me to be bound up by doubts, and yet they remain. I still believe that certain people will never treat me neutrally, but that's their problem, not mine.

If I give all of myself to my pursuits and to the people I'm most passionate about, there should be no mental capital left to spend on playing the paranoid guessing game. I can't be both Zane Williams trying to live my life and Sherlock Holmes trying to uncover the intent behind every action that affects me.

I've learned that my position in the world is a catch-22: by trying to make my race a nonfactor, I deprive myself of an essential facet of being that everyone is entitled to: cultural heritage. In constantly viewing the world through the cracked lens of racial injustice, and dare I say white supremacy, I exempt myself from one thing that matters most in life: happiness. I should resent that society forces me to make an impossible decision, and I do, but it's incumbent on me to focus my energies on what I do have control over. Resentment is not productive.

I'm just going to live my life, take a breath and be free; I'm confident now and I plan to be me.

## Reference

Baldwin, James. *Notes of a Native Son*. Boston: Beacon Press. 1955.

# 6 Finding Blackness

*Samiir Bolsten*

"When Black people marry outside of the race, it waters us down, it is destroying our race," my friend's mother claimed while stopped at a red light. Her head slightly turned so that my girlfriend and I could hear her in the backseat. My friend's mother, a Black woman in her late thirties, was driving my Black girlfriend and me home. Accelerating again as the light turned green, she continued, "That's why it feels so good to see a young Black couple. We start marrying their men and they start taking ours. It's ruining our race." At this point I had to make this woman aware that I was not comfortable with her sentiments, considering the fact that my mother is white.

"Actually, ma'am, I am the product of an interracial relationship and marriage," I started to say, as the car was coming to a halt in the parking space outside the train station. "I'm half white." I saw the disbelief on her face as she turned to look at me.

"No," the woman said, clearly startled. She looked me up and down as if to understand how she could have overlooked something that should be so obvious. Her problem was that my white heritage is hard to spot at first glance, as I have a relatively dark complexion for a mulatto. At a loss for words, she continued to study me before stumbling over three or four apologies. As I sat in the back of the car listening to her incomplete sentences and halting attempts to backpedal, I could only reflect on the fact that I was in familiar territory.

I was used to dealing with awkward and offensive situations related to race, having grown up with my dark complexion in predominantly white Denmark. Later on, as my family moved to more diverse environments, perceptions of me changed—both in my own eyes and in the eyes of others. It seemed that because of my unusual family situation and racial makeup, I was always perceived as different from the norm, no matter where we relocated. Although this led to issues of low self-worth and some turbulent times mentally, I eventually became comfortable with always being different. Much of this comfort came from realizing that norms were by no means rules, and that all people had some way in which they were different.

A stereotype or norm can never define a person completely, and every identity has a story behind it. Regardless of how much one adheres to social norms, the emotions and struggles we carry inside create a unique human. I

DOI: 10.4324/9781003376255-8

eventually saw my struggle to fit the norm as a chance to understand the world better, as well as myself. My unique background forced me to realize that norms did not apply to me, and I eventually used this realization to gain a deeper understanding of myself beyond the pressures of stereotypes. This required me to begin viewing myself and others outside of the racial scope in order to get a deeper appreciation for individual identities. Because discounting race contradicted how it first shaped my identity in every way, the road to self-understanding was long and arduous.

My mother was born and raised in a middle-class family in Ballerup, Denmark, a town of about forty thousand with a very small colored population. Because of her strict upbringing, she focused on working and moved out on her own as early as she could. High school was my mother's highest level of education. During her late teens, she went on vacation with her mother and sister to Morocco. My father, who is only one year older than my mother, was selling souvenirs to tourists in Casablanca. He spent his days standing on a street corner, selling cheap ceramics and pickpocketing tourists who appeared rich. From what I understand, this is where he met my mother.

Given the bits and pieces of the story that I have picked up from my mother and father throughout the years, it appears that their interactions were nothing more than a teenage love affair. To this day I am unsure how they communicated, because my father's English is very poor and I know my mother never spoke Arabic. Regardless of how they communicated, my father gave my mother a souvenir she was not expecting: my older sister, Farrah. I am not sure exactly what happened over the next few months, but I know that my father moved to Denmark and eventually wed my mother. The circumstances under which my parents met did not exactly provide a stable foundation for a relationship or marriage.

My father had a rough upbringing in Morocco as the youngest of seven children. Being the youngest left him essentially forgotten by his parents, and he seldom had his needs met. At times he did not even own a pair of shoes. My father was rather uneducated, which may have contributed to the poor quality of his life. By the time he was twenty, he had completed the Danish equivalent of middle school with a passing grade in all his subjects.

When my father immigrated to Denmark in his late teens, he had problems finding work and turned to a life of crime and drugs. During a psychotic episode brought on by drugs, my father caused a ruckus in a nightclub by wielding a large kitchen knife. I never fully understood how this story ended, aside from the fact that he was apprehended, deemed mentally unstable, and sent to a mental health institution rather than a regular prison. Because of this, for a period in my childhood I barely saw my father, who was virtually the only Black male influence in my life at the time.

I was born on February 10, 1986, in Ballerup. It ultimately turned out that my mother and father were not meant for each other, and they divorced less than a year after I was born. My father still lived in the same town, but he did not provide much support for my mother, who was now alone and raising two

Black children in a predominantly white town. She once told me that people would approach her to compliment her beautiful children, assuming she had done a good deed and adopted them from a Third World country. My mother has vividly described on several occasions how these people's facial expressions changed from admiration to disgust once they found out she had given birth to these two dark children. As my mother described it, their view of her instantly changed from a noble humanitarian to "someone who fucked a nigger." Before I was even able to comprehend the issue of race, my mother had suffered on my behalf, being judged and labeled by others.

Although I was a Danish citizen born in Denmark, and spoke only Danish, my skin color caused people to classify me as an immigrant, or at the very least to associate me with the resentment they had toward immigrants. When looking at me, they instantly felt they were looking at a product of parents from some war-ridden nation who came to Denmark to leech off the state. When they saw me, they assumed that my ignorant immigrant parents were raising me according to their ignorant immigrant culture, which would certainly be detrimental to what Denmark stood for. The xenophobic nature of many Danes reminded me constantly of my skin color, and therefore my inherently subordinate status.

During most of my childhood we were lower middle class, living in an apartment with my mother's boyfriend Jakob (who was white), my mother, my sister, and my half sister (who is also white). Growing up, I seldom had someone to teach me the things that most people learn from their parents, particularly boys: how to treat women, how to drive, and so on. Jakob played the biggest role in raising me, for which I am incredibly thankful. Yet even Jakob's unconditional love could not teach me what it meant to be a Black man, particularly in a town like Ballerup and a country like Denmark. I was completely on my own in trying to figure out what my complexion would mean for my life.

Although we always had food, my mother and Jakob struggled financially, perpetually living paycheck to paycheck below the poverty line while trying to raise three children. My family's financial hardships, coupled with the fact that my skin color was so different from the other children's, made me uncomfortable and self-conscious in school. Most of my friends had parents who were married, educated, had stable jobs, and were significantly older than mine. My school luckily provided free lunch, which hid my family's status on the lower end of the socioeconomic spectrum. Unfortunately, the cafeteria workers went on strike when I was in second grade, and all the students were required to bring their own lunch to school for the year. My lunches, consisting of butter and cheese sandwiches on white bread and orange juice poured into a jar, were rather embarrassing next to my peers' purchased meals of chicken subs and hamburgers, which their parents dropped off for them.

I also dreaded field days, as they were typically ski trips. While my friends were downhill skiing with their brand-new ski equipment or snowboards, I had to cross-country ski using Jakob's old equipment from the 1970s. Sometimes my family situation even affected my schoolwork, such as when we were supposed to do a report on our parents' profession, I had nothing to report on. Even when I began playing soccer, getting dropped off on the back of a bike rather than being driven to practice in a car highlighted the difference between my peers and me. And then, of course, the constant exclamation point: I was "The Black Kid."

As my biological father turned to a life of crime and drugs, his relationship with my sister and me deteriorated steadily. During the early years of my life, my sister Farrah and I would spend a night at his apartment every two weeks. We used to play soccer, cook, watch movies, and sit around while he smoked cigarettes and spoke in Arabic with his friends. At this point I was still too young to realize all the ways in which my father was not fulfilling his paternal duties to my sister and me, and to my mother. The most significant thing I remember him teaching me was how to deliver a headbutt properly— snatching a man forward by his collar and meeting his momentum with a forehead crashing into the bridge of his nose. My father's role as my sole (yet almost non-existent) Black male influence caused me to associate such behavior with what I perceived to be Black masculinity.

My relationship with my father and other colored people gave me no model for what my identity and demeanor should be as a Black person. All I knew was that my identity could not possibly be like that of my peers because there was always something reminding me that I was different and inferior. I faced ridicule in school and on my soccer team, and fought often. Hearing "Nigger!" shouted at me was no rarity, and it came from children both my age and older. Sometimes it made me sad, sometimes angry. Regardless of my external reaction, internally the word affected me the same every time, as it was part of a system of checks and balances that ensured "niggers" would be kept in their place at the bottom of the totem pole. I had no way to find anything positive about being Black, nor anyone or anything to identify with. Instead, I spent the first eight or nine years of my life loathing my skin color and the things that came with it. I remember being in music class in the second grade and looking at my friend's hair, wishing mine were straight like his; dreading soccer practice because my shorts exposed the dry skin on my legs. The other kids did not have to worry about ashy legs because it wasn't visible on their white skin. Ashy skin is of course normally visible on Black children, which is why Black parents know to moisturize it properly. Unfortunately, because I was the only Black child and my mother was white, it only highlighted the differences between my peers and me.

Feeling like an outcast, I spent a great deal of time by myself. I enjoyed activities that allowed me to express my creative side: sports, music, and art. During very early childhood, I often occupied myself by building (not playing) with Legos, drawing, and engaging in just about any form of art that allowed me to express myself. Because I typically excelled at these activities, I felt the most comfortable while involved in them, and in school they gained me social acceptance. Ultimately, however, I was still uncomfortable being Black because I found no advantage in being outside the norm.

Then *The Fresh Prince* came.

In 1990 Will Smith was offered the chance to star in his own television sitcom, titled *The Fresh Prince of Bel-Air.* The show became a huge success in the United States and went on to be broadcast in several nations across the world, one of them being Denmark. Will "Fresh Prince" Smith became one of the first positive images of a Black male I had, and I instantly felt like I should and could relate to his character. I changed my behavior and acted more like the character I saw on the television screen; I could identify with him. Smith's character grew up in inner-city Philadelphia and was uprooted to live with his rich uncle in Bel-Air. Seeing him adapt to his new environment by taking advantage of his status as an outsider intrigued me and inspired me to wonder if I could do the same. Essentially, Smith was creating something positive out of being the one who always stuck out. I concluded that the natural way for me to do the same was to act like he did. I found comfort in being a class clown, using my outsider status as a way to control people's attention rather than to catch their attention unwillingly with my dark complexion or curly hair.

Once I realized that the Fresh Prince was not just a cool person on TV but also a rapper, I instantly took an interest in his music and its genre: rap/hip-hop. I thought rapping was cool mainly because the Fresh Prince did it, and I idolized him mainly because of the show. Rap music remained a loose interest of mine, as it was hard to access in Denmark. So I had to be satisfied with watching shows like *The Fresh Prince of Bel-Air.* I watched *The Fresh Prince* and other American shows so much that I learned to speak English fluently, and I began gaining a deeper interest in music as I started to understand more of the lyrics.

Then 2Pac came.

In February 1996 a Los Angeles-based rapper, 2Pac (also known as Tupac Shakur), released rap music's first-ever double disc, titled *All Eyez on Me.* Because of the album's incredible success, 2Pac's fame extended far beyond U.S. borders and made its way to my television and radio in Denmark. Tupac Shakur was another of my first major influences as a Black male. His swagger, vivid storytelling, and emotional delivery completely pulled me into the medium that he expressed himself through: hip-hop.

After being heavily intrigued and amazed by rap music, I decided that I wanted to create my own, as it seemed like something I could excel at and use to express myself. Because I found the most comfort in the activities I was praised most highly for, I felt that doing them allowed me to be less inhibited as a Black person. I felt that my skin color rendered me so insignificant that there was no reason for me to be around others unless I was doing something worth watching. Rapping appeared to be the coolest thing to do because I had seen those I identified with racially doing it well. I thought I could do well at it too, which would allow me both to express myself fully and to gain social acceptance. Putting my thoughts down on paper allowed me to escape daily reality as a subordinate member of society, and to transform it into a reality in which I held power through my words. I wrote about everything, from my actual life and things I went through to fabricated stories about people in the

United States. I enjoyed transcribing my imagination into rap. As I began jotting down my thoughts, feelings, random stories, and even just things that rhymed in cool ways, something was also changing in the social fabric of my peers: being Black was becoming cool.

Because gangsta rap, now with 2Pac at the forefront, so heavily influenced popular culture, everything represented and described in this music had become the latest fad to follow for millions of people worldwide who could not relate in the least to being Black. The result was that in about 1996, the youth of my hometown, Ballerup, deemed acting like 2Pac the coolest possible behavior: people were imitating the hand signs he was flashing, reciting his lyrics without knowing the true context (or at times even the translation), and trying to dress like they were gangsta rap artists. Everything surrounding the gangsta rap culture became the latest fad. For me, this mainly meant that I could now be comfortable being Black. Between 1996 and 1998 I found ways to be a little more comfortable in my skin. I benefited from the social acceptance that popular culture icons whose color matched mine had gained among youth trying to rebel against their parents.

The character traits of the "cool" Black people, however, were less than admirable, and my peers began to associate blackness with all these negative qualities. While I was simply looking for a way to feel comfortable by having a point of relation in social situations, I had instead subscribed to perpetuating negative stereotypes by equating the characteristics portrayed in gangsta rap with blackness. Immature and ignorant of the implications, I took comfort in the current trend in my middle school that was pushing me right to the top of the social hierarchy.

The question of whether I was "authentically" Black never actually occurred to me because I had no basis for comparison. Because my skin color had caused me so much turmoil and ridicule in my younger years, I clung to the notion that I was Black because it was the only identity I had comfortably adopted. As hip-hop and various other mediums of popular culture set the trends for what was cool and socially coveted, I related many of the hyperbolic images of Black masculinity to aspects of my own personality, believing I had found my pathway to fail-safe social acceptance. This type of comfort grew to the point where my personality began to develop into a loud and outrageous character. I sagged, gestured, rapped, and code-switched my way into feeling comfortable in an identity that I saw as a social safety net. Ballerup, Denmark, did not have enough Black people for me to understand that what I associated with blackness was not a universal reality. I would eventually realize that even in a community filled with Black people, I was outside the norm because of my unique situation growing up.

The turning point of my life came at age twelve, when I was uprooted and had to leave everything I had ever known in Ballerup to move to the United States. My mother had broken up with her boyfriend Jakob two years earlier and now had a fiancé named Enzo. Enzo was a white man of Italian heritage who had grown up in the United States, and my mother decided to follow him overseas to start a new life. Over the next few years our family did quite a bit of moving between different places Enzo had lived before—Philadelphia, Orlando, and then back to Denmark. While these moves taught me to interact with people of all races, it also taught me that I deviated from the norm no matter what type of community I was in. After moving around for a few years, I finally decided that I wanted to move back to Philadelphia to finish high school.

When I was sixteen, I moved in with Enzo's ex-wife, Leslie. Leslie also lived with some of her children by Enzo, who were now my stepsiblings. The house was both crowded and cluttered, a chaotic environment. The three bedrooms and living room were inhabited by as many as nine people, depending on the day and time of year. We also had two flea-infested dogs and an old cat named Missy. For a period of time we also had a friend of the family sleeping in my brother's broken-down Ford Taurus out in front of the house.

Usually someone would be up and using the living room until 3:00 or 4:00 a.m., so I simply had to adapt to noise at all hours of the night. My brothers often had friends coming over very late, and they went in and out of the house to smoke blunts, get drunk, and carry on in the living room. This environment made it very hard to focus on academics and to get a decent night's sleep. My main goals when I moved back to the United States, however, were to earn good grades and finish high school, so I always found a way to get my homework and studying done, even if it meant doing so in a distracting environment. Although I was getting high constantly with one of my stepbrothers, my rule was that I never got high during the week unless I had finished all of my schoolwork. Therefore, the first thing I did when I got home from school was to sit down at the kitchen table and do my homework.

My time back in Philadelphia was also the first time I ever faced challenges to my blackness because of my complexion. As a child, I was always the darkest person around (except for my father), leaving me subject to a variety of jokes regarding how dark I was, how hard I would be to find at night, and so on. In Philadelphia, though, there was a large colored population with a wide range of complexions. During that time I first experienced someone referring to me as "light-skinned." Although I resembled a Negro phenotype, I felt that this comment somehow detracted from the Black image I had fabricated and held so dear for most of my life. I had always clung to the notion that I was Black, visibly Black. If some perceived me as light-skinned, how would that affect my already shaky blackness? Furthermore, because I had grown out my hair during the first few months back in Philadelphia, my status as "other" rather than Black in the eyes of others grew. At this point my lack of fashionable apparel, strange demeanor, curly hair, and different vernacular all contributed to what I perceived as the failing of my blackness.

Once again I found myself differing from the norm. The perception of Black masculinity I had drawn from my father, *The Fresh Prince*, and 2Pac years earlier seemed obsolete, and I was unable to locate a persona to strive for. Rather than seeing one way a Black male should act, I realized that different norms applied to different people. While I wanted to be seen as Black in the eyes of my peers, I still did not drastically change my demeanor to fit the norm. I ultimately realized that I would rather be true to myself and strive for my own goals: attending college and succeeding in life. The stereotypical Black males at school called me a nerd because I spoke differently and spent class time participating and working.

Living in an area where the complexion and demeanor of the colored population was quite broad allowed me to concern myself less with my complexion. Rather than worrying about looking different, I began to realize that I always stood out in some way, owing to my upbringing. I could relate to many of the people who fit the norm in terms of skin color, but aside from this superficial characteristic, our commonalities varied. Everyone had a different way of dealing with being Black in modern society. When color started having less significance in my mind, I was able to concern myself with getting to know myself as a person rather than as "a Black person." Although I still wanted to be accepted by my peers and to earn the title of "being Black," as I grew I became more concerned with learning about myself as a man than with being among the in-crowd. I felt I was repairing my identity to compensate for the damage caused by all the confusion in my early years. Part of this reparation involved reassessing my relationships with my early Black influences and understanding more about their identities. The very first of these influences was my father, and I felt a need to get a deeper understanding of what had shaped the outcome of his life and identity.

Once I finished high school and started college, my father and I did not maintain steady contact. I never really spoke to him over the phone, and he did not have a computer, so we couldn't communicate through email. During my junior year, however, my father sent me a letter. I opened it and immediately was filled with a sense of nostalgia for my childhood. Every birthday and Christmas card had been scribbled in the exact same way—over two entire pages. The penmanship was visibly that of someone unused to writing, which made sense, considering my father's middle school education. It appeared that he had spent extra time formalizing the letter, skipping every other line to simulate the double spacing in a computer document. Through run-on sentences and poor Danish, I sensed a father's genuine attempt to connect with his son.

About halfway down the first page, he truly tried to reach out to me:

> Samiir it's the first time I write to you we have never SpokeN with Eachother as father and son but I think you have dun very WEll I am ProUd over you but one thing I want to say that you should foCus on your sTudies so you can get yourself a good eDucation hope you don't dislike or afTer all these years I should come and decide over you Samiir I write these lines because I want us to start keeping contact by telefone to begin me or that you come n live with me a few days when you come To Denmark we have to start spending time or more specifiCally speak to eachother once a month per Telefone.

While I was reading the letter, tears started streaming down my face. I felt a sense of happiness and pride that my father had reached out in an attempt to connect with me. I saw my father's vulnerability in this letter and began realizing that he did not have all the answers. This was not a man who had been guiding me through Black masculinity as a child; this was a man who himself was young when his life had been turned upside down with the sudden responsibility for a life other than his own; a man who in his teens had left everything he had ever known to go live in a foreign country where he was in the minority. His life and identity as a Black man had been shaped by confusion and instability, so for me to base my early identity on his example was illogical. At this point I wanted to see my father as badly as he wished to see me. I wanted to look deeper into his personality and life in order to understand myself better.

The next time I went to Denmark, I lived with my father for most of the time. During this visit I got to spend time with him and see his daily routine of drugs and alcohol. On one occasion I sat down and joined in these activities. It was a Thursday afternoon, and I was sitting around the apartment lounging in my robe. One of my father's friends, who couldn't have been older than twenty-five, came by with a bottle of liquor and immediately began drinking. After about ten minutes, both he and my father snorted a line of amphetamine off the table. Although on some level I felt hurt that my father was living this lifestyle, I also felt a certain sense of connection and pride that our relationship had grown to the point where he would allow me to see this side of him. I poured myself a drink from his friend's bottle of liquor and took a sip. As painful as it was to see his destructive lifestyle, I realized that I could have been in the same position if a couple of circumstances had been different in my life. As we became more and more inebriated, I became increasingly comfortable with seeing and connecting with this side of my father. After about an hour, I joined them as they smoked some hash.

It was three in the afternoon and I was already quite intoxicated. I sat back on the couch, feeling the liquor in my system while listening to my father and his friend converse. Peering through a cloud of hash smoke, I wondered what the two could possibly be speaking about that was of any importance. These were two individuals divided not only by generation but also by race. Were drugs such a point of connection that two individuals from such different walks of life could use them to connect with each other? After pondering this for a few minutes, I realized there must be some sense of kinship around these substances, considering that I was just now connecting with my father at age twenty-one because of them. I felt as if I had been inducted into a fraternity of substance use, sitting there drunk in a hazy room, watching two people of different backgrounds do lines of amphetamine. While it was a strange thing to see, I still felt a sense of resolution in finally being a part of the type of life my father had chosen for so many years over connecting with his family.

I had succeeded in viewing my father just as a person, rather than as the figure who was supposed to teach me how to be Black. I was trying to disprove the notion that being Black trapped me in a set behavior or thought pattern. This would help me contextualize myself and gain comfort in straying from the norm instead of being depressed by it. I wanted to see myself as Black, but I was slowly learning to accept that there was not just one behavioral pattern I had to adhere to. The range of complexions, experiences, and demeanors of Black people was vast, and not everyone would stand under the same umbrella. I strove to view people as humans, rather than determining what race they belonged to. The complicated part came when people dictated their behavior on the basis of race and racial stereotypes.

When I first arrived at Dartmouth College, a prestigious liberal arts college in rural New Hampshire, I did not really know what to expect. During the course of my life, I had encountered several different types of Black people: people who seemed to subscribe to the stereotypes portrayed on television and people who were Black but had nothing to do with the stereotypes on television. I wondered what types of people I would encounter at Dartmouth.

What I found in college was that not many people shared the "Black" experience in terms of what it stereotypically implies: lower socioeconomic status, an urban environment, and so on. If the aforementioned implied anything about blackness, then I found that I, in fact, would seem to be one of the blackest people at the school. I did not fully subscribe to the stereotypical behavior that accompanies such experiences, because I was growing accustomed to concerning myself with my natural inclinations rather than adhering to how people expected me to act. Much as I had determined in high school, there were certain types of behaviors that signified "blackness." It was my assumption, however, that those who subscribed to these behaviors did so because of their life experiences. My assumption turned out to be incredibly wrong; it seemed that many of the Black people at Dartmouth who acted "Black" appeared to do so in order to legitimize their blackness. Many of them used inner-city slang, wore urban attire, and generally had an inner-city demeanor. My impression was that these people were trying to establish a new identity while at college—one they hadn't had access to in high school. Perhaps they had been like me, considered nerds because they weren't Black enough, and were now trying to escape that label. The difference between them and me, however, was that I had actually lived many of the experiences that created these signifiers of an authentic Black experience. I simply chose not to act them out because I was finding comfort in straying from the norm and focusing more on myself.

Because of the way I perceived many of the Black people at my college, I continued to be somewhat of a loner. I had friends, but I did not let too many people get close to me. We were at a privileged school like Dartmouth, so why would they want to hear about the drug charges my brother back home was facing, my father's drug problem, or my family's money problems? I did not disclose much information about these things because I figured people would place me in the same box with many of the other Black people at Dartmouth, assuming I was disclosing these things only to legitimize some form of blackness related to the struggles commonly faced in urban environments.

I found that those I got along with best were those who did not concern themselves too much with how they were perceived by others, but rather were true to themselves and simply focused on enjoying college and getting an education. My diverse life experience had finally made me as close to color blind as one can be, and I selected my friends entirely because of their demeanor, and in no way for their skin color or social class. As I grew more comfortable at Dartmouth, I began to understand the value of my life experience more fully. All of the places I had lived and all my struggles had made me a person who could relate to and communicate with almost anyone, no matter where a person was from.

Just as Blacks had been portrayed in their first cinematic representation in *Birth of a Nation* as lazy, good-for-nothing slackers, many Blacks at Dartmouth would try to embody this stereotype in an effort to claim their blackness. Rather than bragging about who had the best grades or who performed best under pressure, many conversations would lead to a competition over who could convince the other that he was a worse student—whether these claims were true or not. Realizing this, I became comfortable with what I was and whom I had become for one of the first times in my life. Not only had my unique and incredibly diverse life experience helped me adapt to college and gain acceptance from my peers and interest from my professors, but also it embodied the struggles that so many Black students for some reason wished they had experienced, which gave me further legitimization in the eyes of those who actually gauged this as something important.

While I was thankful I had endured the circumstances I had, I would never want to do that again. When I was embarrassed because my family did not have as much money as others or when I had to see family members deal with substance abuse, the last thing I thought about was how it might legitimize me at a later point; all I wanted was to overcome it. Once I finally made something out of myself and matriculated at an Ivy League school, my previous struggles and failures became marks of pride as opposed to points of shame.

I have been called "nigger," been on the receiving end of racial jokes, and struggled with my own self-worth solely because of my skin color. Regardless of how strange I seem to my peers and how little I fall within the scope of stereotypical blackness, my life and identity have been dramatically influenced by my complexion. How could anyone tell me that I am not Black? Limiting blackness to a number of stereotypes and negative behaviors is ignorant and disrespectful to the race as a whole. So while I consider myself Black (well, half Black), I will never again allow this label to dictate the way I interact with others or present myself to the outside world. At times it will change how I am perceived and treated, but as a man who has endured this label my entire life, I shall not let myself be affected. Through the same actions, thoughts, and expressions that make me so hard to define, I will continue to prove to those around me that it is best to define me by my character and not my complexion.

(A follow-up life story by Samiir appears in Part IV of this anthology.)

## Part III

# Becoming: Growing Into Adulthood

# 7 Metamorphosis

*Andrew Nalani*

If you'd met me six years ago, you'd think I was born in church and never left. I carried a Bible with me every single day, a large one in my bag, another so small it fit in the pocket of my school uniform shirt. Everything about my life—the questions and uncertainties, my hopes and fears, how I understood myself—had a reference point in the Word of God or in a particular interpretation of the Word that I'd learned from a man of God. I was sixteen years old then, and sure of where I stood in life.

My self-assurance was a double-edged sword, at once a blessing and a setup. I found security by conforming to whatever shape the community I grew up in wanted me to take on. At home, my mother saw me as more feminine than my older brother, for which my siblings shamed me. Meanwhile, I imitated my father's roles, the roles of manhood, always vying for the driver's seat in mock car games, and I was obsessed with the way dad dressed. In school, I listened to what the authorities said a good student was like and conformed to what they said I should be. I became a well-mannered boy, an example for other students to emulate, and I even took on the role of a priest. I also conformed to what my peers needed me to be for them: a friend, helper, advisor, and spiritual leader. I was locked into the models my community defined for me and found a sense of belonging by not veering from those expectations. When I felt I belonged, I felt relatively safe, but my sense of belonging and safety began to crumble when I left home to study in the United States. My self-assurance became self-consciousness that turned into defensiveness, which in turn morphed into questioning. My questioning led to rebellion, and heartbreak, which opened me up to seeing the world through a wider lens and gave me a broader sense of my own identity. For the first time in my life I became aware of my blackness, my prejudice, my overly sensitive nature, and the impact family violence had on shaping who I am. I have changed since leaving home, and this is my story of transformation.

I was born and raised in Uganda, where I grew up in a family of six: my mother, my father, two older sisters, and an older brother. We lived within a housing estate in the suburbs about a half-hour from the capital, Kampala. When I was four, my mother often made me wear my older sisters' dresses, most often a red one with a white flowery lining. I will never forget how

DOI: 10.4324/9781003376255-10

humiliated I felt when my siblings laughed at me. When I look back, I see that my mother encouraged my feminine qualities by dressing me up as a girl. I was her last child, and she treated me like a daughter, not a son. I was closer to my mother than my father, as she spent more time at home. We laughed together, she comforted us when we cried, she helped us with our homework, she sang hymns with us when the electricity was out and there was no television, and she prayed with us before bedtime. She never hesitated to spank us when we went astray, but her warmth always drew us to her.

My father, on the other hand, is a man I both liked and feared. He spent most of his time away from home. When he returned from work each day, my siblings and I would scramble to put the house in order before he opened the door. After we'd greeted him, each of us would find our own refuge far from the living room, where he sat watching television. My brother and I would pretend to be doing homework, even though we wanted to go outside to play. Our friends often commented, "Your father is a tough man," and they weren't far from the truth. Thus, I came to associate femininity with physical and emotional closeness, and masculinity with physical and emotional distance, manifested as toughness. Home was my first school, the place where I learned what roles men and women were expected to play.

One night my father returned home an hour after we'd finished dinner. He argued with my mother about the food she had left for him. I went to bed and soon awoke to the sound of my parents fighting. I stumbled out of the children's bedroom and saw my mother headed toward their bedroom with a long thick stick, yelling, "I'm going to kill you. I'll kill you." Father rushed out of the bedroom to stop her, stepping on my toe as he fumbled to take the stick from Mother. Blam! Blam! Blam! Mother's clenched fists pounded on Father's back—I had never seen her so furious. I was drenched in tears. My brother came out and put his arm around me; in that moment it seemed as though my brother and I did not exist. Later that morning, as if to reassert his authority after things had cooled down, Father stormed into the bathroom where Mother was brushing her teeth and pushed her head into the bathtub. He grasped the back of her neck and held her under the water running from the tap: he was taking his revenge.

We never talked about this incident, but I would learn many years later, simply by connecting the dots, that my mother had learned that my father was seeing other women. Outside the home, everything in our family appeared to be all right, and my parents' fights remained a secret between my brother and me. I was marked deeply by the violence that morning and did not know what to do; I never forgot. Even though my parents treated each other cruelly, I felt it was unfair for my father to be violent to my mother. I had already come to associate maleness with toughness, and now I added violence to the association. I vowed to be a different kind of man from my father.

However, even though I feared my father, I sought his validation; when it was lacking, school became the substitute. I've always drawn attention from my teachers at my Catholic primary school, St. Kizito. During one parents' visit, my third-grade science instructor, Teacher Mercy, mentioned to my mother that I was different from my peers and was destined to become a priest—even though I was not Catholic. Perhaps what Teacher Mercy saw in me was my quiet, reserved nature, but whatever the reason for her prediction, it captured my imagination, and from then on when asked what I wanted to be in future, I'd always emphatically respond, "a reverend." One Christmas, my father even gave me a Black button-down shirt that was similar to what a reverend would wear. Saying prayers before all the big eating events at home became my responsibility, and each Sunday I gave an account of what happened at church—never mind that I hated Sunday school and used money meant for the offertory to buy ice cream. I never questioned whether I *really* wanted to become a reverend, and I realize now that what attracted me to the idea was the sense of purity that surrounded ministers and the respect they were accorded. I thought that becoming a priest meant having no blemish, which would earn me the respect of others. But the main force behind the attention I sought was my need to belong, to be seen and appreciated. Therefore, I presented myself as a priest-to-be, and many people in the schools I went to after St. Kizito came to perceive me as one.

My academic performance soared at boarding school, and many teachers asked my mother, "How did you raise such a disciplined, humble, and hardworking boy? You must be very lucky!" This praise made me work even harder to please my teachers, which became a self-reinforcing cycle. My teachers often told my peers that I was an example to be emulated, and, surprisingly, rather than responding with spite, my peers nominated me for various leadership positions and other responsible roles, such as class captain in primary four. I remember one particular incident that year: my social studies teacher walked into class and found students talking—what we called noisemaking. She asked me, the class captain, to give her a list of the noisemakers; I did so, although my feelings were conflicted. She called the noisemakers to the front of the classroom, holding in her hand a smooth yellow-and-black bamboo stick about a meter long. She handed me the stick and asked me to cane my classmates. I felt even more conflicted than when I wrote down the names, but, because I was a good student and didn't want to disobey authority, I did as my teacher wished. I swung that stick with skill and precision, never once wincing. It felt like the right thing to do; after all, the teacher approved and it made me feel important. Afterward, however, I returned to my desk with eyes on the ground, feeling uneasy for having punished peers I knew I ought to care about. I did not know what my classmates thought of me, but if I had, I'd have been torn with guilt. Three years ago, one boy I caned wrote to ask whether I remember caning him, and I thought how pitiful it was that friends have this particular memory of me. I shake my head when I think of those days, and my actions now seem pathetic. However, they also shaped how I understood myself, enjoying the attention I got from my teachers and the respect my peers consequently accorded me. I was more eager to please and gain acceptance than to rebel and risk losing everything that gave me a sense of identity. School had become the place where I got the validation I lacked at home; this became even truer when my mother lost her life to cancer of the cervix in 2004.

When mother passed, our home became a wasteland. Her passing left a hole in my heart, for I felt no one could understand me as she had. For the first time I became acutely aware of the distance between my father and me, and although my siblings and I had grown very close, we were all studying at separate schools so our bond gradually weakened. We never spoke about mother's passing after we buried her—but how could we? We didn't know how to handle the loss, nor did our father, whom we saw less of thereafter. We found solace in prayer and in church, and the church and school became my refuge. I was eleven years old then, and my sisters, who had become strong Pentecostal Christians, introduced me to the faith and to their friends in the youth fellowship they attended during holidays. After that, I never missed a chapel service at school and I read the Bible often. Gradually, my peers came to know me as a "man of God." I carried a small blue pocket Bible everywhere I went, and another in my school bag.

My second older sister had passed her old Bible down to me. It was big. It was old. It was Black. Its covers were falling apart and I'd lost the first twelve chapters of Genesis. Yet whenever I pulled out this Bible, I felt more knowledgeable and wiser than my peers, as the old torn Bible was proof that I spent a lot of time buried in the pages of this Word of God; like our preacher said one Sunday, you can tell a true Christian by how old his or her Bible is. I quoted numerous Bible passages from memory, which gave me a sense of belonging and distinguished me from other boys in school, who defined themselves more through their athletic abilities. Over the next four years, I was chosen to lead my Christian fellowship class and became an assistant choir leader for the Scripture Union at my school. So, while many of my peers spent their free time playing sports, watching movies, or hanging out with members of the opposite sex, I busied myself with the works of God, attending prayer meetings, preparing for the next Bible study, and meditating on the word of God. The priest in me—or the caricature of it—was bringing me attention and, thus, a sense of belonging.

While preparing for Bible study during my third year of secondary school, I came across an interpretation of the gospels and the New Testament that differed radically from what I'd heard the school chaplain preach from the pulpit. Chaplain outright condemned anyone who was not "born again," and at one point he mentioned that the Seventh Day Adventists and Muslims ought to come to chapel on Sunday. "If you dodge chapel, you'll find yourself begging God for forgiveness when you see failure on your school report, heh! Even you who 'dark corner', you should repent." I struggled with Chaplain's legalism, while back home my sisters' radical commitment to Pentecostalism did not ease my situation. They attended the youth fellowship during holidays, and while I did not feel on a par with their friends (I did not have friends of my own), I felt obliged to attend faithfully, as they did. During one holiday period, we went door to door in the housing estate where we lived, which was not far from the church, to evangelize. I felt awkward, but that was what the Bible commanded us to do: "Go out and make disciples of all nations." Besides, I enjoyed the conversations. When I stumbled on a new interpretation of the Christian faith, one that emphasized that God did not condemn me and loved me unconditionally, I responded strongly to this Gospel of Grace and began teaching it to my peers. Many of my peers who shunned chapel were drawn to the message of the Bible studies I led. Chaplain asked one of my friends to tell me I was teaching the wrong message, but that did not deter me. I think I was looking for a freedom I did not yet know.

My classmate Patricia and I frequently discussed this newfound Gospel of Grace. We met often in the chapel to talk and grew fond of each other. I gradually developed an attraction for Patricia, and after a year-long inner debate, I wrote Patricia a letter to ask whether she would like to be in a relationship with me. I was really nervous about making my intentions known, and hoped it would work out. Meanwhile, I'd submitted an application to study in the United States, although I didn't expect anything to come of it. I had mentioned the application to Patricia, but it didn't seem to interfere with the feelings growing between us. Despite the positive direction our friendship was heading, I was overly conscious and cautious whenever I was with Patricia because it mattered to me what other people thought was going on. I wondered if they were saying, "There he goes, man of God, breaking the law...setting a bad example..." I was careful not to express my romantic feelings physically, let alone mention to anyone else how I felt about her.

In April of my sophomore year of high school, I received the news that I had been granted a scholarship to spend my last two years of high school in the United States at the United World College (UWC)—a school that brings students between ages sixteen and twenty from all over the world to study for the International Baccalaureate. The school's mission is to use education as a force for peace and to unite people from diverse cultures. I'd never imagined studying outside Uganda; the farthest away from home I'd been was the border with Kenya. When my father heard the news, he had me leave my local school and stay at home, as he didn't have the money to pay school fees for another term. So, for the next three months, I remained at home while the rest of my peers, Patricia included, were at school. Patricia said yes to my request about a relationship, so from then on we spoke frequently by phone. I ardently laid out plans for how our relationship would blossom, despite the distance, and fantasized about our future marriage; my life course was all set. Meanwhile, to prepare me to study in the U.S., my father asked two uncles to "advise" me on how to lead my life away from home:

> "Those people live differently, heh, don't allow them to change you..."
> "You'll see strange buildings...you've seen those skyscrapers on TV.... don't get distracted, just concentrate on your school work."

And Father interjected:

> "They also use words like 'bullshit' and have gangs…but just stay concentrated."

Because I had no emotional trust with my father, these words simply glided over me as I crafted my own version of the future. I read in the FAQ section of the UWC website that "nothing can prepare you for a UWC education. You simply have to be open." I scoffed. UWC didn't know that I served a God who was capable of preparing me for anything—I believed that UWC was in for a treat. From April until August, I sat in my bedroom daily, meditating and studying the Word of God until I could recite scripture from memory. I imagined I would soldier my way through it all with my faith, which could move mountains. I knew exactly what to do at UWC, I knew whom I'd marry, I knew what I was going to do with my life. I was only seventeen years old then and believed that my life course was set in stone. I was in for a big surprise. Little did I know that I had begun a journey that would raise many questions and lead to my radical unraveling—and, eventually, a personal transformation.

I never was Black until I stepped off KLM flight DL9319 in Amsterdam, en route to the UWC site in New Mexico. This was the first time in my life I'd been off the African continent or even outside Uganda. Up to now I had been surrounded by people who looked like me, who spoke with the same accent, and whose beliefs did not differ drastically from mine. But when I got off my flight, I saw more white skin than dark skin, and for the first time I was acutely conscious of myself as a Black person in this *muzungu* (white) land.

In my first year at UWC, I was first and foremost international, then Christian, then African. "Hi, my name is Andrew and I'm from Uganda." This is how I introduced myself to my fellow students, as they did with me. Back home I had identified primarily with my faith, and my Pentecostal Christianity was central to my identity. At UWC, however, I found myself embracing my Ugandan identity—after all, I was representing my home country. At the welcoming ceremony that began my UWC experience, I wore my *kanzu*—a long white robe that is one of the traditional dresses men wear in Uganda—a sisal hat, and carried a Ugandan flag. I had worn a kanzu only once in Uganda, at my sister's traditional wedding, and my peers in Uganda would have ridiculed me for wearing the robe, as it was uncommon to wear one in the urban areas of the country. At UWC, however, it seemed imperative that I put one on, as I thought wearing my plain kanzu and sisal hat made me appear more authentically African.

Because of the culture of international understanding central to the UWC mission, I was less conscious of myself as a dark-skinned person in muzungu land than I had been in Amsterdam. Looking back, I realize that the idea of Africa my peers from the continent and I nurtured while "representing the motherland" at UWC was closer to the nostalgic traditional Africa in Achebe's *Things Fall Apart* than the westernized urban suburbs where most of us had grown up. As I write this, I think of my father, who was the only one in his immediate family to leave the village for the opportunities of the city. Once established in the city, my father drove four hours eastward to visit his village homeland every Christmas, and our whole family traveled with him. In a way, he lived his life with one foot in the village and the other in the city. But for me, the city is where I was born, where I spent most of my time growing up, and where I received a formal Western education and instruction in the Christian faith—that is what being African meant to me before I left Uganda. However, as I traveled through Europe and North America before arriving in New Mexico, being African became associated with "blackness"; at UWC, Africa became an exotic phenomenon to be celebrated on the one hand, and to be criticized for its history of colonial bondage on the other.

My first outright conversation about race took place in my social anthropology class at UWC. I had to read a book on some social aspect of culture and write a critical review of it.

Since many of the entries in my social anthropology journal concerned race, I strolled into the school library looking for a book about that topic. I stumbled upon Beverly Daniel Tatum's *Why Are All the Black Kids Sitting Together in the Cafeteria?* As soon as I read the title, I knew this was the book I wanted to review. What I read in Tatum's book resonated with me on many levels, and her exploration of the psychology of race articulated an inner conversation I was having with myself. There was in fact an "African table" in the cafeteria at UWC, which was where the Africans, some students from the Caribbean, and one African American sat during lunch and often at dinner. This group was known for its loud conversations and arguments, and the Africans' obsession with Fanta soda.

Although I knew it was important for me to connect with my African peers, I did not feel comfortable at the table. I thought it felt exclusive, and, in fact, my non-African friends who sometimes joined me at the African table felt a little left out of the conversations and jokes that cracked up the rest of us. I was always deeply aware of this, and would consciously steer the conversation around to include these friends. I felt left out too, as I did not see myself as a loud, extroverted individual always ready with a joke, and I thought my counterparts considered me too serious or overly sensitive—maybe both. Now that I understand my highly sensitive temperament better, I know why I was uncomfortable at the table. I preferred less noise and warmer conversations in much smaller groups, and I felt the other African males were more macho than I, with their extroversion and apparently carefree conduct. I was more reserved and soft-spoken. I wanted to connect with them, but felt an emotional divide when I tried to do so. Consequently, I sat with my non-African peers and made some close friends, among them folks of Asian and Middle Eastern origin, and a few Latinos and Americans. Most of the people I connected with deeply were quiet and introverted, like me. In fact, with them I sometimes felt like an extrovert.

However, I felt that these new friends could not fully identify with me or understand the complexities of being an African living in the U.S. I was unable to have certain conversations with them because it would take so long to explain certain contexts, or because I feared I would not feel fully understood. When I reached out to my African friends, I did not find the depth of understanding or intimacy that I sought. I felt exactly like the middle man, the "oreo" as Tatum calls it in her book, the one who dances between the world of the whites and that of fellow Black students. Her ideas opened up a new world for me, one marked by thinking critically about religion and colonialism. The book review I wrote, which I still keep in my file cabinet, started me off on a journey of asking questions about race and religion.

As I started to ask probing questions about my religious affiliations, my church attendance began to deteriorate. Many of my African friends attended church regularly, and when I stopped going to church every Sunday, I lost another avenue of communication with other Africans. I also found it difficult to initiate a dialogue with them about my many questions for fear of being ridiculed for "being brainwashed by the whites." My friends probably would have shown a good degree of tolerance, but I didn't have the emotional connection with them to trust opening up. I had never put much importance on my ethnicity before coming to the U.S., but once I arrived here I felt more and more that I had to claim my African identity. And yet, I did not feel fully African in terms of personality and gender.

The religious identity that had been so central to my sense of self before leaving Uganda was no longer at the forefront; my blackness and my maleness began to take center stage once I arrived in the United States. This change was gradual. When I arrived at UWC-USA with my fellow first-year students, the second-years received us with warmth and open hearts. Despite their hospitality, I felt threatened the moment I stepped off the bus in the small town of Montezuma, New Mexico. I felt threatened because I quickly perceived that not everyone shared my religious beliefs. For the first six weeks of school, I spent most of my time alone in my dorm room, trying to make sense of my transition using what I'd learned from the Bible and from other "men of God." Nothing resonated, not a single word. My preparation for this new experience did not give me the sense of security I thought it would provide, and I was devastated.

Near the end of the term, I participated in an interfaith dialogue where I met students from different faiths and belief backgrounds. We debriefed on a previous activity on identity in which partners had to take one pipe cleaner away from each other's identity models, which each of us had made from five pipe cleaners. My partner was Malak, a student from Palestine. At the center of her model was a green circle that held the rest of her pipe cleaners in place; mine had a red cross that held the other pipe cleaners. During the activity, I removed the green circle that held the other pieces of Malak's model, and she said during the debriefing, "Andrew, when you removed the green pipe cleaner from my model, it felt like you had ripped my life apart because you took my Islam away." I remained silent, but I never let her comment stray far from my mind.

Soon after, following a discussion about heaven and hell in my English class, I walked up to my atheist instructor and tried to convince her of my beliefs. She shunned my attempt, saying, "Do not even talk to me about it, Andrew." I was nothing but bewildered by her response. In Uganda I was the "Bible Guy"—everyone listened when I preached—and here I was, figuratively slapped in the face for trying to evangelize a seventy-five-year-old atheist! I realized for the first time how my constant urge to evangelize made me fail to respect and honor other people's belief systems and traditions. Before I came to the U.S., evangelizing had helped me belong. Now, seeing the impact it had on other people's strongly held beliefs, the evangelist in me began to crumble. What had given me identity and a sense of belonging in Uganda would not work for me in this new place. Before leaving my home country, I had thought UWC was in for a treat—my arrival on campus. Three months into my experience in New Mexico, I knew I was wrong.

At the end of my first year at UWC-USA, I represented the school as a youth facilitator for the Pearson Seminar on Youth Leadership (PSYL) in Victoria, British Columbia. David, the adult coordinator who received me at Pearson, had a bald head and pierced ear, and he wore a tie-dye T-shirt, thermal underwear beneath his jean shorts, and mud shoes. I thought he was wearing women's leggings and said to myself, "Oh my gosh, I'm going to be taught by a bunch of atheists and homosexuals! What have I thrown myself into?" I felt an aversion to David, and to ward him off I said to him sternly in our first conversation, "I am a born again Christian." I said this thinking he was gay, as I tried to interpret new situations through the only lens I had—my old and only strand of identity. Upon meeting David I could not have imagined what PSYL had in store for me.

While at PSYL, I shared a conversation about faith with Valerie, an atheist Caucasian American who was another of the youth facilitators. After speaking at length about the salvation in Christ, I paused. Then Valerie spoke: "Too bad for people like us who were never raised Christian. I guess there's no option for us but to go to hell." Even though Valerie might have been mocking my beliefs, I did not see it that way. I took her words seriously, and when I sought solace in the woods that evening, her words haunted me. They pierced my heart and made me question the very framework that had given my world meaning, that had given me a sense of belonging. Could it be true that all these people at the camp, most of them non-believers whom I'd come to love so much, would go to hell for having their own beliefs? Trembling, I scribbled in my journal: "God, I do not know whether you've created a heaven or a hell, but if you have, I reject your heaven; I'll go to hell and love people out of it." I felt the blood rush to my head—I almost thought my brain would burst for writing such blasphemy. That evening, the priest in me became a rebel. My rebellion would later reveal a heart broken by coming to consciousness.

David, who had so put me off with his appearance, facilitated key workshops on gender, environment, and social justice, which is where I began to understand myself, and the world, in a whole new light. During Gender Day at PSYL, all the men and women spent time in separate programming for a full day, exploring the question, "What does it mean to be a woman or man in the 21st century, and what does each need in order to thrive?" It was the first time I was talking and participating in experiential activities with a group of male peers, where we discussed the concerns, questions, and difficult experiences each of us carried. I have never seen such a level of honesty, compassion, and vulnerability expressed by a group of men. We shared stories about our relationships with our fathers, about our emerging sexuality, about male-on-male violence, and how we could support one another instead of competing. I had never participated in such conversations.

Because of the trust we built that day, I opened up about three key memories I had never shared with anyone: my mother's death, my relationship with my father, and my Christian upbringing. With this opening up came a sudden burst of tears and pain. I'd never really grieved my mother's passing because I claimed that Jesus Christ had taken care of that, and I had needed to have hope. I also realized how the distance between my father and me drove me to find solace in church. In church I had initially felt safe to be the "emotional male," but in fact I never felt as tenderly supported as I thought I would; instead I felt judged and shamed, and thus I sought interpretations of the Bible that offered me some validation. At PSYL, I felt that tender support and truthful speaking I had been seeking for the very first time. I felt cheated by my background, and that I was now finally fitting into my own skin. At that moment I also realized that my old way of being and belonging could not support the tumultuous transition I was going through, both physically and psychologically. I was drenched in tears, and David embraced and whispered in my ear, "I got you, brother. I got you." At PSYL I finally found the support I needed to choose to be my true self—to show my vulnerability and emotion, to talk about "touchy-feely" stuff, to be quiet and introverted, to drum and make music without fear of judgment. I resolved not to look back.

Post PSYL, I read *Men and the Water of Life*, a book by mythologist Michael Meade (1994) in which he talks about male vulnerability and the relationship between fathers and sons. Meade's work helped me confront my difficult relationship with my father. I'm not fully healed and may never be, but being conscious of the wounds caused by my family background is already a thousand steps in the right direction. I also read works by Jungian analyst Robert A. Johnson: *We: Understanding the Psychology of Romantic Love* (2009); *He: Understanding Masculine Psychology* (2020a); and *She: Understanding Feminine Psychology* (2020b). These books validated me and helped me cultivate a capacity for vulnerability, which the masculine examples in my life before PSYL had completely disregarded. I also began to reflect on my relationship with Patricia, the girl in Uganda. Besides the strain that distance had put on our relationship, I was changing at a very fast rate, and my priorities were changing too. I realized that I no longer had the strength to maintain my commitment to Patricia, and that it would be too difficult to explain to her all the radical changes I was going through. So I did what I'd promised never to do, and what my church would utterly condemn (or so I reasoned): I picked up the phone and called Patricia to end our one-year relationship. I walked away, leaving her heartbroken. Soon after, I also walked away from the Pentecostal Church I was attending in New Mexico when the pastor said one Sunday morning during his final blessing, "Let's preach the gospel of Christ to all the world; we must never rest. Let's bring into the body of Christ even those who worship Allah." My knee jerked when I heard these words. I thought of Malak. I remembered David. I saw Valerie. I stood up, gathered my belongings, walked out the door, and never looked back.

The journey of reflecting on the multiple strands of my identity that began during my time at UWC continued when I got to college. My college application process led me to Dartmouth, in part because of the financial aid the college offered but also for the stellar academic experience I expected to have at the school.

The moment I stepped off the Dartmouth Coach in Hanover, New Hampshire, I knew Dartmouth was going to be my home. In April of my final year at UWC I had visited the school to attend the Dimensions Program, which is held to enable students admitted to the college to gauge whether Dartmouth is the right fit for them. My host, Stephan, was an African American first-year student. When signing up for a host before my visit, I'd indicated "Black" as my top preference. At UWC, being Black was synonymous with being African, therefore I expected to get a student host from Africa, so I was surprised when I found out Stephan was African American. We got along very well and still meet up; however, it never dawned on me until later in my first year at Dartmouth that Black was synonymous with African American, and that Africans were considered first and foremost international students. Contrary to what I had expected, Africans and African American students were two distinct communities on campus. I now know, of course, that my narrow assumptions reduced both groups to a skin color. I'm now aware that many differences, allegiances, and histories exist both within and between these two groups.

The classes I have taken make me realize, however, that it is important for me to remain aware and stand in solidarity with other Black people, whether they are African American or African or Jamaican, in this country and elsewhere where white people are more privileged, especially at the expense of colored minorities. Claiming my own blackness has been gradual and still is in its infant stages. Although I have experienced some racial incidents, my connection to my own blackness has come about not through a direct act of discrimination but through my intellectual exploration of issues of social justice and equity. I am also acutely aware of how Black men are represented in the media. From basketball commercials to TV shows, Black men are depicted with buff chests and biceps, as tough and unyielding, or as eloquent intellectuals who shepherd the rest of the "Black herd" into a promising future.

If I had not developed crucial social-emotional and critical thinking skills at PSYL, UWC, and Dartmouth, I would have bought into the stereotypical male created by a media industry dominated by white males, and I would have felt less of a man as a result, just as I felt less of a man by trying to meet the standards my father set when I was a child. I am quite thin-skinned, overly sensitive, and mostly soft-spoken, a lover of literature rather than an economist, political scientist or engineer, as are many of my African male peers. I am not the kind of Black male glorified in the media or the kind of male heralded in my father's culture back in Uganda—in fact he never tired of urging me to study medicine. I do not feel comfortable performing some of the stereotypical roles expected of the male. In fact, while I was still in a relationship with Patricia, my brother joked that if we'd ever have children, I would be the kids' mother and Patricia the father. I think he was referring to my soft-spoken, sensitive nature, which is usually associated with femininity, especially in Uganda. In my sophomore year of college, I came across *The Highly Sensitive Person*, a work by psychologist Elaine Aron (Aron & Moorjani 2022). This work helped me reframe my thin-skinned nature, which I had felt ashamed of, in a positive light, and offered a model of self-care that has enabled me to live well in my relationships, and in an intense place like Dartmouth.

Although I would now describe myself as Black in terms of the color of my skin, I was unlikely to do so until recently because of the complex issues surrounding the word and my lack of shared history with the Black people who call the U.S. home. And yet, if I were to completely disassociate myself from the Black struggles in this country, I'd feel guilty. Somewhere in my memory the words of my Ugandan uncle, who is now an immigrant resident of the United States, ring loud and clear. When I told him I intended to do psychology at Dartmouth, he said, "Andrew, what are you going to do with that? Why not economics, medicine, or engineering? Remember, you are a Black man in a white man's country." If these words mean anything to me today, it is this: the story of Black maleness is a story of survival in a world constructed by and for white male supremacy, and perhaps careers in economics, medicine, and engineering are the tools that give Black males a chance to be in power and to thrive, and to create a world in which they are seen as human—to overcome the subordination white power robs them of.

I cannot be fully separate from my father, his blackness, his history, and the colonial legacy in which his life is embedded, so perhaps I also cannot be separate from my fellow Black folks in the U.S., regardless of heritage. The issues of race in this country are my issues too; the issues of blackness are mine to own. My maleness, too, and how I belong to it is both a statement of authentic selfhood and one of resistance. I have learned a lot about oppression and resistance from the classes I have taken at Dartmouth and UWC on identity, gender and feminism, religion, colonialism, and social change. I have learned about my own psychological makeup, my strengths and limits, and that my Black, sensitive masculinity cannot be separated from the sociocultural web in which it is embedded. Being conscious that I belong to both my thin-skinned nature and to society, and that I need to make choices that enable me and others to thrive, is indispensable—it is the work of a lifetime.

At Dartmouth, I continue to reflect on my journey of transformation with a mixture of wonder at how critical incidents in my life have formed me, remorse and regret for some of the ways I sought to gain attention, and gratitude for the supportive adults in my life who have helped me develop critical social and emotional skills. I am also indebted to the education I've received at Dartmouth, for without my intellectual journey at both UWC and Dartmouth, I would not have been able to come home to a self I feel is authentic—a self I can claim as my own. Whereas I previously said yes to whatever society wanted me to be—a priest, an ideal example, a less-than-masculine man, an oppressed Black male—I have gained a critical ability to reject self-defeating caricatures of myself and embrace my authentic self. The protection of the college campus has given me a safe place to cultivate that self.

Because of my experiences, I've devoted my time outside the classroom to help my fellow youths discover their authentic selves. Each summer I work at youth empowerment art camps, and I recently designed and directed my own youth leadership camp in Uganda. Even though I have rejected the image of the pious priest that I conformed to early in my life and the earlier expressions of my religiosity, I am a religion major at Dartmouth, which enables me to explore the intersections of gender and power, spirituality and ecology. In my personal life, I have developed a spirituality comprising an appreciation of poetic language, nature, and mystery. I want to find a community of practice in which my intellectual and personal interests can flourish, and in which I can work to advance social justice and the greater good. However, I am not in a rush to belong to a particular religion. The guiding ethos of my personal and intellectual journey has been inspired by the very first assignment I received from my Dartmouth writing professor: "What questions keep you awake at night?" I've since structured my academic experience around the questions that have kept me awake at night: questions of identity, transformation, and the possibility of peace and social equity.

I have more questions than answers about my own evolving journey and identity. It has been a journey of making, being unmade, and remaking myself. For now, what I'm sure of is this: I'm stepping out of the red dress of shame I had to wear during my childhood because I displayed "feminine" characteristics. I'm also stepping out of my father's shoes, dress shirts, and cufflinks—the trappings of a single story of being masculine. Even though I know that some of my father's struggles are my own, I am seeking a different way of belonging in the world as a man, choosing something other than violence. I left home six years ago to embark on a journey of transformation, and I have changed. Now I am arriving in a new home. I am coming home to my ever-evolving self.

## References


Aron, E. N., & Moorjani, A. *The Highly Sensitive Person By Elaine N. Aron, Sensitive Is the New Strong By Anita Moorjani*. 2 Books Collection Set. Broadway Books/Atria/Enliven Books Ltd, 2022.

Johnson, R. A. *We: Understanding the Psychology of Romantic Love*. HarperOne, 2009.

Johnson, R. A. *He: Understanding Masculine Psychology* (Revised). Harper Perennial, 2020a.

Johnson, R. A. *She: Understanding Feminine Psychology* (Revised). Harper Perennial, 2020b.

# 8 The Big Chop

*B. Coombs*

I was born in Baltimore on August 18, 1988. I am the only child of my mother Wanda and my father Ronald—two people who are Black in two completely different ways.

My mother is Black in the sense that most people understand the term: she has a dark brown complexion, tightly curled hair, and a broader nose, much like her mother and father. She was raised in Baltimore, a once predominantly white city that is now, sadly, mostly famous for negative social conditions that are often associated, in Western culture, with blackness, such as a high crime rate and poverty. When I was a child, my mother visited an elderly relative of ours and mined her for information about our heritage, information that had been passed down orally for generations. This relative told her that we are descended from a woman who was born in Madagascar many centuries ago. According to official records, her name was "Sofa" (most likely, it was the Anglicized "Sofia") who was brought to America and put to work by the Beckwiths, a white slave-owning family in Virginia, whose blood still runs in us today.

My father, on the other hand, is Black in a more technical sense. He is tan-complected—a dark yellow-peach—and his hair, though now barely there, is straight and fine. His features are not what is typically considered Black or white; he looks like he might be the son of a white person and a Hispanic person. His late parents had the same look, as do many people on his side of the family, from which I am now, unfortunately, somewhat estranged. My father knows little about his mother's side of the family, except that it apparently was connected to Latin America, perhaps Cuba. He considers himself Black mostly, I think, because his paternal ancestry can be traced back to Jamaica and Haiti. Through my own research, I have been able to discover that my paternal grandparents married and immigrated to the United States, from where I do not know, shortly before my father's older sister Joanne was born, ostensibly to ensure that their children would be born American citizens.

I have always considered myself Black, which is a silly statement to make in some ways, since race (as I only begun hearing when I started college at Dartmouth in 2006, and as I now agree) is a social construct. This popular axiom was born not only to emphasize the meaninglessness of race but also to highlight its

DOI: 10.4324/9781003376255-11

"bigger than us-ness." In other words, I could not wake up tomorrow morning and decide that I am white, when a world full of people would see the contrary. Nevertheless, I am a combination of my mother's and my father's blackness in the sense that, to others, it seems I am at the same time obviously Black and still not-quite-black. My face is much like my mother's, but with a thinner nose. My hair and hers are kinky and thick and strong. The kicker is my complexion, which has always been the source of confusion for others and for myself. My skin is a dirty yellow or butterscotch. My nose turns red when I am sad and my ears turn red when I am angry. The blue of my veins is visible. In the summer I am quick to roast to a light brown, but in the winter I pale considerably. I am lighter than my father, and lighter than some people who are classified as white. I have been told more than once that, were it not for my hair that I now wear in an Afro, people would have no firm idea about my race.

Many enlightened non-black people can probably understand that, after centuries of physical and psychological torment, Black people care a lot about complexion: their own and those of other Black people. However, I do not know if those same people could guess the extent to which the Black community is absorbed by this concern. "Color struck" is what Black people call other Black people who are hung up on complexion. The term often alludes to Black people who prefer to date other Black people who are not darker than a certain shade, but it also refers in a general sense to Black people who make conclusions about others based solely on their skin tone—who trust or admire more those who are brighter than the coppery brown common to Black Americans. The first time I heard the term I was age ten. My mom was trying to explain to me why a distant cousin had asked when I had been adopted. Not if.

Color-struck thinking is prevalent in our community. It's a vestige of slave days, a holdover of the mentality that once shaped what it meant to live as a Black person in white society: if white is right, then lighter is righter. Although the majority of Black Americans have white ancestors, the light-skinned among us whose color most reveals that whiteness are often placed, misguidedly, on a pedestal. Many light-skinned folks are incorrectly assumed to have a white parent—an assumption that has plagued me my entire life. People who've barely known me have asked about my heritage, and while such intrusion does take a certain gall, it stops very few people. The worst part is I tend to feel awkward and apologetic when I have to explain to these bright-eyed inquirers that, despite my light color, I do not have a white parent.

"But," they beg, "there is some white in you, right?" I guess their hope is their worldview on Blacks and melanin will not be fundamentally challenged. I sometimes dutifully say yes, but remind them that most Black Americans have white ancestors.

I have been asked, "What are you?" or some version of this question hundreds of times. In high school I was asked by brown-skinned girls who were more extroverted than I was and who teased my "yellow ass" about this or that, or who asked me loudly why I was "so yellow," as if I was obligated to explain. In college I was asked more gently, but no less often, by romantic interests or friends who felt we had become close enough. (Usually they revealed that they had been dying to know all along.) I remember being asked by a classmate at Dartmouth, as the summer sun bounced brightly off my thigh, "Why are you so pale?"

But the fact is, my color is me. It represents a long line of individuals and cultures of which I am part. I cannot help but love it, and today I would not change it, even if I could. But this was not always the case. I suppose the reaction my complexion often causes in others is the peculiar thing that has made me sensitive and alert, in the past, to questions about my background. This sensitivity began when I was about four years old, two years after I enrolled in a unique but flawed school that would change my life.

For 11 years I attended Maarifa, an Afrocentric elementary and middle school on the outskirts of Baltimore City. Maarifa means "knowledge" in Kiswahili, a Bantu language spoken in East Africa. (Through genetic tests, I would later learn I am descended from the Bantu people.) As Maarifa expanded over the years, so too did its name, until it eventually became known as Maarifa Shule ya Mzingi Upili, which translates to Maarifa Elementary and Middle School. Maarifa was almost as young as I was when my parents first enrolled me. The school was founded in the 1980s by a Black husband-and-wife team who envisioned an institution that specifically catered to the needs of children of color—children who desperately needed to be told that they could succeed in American society, that they too could be writers and scientists and inventors if they studied hard and set goals.

Maarifa was a lovely dream, and it did a lot of things right. It instilled in me a racial and personal pride that endures to this day and that I will carry with me forever. Not everyone who is born Black is automatically proud of that fact; many are ashamed. More common is an ambivalence toward being Black that is not based in a progressive, post-racial mindset but in a willingness to be distant from a gut-wrenching history. It is likely that I would have found pride in my blackness even if I hadn't attended Maarifa; my mom and her family—my brown-skinned aunts and grandmother who grew up before and during the civil rights movement—would have ensured it. But Maarifa took things to another level—one that was not always healthy or fair.

Each grade at the school had a name that corresponded with an African tribe: the first graders were called the Masai Class, for example, and the fourth graders the Igbo. Every classroom also had a red, Black, and green flag, the colors of the Pan-African movement that, respectively, symbolize the blood shed in the fight for freedom, the Black race itself, and the land of Africa. At school we called our male teachers "Baba" and the women "Mama," the Kiswahili words for father and mother. Hand-sized people cut out of brown construction paper lined the walls of our classrooms; and when doing a science project, we had to explain not only how such-and-such technology or invention or discovery would benefit humankind but also how it would benefit Black people specifically. The science fair prizes were named after famous Black engineers through history, like Imhotep, Benjamin Banneker, George Washington Carver, and Mae Jemison.

We began each school day by gathering in a circle and singing this song: "Maarifa, Maarifa, dedicated to knowledge; Maarifa, Maarifa, dedicated to knowledge; We go there each day, to work in our way, to build a strong African nation!" Then we usually sang "Lift Every Voice and Sing" by James Weldon Johnson and John Rosamond Johnson: a treasured song in the Black community (some call it our "national anthem") for over a hundred years, which featured prominently in the civil rights movement.

My attending Maarifa helped both me and my mother, who told me she had privately fought for years against the sting of childhood encounters that had made her believe that, as a Black person, she was innately inferior to others. She particularly recalled a white person having spat at her when she was a little girl because she'd had the audacity to walk beside him on the sidewalk. My mom, therefore, was deeply invested in my education at Maarifa. She was learning and becoming enlightened right alongside me, grateful that her child had been given the chance to feel not cursed but blessed to be born a Black person. Looking back, I too am grateful. With its academic rigor, Maarifa laid a strong foundation that prepared me for the hard work it would take to succeed in challenging schools later in life. More importantly, it engraved in me a sense of self-respect and dignity that I could not shake today, even if I tried.

However, despite Maarifa's admirable core, it also had deficiencies that contributed in no small part to my self-consciousness about my skin tone. Maarifa was prone to political incorrectness and insensitivity, and there was something subtle but ugly about the information we were given and the impressions we were encouraged to form. The school walked a fine line between teaching personal pride and denigrating the heritage of others. I grew up feeling more than simply proud or happy to be Black; I was taught that Black people are better than everybody else. This evolved into my conviction that brown-skinned blackness was, in fact, the ideal. I mentioned the brown construction-paper people that lined the walls of our classrooms—a nice enough idea, but what about the millions of Black people in the world who are not coppery brown? My mother—Mama Wanda, as she was affectionately called by the students, teachers, and other parents—was floored when I admitted to her one day that I wanted to have dark brown skin like she did.

It should have shocked no one that I came to think poorly of myself merely because I had light skin. Teachers at Maarifa often told us young students about "scientific studies" that showed a link between more melanin and greater intellect. I now can see that this was their attempt to build up our confidence, since the majority of us were indeed coppery brown or darker. I also know that brown-skinned Black people may need to be assured more than their lighter-skinned compatriots that their skin tone is all right in a lighter-is-righter world. At the time, however, I was one of perhaps three light-skinned children in the school; and an institution that was dedicated to the liberation and strengthening of Black minds should not have compromised that effort by overtly focusing on skin of a certain shade. My peers, who were encouraged to draw people only with brown crayon, treated me like an outsider.

My mom saved the day. Wise to the propaganda that my teachers were trumpeting, which worsened as the school and I grew older, she bought me a set of crayons called People Colors, which I still own to this day. While at school I was taught that brown was the best form of blackness, at home my mom went to great lengths to ensure that I never felt as inadequate about my lightness as she had once felt about her darker complexion. People Colors came in flesh-colored tones like Chestnut, Wheat, Pecan, Sand, and Olive. I brought them to school to share with my classmates and was delighted to see them enjoy the crayons as much as I did. What I did not understand was why our teachers did not seem happy about the drawings we made with them.

One of my most distinct childhood memories occurred at Maarifa around age four. Despite the People Colors, after school one day a brown-skinned classmate asked me if I belonged to the race that we had, in essence, been taught was our enemy. "Are you white?" he blurted accusingly, staring at me from a few feet away as he beat on an African drum. I still feel my indignation! I flinched and responded with a shriek. "No!" When my mom picked me up from school that day, I asked her how people are supposed to know the difference between white and Black people. Despite her constant interventions at home, at school I was still being taught that Caucasians were, as a group, racist and untrustworthy. I did not understand how or why anyone could mistake me for a white person when I knew I was a good person.

> "Don't worry," she said with a laugh. "One day you'll be able to tell from a mile away."
> "How do you know?" I pressed. "Are you sure?"
> "Yes," she said, "All white people are not bad and all Black people are not good."

That is a phrase she would repeat many times in my years at Maarifa.

Questions about my skin color and heritage persisted when I entered the prestigious Western Senior High School, a formerly all-white school for etiquette instruction. By the time I enrolled it had a predominantly Black student population, but also some whites, Asians, and Hispanics from local neighborhoods. For me the most important thing about Western was not its racial composition but the fact that it was an all-girls school. I chuckle now, but at the time I did sincerely want to be able to concentrate on my studies without the distraction of boys. That was well and good; but my knowledge of men and relationships would be set back four critical years in ways I would not understand until much later, including the connection between race and modern dating.

Dating opportunities were not abundant during high school, given the estrogenic atmosphere, but I also did not have much interest. I became close with only one young man during my adolescence, a tan-skinned guy with tiny ringlets in his hair, whose Black father and Hispanic mother were estranged.

Many girls at Western thought he was my brother, and they would say how cute he was and ask if he was seeing anyone.

One day, as this friend and I were riding a bus to downtown Baltimore to see a play, I casually mentioned in conversation the fact that he was a Black person. "I'm not Black," he interjected, disgust in his voice. This moment gnawed at me for the rest of the time we saw each other, as I had the impression that he—like so many Black people—was all too eager to shed the label.

At Dartmouth I made more strides in understanding myself in relation to the opposite sex. Maarifa had discouraged its girl and boy students from forming close friendships, and at Western I had never had or even desired a boyfriend. But in the wilderness of New Hampshire, while I still remained boyfriendless, I was pleased to discover that I did have something to interest and offer other people.

I quickly learned that what my mother had told me in defiance of Maarifa's apparent credo was true: not all white people are bad! Surrounded by them as I was for the first time in my life, I soon realized that in many simply human ways, white people are no different from me. Some people happened to be prejudiced or entitled or selfish, incidentally in line with my middle school teachings, but of course many were as kind, funny, and hard-working as I imagined myself to be. This enlightenment transferred to dating. While I did not have a boyfriend during my undergraduate years, I did come to understand that white men could find me attractive and that I could be attracted to them. I went to movies with white men, had lunch and dinner with them, and enjoyed walking and conversing with them. At Dartmouth I met one of my dearest friends, a self-described "white-ish" Native American man. Another white male friend who hailed from Kansas seemed to prefer the company of Black women. All of these were firsts for me, and I welcomed them.

After graduating from Dartmouth and moving to Washington, D.C., to enroll in a master's program at Georgetown, I learned even more about myself. In an effort to test the waters, I created a profile on two dating websites in which I tried to advertise my genuine self. I mentioned how much reading, writing, and researching I did as a student and a part-time reporter; I spoke of my passion for philosophy and religion; I described myself as earthy, compassionate, and wry. I listed my race as "Black, Hispanic/Latin," but my profile screamed blackness: I told the world that I was reading *The Autobiography of Malcolm X* and admitted the uncanny ease with which I can quote from *The Boondocks*, an animated television show centered on a militant Black boy with a huge 'fro. Interest came rapidly from men of all races, ages, and occupations. Many of these men commented on my "awesome" or "impeccable" hair as an icebreaker—charming, if also a little predictable.

Despite this ego boost, I soon found that online dating reflects certain assumptions many people harbor about race and romance. A study published by one site I used cross-examined each gender and race to determine how often each subgroup contacted every other subgroup, and how often members of a targeted subgroup responded to a first message. The study found that Black women received the fewest first messages and were the least likely to receive a response after making first contact.

Can anyone be shocked by these results? I believe that most people would agree that Black women have it the roughest in the real world, including in terms of the dominant perceptions of beauty. Comments by site users ran the gamut, but one person wrote bluntly, "So what we have learned is that white men are dicks." Others said the numbers simply echoed statistical odds—more whites than non-whites live in English-speaking countries and can afford the time and money for computers and dating websites. A smaller percentage of users said everyone should face the facts: the white standard of beauty and the white superiority complex are so deeply engrained in Western culture that they of course show up in a study of behavioral patterns. This was right on in my mind, as most of the people who commented on the study did seem to be groping for a way to rationalize an ugly truth.

This truth was manifested even more clearly on the second dating site I joined, on which users were able to specify the physical and mental attributes of their ideal mate—their level of schooling, their religiosity, and, naturally, their race. This site was dominated by white men, the vast majority of whom wanted nothing to do with Black women, as indicated by the fact that many had checked every box in the "preferred race" category except African-American. My guess? Many white men who are opposed to dating Black women are perhaps put off by the images of Black women lazily and offensively propagated in American pop culture: the "welfare queen," or some other gaudy, crass ghetto caricature.

As double minorities, Black women deal with expectations and a level of scrutiny no other group can imagine. Probably the best illustration of this is the lengths to which we go to straighten our hair, which many of us do to gain the hegemonic approval of others. As early as age three or four we glean—usually from our mothers or other female guardians—that our naturally kinky hair is childish, wild, and embarrassing, something to be hidden or fixed. We learn how important it is for our hair to look "normal," as defined by what the majority has and understands, and the majority of the world neither has nor understands the hair of Black people.

Black girls and women have four options for fitting the hair mold: wearing wigs, wearing weaves, pressing our hair with grease and a hot comb, or getting a perm—what Black folks call "relaxing" our hair. Most Black women, young and old, get perms, which remains the standard. Having had a perm for most of her life, my mom now wears her silver hair naturally, but she is an anomaly. My 83-year-old maternal grandmother continues to relax her hair, which is reflective of the norm. Most Black women, however, are perpetually dissatisfied with their hair, even if it has been permed, and thus find themselves running in a stressful loop, all their lives, in an effort to get the hair they desire (and our society, for the most part, mandates).

I got my first perm when I was thirteen years old. For years my mother had disallowed the procedure, knowing the pains both psychic and literal that awaited, but she finally relented on my nagging insistence. I had worn my hair naturally in my early years at Maarifa and thought nothing of it, as I did not specifically associate my curly hair with pride in my race or in myself. Like most unpermed Black girls, I simply knew that my hair would be straightened for special occasions with a hot comb most likely warmed on the kitchen stove, with it sizzling as it sliced through my thick brown curls and filling our home with a sickly sweet aroma as it, essentially, cooked and burned my hair.

If I had gone to a mainstream school with other little Black girls whose mothers had straightened their hair, my kinks likely would have bothered me sooner than they did. But at Maarifa, where Black was beautiful and many girls wore dreadlocks, I never felt ashamed or self-conscious about my natural hair, which I wore in tight, beaded twists until I was a preteen. I could have chosen a more conventionally "feminine" style, but then again I lived in a neighborhood full of boys who I raced against and biked with and caught bugs with, so I shunned the un-fun care of a delicate hairdo.

By the end of middle school, however, a vague notion that I had been harboring since childhood finally came to the surface. For years I had imagined that I had existed in a kind of cocoon, and that one day I would emerge from that cocoon with the markers of conventional white beauty. This weird idea grew out of my childhood confusion over skin tone and the way Maarifa had shamed me as a light-skinned Black child. Although I always knew I was Black, simultaneously I believed that Black people were always brown and that people who weren't Black were always lighter than brown. And, since I also knew that Black people have tightly coiled hair while people who aren't Black typically don't, quietly and subconsciously I came to believe that I, as light as some white people, was destined to have long, slick, straight hair.

Twisted, I know.

This impulse drove me to get my first perm, which I can remember clearly. The night before the big day, my mother oiled my scalp with Bergamot hair grease: a sweet-smelling blue goop that has been her favorite (and the favorite of many a Black Baby Boomer) since she was a child. She untwisted my already fairly long, thick hair, carefully combed it into sections, then dipped her fingers into the grease and rubbed it into every inch of my hair. The next day her friend Ms. Lois massaged mounds of a cold, white and smelly compound into my scalp, letting it sit until the lye took hold and really started to make me feel like my whole head was on fire—a sign the process was going well. The longer the burn, the straighter your hair at the end! When I had taken all I could, Ms. Lois rushed me to a sink and washed it all out. I gazed up into the mirror above the sink, and I stood awed and blinking—I knew the face that stared back at me but not the damp, limp hair that hung around it.

At first, I was in love. As Ms. Lois blow-dried my hair, it whisked about with feather-light ease. In the coming weeks and months I could not stop marveling and touching it, petting and combing it. It was as if I had finally emerged from that cocoon and was moving toward the appearance fated for me as a person who did not have brown skin. But shortly after this essential rite of passage for most Black women, the illusions started to fall away. I began to understand the depressing reality of what it means to be a Black woman who has permed her hair.

I struggled to adjust to the never-ending routine of maintaining the perm, of keeping it looking healthy and freshly done—which, as any Black woman can attest, is no easy feat. Every night, I had to pin up and then wrap my hair with a kerchief so that it would have a natural-seeming curl the next morning. Every other day I had to apply hair grease to my scalp, so that my hair, made brittle by the harsh chemical process of the perm, didn't get dry and break and maybe even fall out. Every two weeks I had to go to the beauty salon to have my hair washed and conditioned by a professional, and every six weeks I had to have a "touch-up" to re-administer the lye to the new hair that had grown in since. And most of all, I had to avoid any type of moisture—humidity, rain, even sweat from physical exertion—a first for me.

A tomboy by nature, initially I took it as a personal challenge to maintain my perm, if only to prove to myself that I could succeed with a regimen so discouraging. In short order, though, the situation became ghastly. Scabs formed as a reaction to the perming chemicals. My hair thinned and lost volume, and I became plagued by split ends and dandruff—all problems I'd never had before. I spent every other Saturday in a gossipy beauty salon, while my mom shelled out hundreds of dollars for a procedure that was embittering me. Moreover, I was never happy with my hair anymore. It looked less creative than my Maarifa-era twists, and less full and lustrous by far than my special-occasion hot comb "dos". I took personally my failure to succeed in one of the quintessential regimens of Black womanhood, and felt more dissatisfied in my appearance than ever before.

By the time that I left for Dartmouth, I knew I wanted my kinks back—but this can be a tough thing for a Black woman to do, as we have largely been made to internalize the idea that unprocessed hair is not acceptable. I am not the first person to realize that having a perm costs a lot, both monetarily and psychically, but most of us do it anyway, fearing the social consequences of wearing our hair naturally. I endured six more years of what can only candidly be described as misery before I worked up the courage to cut off my straight, shoulder-length tresses.

I made the big chop, as they call it in natural hair circles, in May 2009, during the summer between my junior and senior years of college. Up to then I had let my hair grow during the months I was on campus, so that my usual beautician, Ms. Maria, could straighten all the new hair during visits home to Baltimore. But in my junior spring I took a class on television history, during which I unexpectedly became a fan of the 1970s Black sitcom *Good Times*, a show in which several female characters sport voluptuous Afros. That moved the needle—I finally felt empowered to make the long-overdue switch. I took the train back to Baltimore late that spring and unveiled the huge mass of kinks and curls I had been saving up for Ms. Maria. But this time my request on what to do with them was different, and shocked Ms. Maria and the whole salon.

"I'd like you to cut off all my permed hair," I said, anxious but certain.

I felt the heat of eyes on me. "Are you sure?" she asked. I confirmed.

It is hard to describe how I felt as I heard her scissors snip and snip (an unfamiliar sound) and watched in the mirror as eight years of posturing and frustration fell in bundles on the floor. Even then, at the point of no return, I feared I was making a terrible mistake. But when she stopped cutting and handed me the small blue mirror, I was relieved right down to my soul. I had done something that scores of Black women might dream about but never do: I had defied expectations and forever left behind the maddening cult of processed hair.

Since the big chop, I have noticed that young Black women interact with me differently. Most noticeably, there is no tension over just what the other is doing with her hair, which normally can occur between two Black women who so much as pass in the street. I do occasionally encounter a nervous glance downward instead of eye-to-eye contact; I wonder if that is because my Afro reminds some women of their own suppressed inner itch to go natural.

I return to the quandary I laid out at the start of this piece—that race is both internal and external, a product of our acceptance of elements that are given weight by other people. I am a self-identified Black person: one who may seem blackish to some, non-black but for my hair to others, and unequivocally Black to countless more.

Early in life I struggled as an Other in my own community. But today, I have different tools at my disposal: tools more metaphorical but no less useful than the People Color crayons I was gifted in middle school. Today I am equipped to understand and, sometimes, deflect (with what I hope is a measure of grace) those inquiries that pry into my heritage, whether they come from friends or colleagues or strangers—anyone who looks at me and has to sort through some confusion, steeped in centuries' worth of racial thinking that performs othering.

Today I am glad to know that, in time, I was able to learn how wide the Venn center is between self-pride and misconception. At twenty-three years old, it feels good to be comfortable in my own skin.

# 9 Gotta Keep Climbin' All De Time

*Candice Jimerson*

"Mom, Mommy!"

"Call the ambulance, Chantal! Tell them your mother can't breathe. Give them our address!"

My footsteps shook the glassware on the buffet table as I ran to the phone. After hanging up, I returned for more instructions. My mother's body lay on the floor, her back against the flowered love seat. My father, with his arms around her, knelt by her side talking nonstop.

"Stay calm, Anne, you'll be okay, don't worry. Chantal, go get Mrs. Smith, tell her to come over right away!"

Pain shot through my cold knuckles as I knocked on the wooden door. "It's Chantal," I said to the groggy voice that answered the door. "It's my mom, she can't breathe. We need your mom to … I, I." Tears rolled down my face as my body lost its strength and fell into a chair in the house.

The next thing I remember is kneeling next to a bed in the Smith girls' bedroom. One of the girls tried to reassure me, "Don't cry, Chantal, God will take care of your mother." The girls prayed with me, and I prayed by myself. I cried myself to sleep at the Smith house that night. Early the next morning, I woke my younger brother (I cannot remember how he got to our neighbor's house) and walked back to my house. My uncle was inside on the phone, and my father sat in the back of the house. He stood up and said to me, "We lost her Chantal, she's gone." He embraced me as I stood motionless for a few seconds, then I returned the embrace and said, "Well now, she won't have to worry about the folks at church anymore." No tears fell from my eyes, yet something inside me had changed. I felt empty, incomplete, and numb.

Against my father's wishes, I went to school that morning. In the middle of eighth-grade algebra, it hit me. I went to the bathroom and cried without ceasing. One of my best friends followed me into the bathroom, where I told her of my mother's death. She told my algebra teacher, who was a pastor at a local church. I will never forget how he took me into the computer room and talked with me. He explained what God had planned for my mother and how I must understand God's will. I told him that last night while I prayed, I knew she would die; God had told me. I was now afraid of what life would be like

DOI: 10.4324/9781003376255-12

for my family and I was angry that this had to happen to me. God had something in store for me, my teacher said. I now believe that He does.

My father's mother helped me to understand the death of my mother, and her guidance and wisdom influence many of the ways that I look at life and our existence on this earth. She told me often that we all must die and that God has a time, place, and reason set for our death. One must not try to defy God's will, but to be thankful for all the other blessings that he bestows upon us daily in both small and big ways. My grandmother was a symbol of stability in my life; I could always count on her, she would never leave us. Of course, I realized as I grew older that she, too, must die, but I felt that one of the reasons that God kept my "granny" alive was to help us survive this tragedy in our lives. She was also the repository of traditional Black culture in our family; her cooking, folktales, and stories about the past grounded me in my heritage when I was being attacked by nonblacks in my life. This knowledge and pride remains with me today.

I only survived these past six years through the grace of God. I owe all of my success to Him and to my parents. My mother gave me the foundation of my first thirteen years, from which I draw most of my values, while my father reinforced those values as well as supporting, advising, and loving me. My father and I did not have a close relationship before my mother's death, although I loved him dearly. However, since her death we have become best friends. We talk about everything: politics, religion, people, relationships, the world. And although I have learned to disagree respectfully with him, our talks strengthen my character. My mother's death caused my father to be more attentive to the needs of my brother and me and to play a more active role in our lives.

My mother's death has changed my entire outlook on life. I feel I skipped my adolescence, a time, in my eyes, of careless abandon, silly mistakes, and independence. Instead, I found myself overwhelmed with sorrow, depression, and responsibility. My brother, who was six at the time of my mother's death, and my father, who was psychologically devastated by it, both depended on me. I resented having this responsibility during my teen years; I felt that it wasn't fair that I had to clean up "all the time," that I had to worry about my brother's clothes, homework, and discipline while the majority of my friends did not have to deal with these issues. In retrospect, I realize that I was exaggerating my plight. Mrs. Smith, our neighbor who helped us during the night of my mother's death, worked for us as a sort of housekeeper. She cooked breakfast for my brother and me, washed our clothes and dishes, and cleaned house for us for the next four years. Until I could drive, she drove me to my numerous school activities. Yet I perceived myself as the new woman of the house, therefore causing myself undue emotional stress. I pitied my father for having to work so much in order to compensate for the loss of my mother's income, so I cooked dinners whenever I could and tried to keep all domestic needs in check.

My brother, Ryan, also became my son. In effect, I tried to take my mother's place in my brother's life, while simultaneously trying to forget her absence in my life. In hindsight, I realize that I was probably overbearing, almost paranoid, about my brother's life. However, at that time I felt that I had to ensure my brother's success for the sake of my mother, for she would have made Ryan a success. Now I appreciate my higher levels of maturity and responsibility, which in part have enabled me to be so successful. At present, I have a unique position in my family. I am at school for three-fourths of the year, so much of my influence occurs over the phone lines. I think that I have gained more confidence in my father since I have been at college. My college experience has helped me understand many of the things with which my father struggles. Therefore, we talk at length about subjects he cannot discuss with many people. For my brother, I try to be a cheerleader, a friend as well as an advisor. I tell him if he needs me, I'm only a phone call away. I scold him if his grades fall and I encourage his athletic pursuits. I still feel a large responsibility for my family and I ensure that things I do at college will not jeopardize my family's economic status nor bring shame to my family in any way.

I learned my sense of family responsibility from my parents. I learned that what I do in society reflects on my family, particularly on my parents. I work to succeed because my parents taught me to always do my best. I want to make my family proud and to become a success to honor my mother. My mother inculcated this ambition in me throughout my first thirteen years of life by pushing me beyond my limits. Her description of the subordinate position of African Americans and women in the United States forced me to realize that I would always have to fight in this world, but that my battle could end in a much sweeter success through hard work. I will never forget one of my mother's first long lectures about being Black in the United States.

I thought that earning a spot on the National Junior Honor Society would disprove those teachers who doubted my ability because I was black. When my mother and I left the induction ceremony, I felt wonderful. My mother, however, looked disgusted. During the ride home, she told me why she was so angry. She had spoken to my math teacher, Mrs. McGuire. "She was just so impressed with you. She said, 'Chantal is so polite and intelligent. She's a hard worker and doesn't give me any problems in class. She's so clean and dresses so well.'" My mother's face wrinkled, and her voice cracked when she said, "What did she expect? Did she think you would come to school dirty and badly clothed! Did she think you were stupid and undisciplined?! No, I know what she thought! She saw your little Black face on the first day and thought, 'Here comes another one of them niggers.' It is unbelievable to her that you, a Black girl, could be as good or better than those white kids! She kept saying, 'Chantal is so different, she's not like the other kids.' She meant you're different than those other Black kids or what she thought other Black kids were like. Tell me white folks ain't a trip!"

Then my mother turned to me and said, "Remember this if you don't remember anything else, Chantal. You have to be twice as good as any white person to get the same recognition! None of them will expect you to succeed, but you do it in spite of them. They'll call you nigger, jiggaboo, blackie, pickaninny, and anything else, but you fight them tooth and nail, and make them know that you deserve a place on top as much as, if not more so, than they do. Don't ever stop fighting for your people, because they have never stopped fighting for theirs." I didn't quite understand her anger then, but I will remember the incident always and I have used her thoughts to push me even further when racism hits me in the face.

Thinking back on this incident helps me realize that one of the many characteristics my parents instilled in me was racial pride. I knew from childhood that I was different from the majority of my classmates, who were white, and that this difference made me special. My classmates made my difference known to me almost daily, through their endless questions about my hair, church, music, and other Black students. To combat the frequent cruelty and ignorance, I used my brute strength. I was already a "tomboy" and one of the tallest children throughout my elementary years, so I acted tough and pushed some people around occasionally in order to prevent any incidents from occurring. I would blow my top over "the N word" and anyone who criticized Black people. I don't think I changed many minds regarding Blacks, but I thought that at least I had shut them up. Now I fight my battles with knowledge and words. Life as a Black girl was hard where I grew up not only because I was one of a few African American kids in my school system but also because the area contained white working-class people. I was thus also a part of the "white trash" school system—I was the nigger among them.

There were never many African American teachers in my primary education (I remember only one African American male teacher in elementary school), but this did not seem to bother me. I was fighting students' racism too much to worry about the teachers. Once I established myself as a good student as well as a tough girl, I focused my attention on what type of education I received and from whom I was receiving it. However, that did not occur until junior high. Establishing myself was strange because I always had to prove that I was "really" Black (because I didn't "act like Black people"), or prove that other Black students could also do well and that I wasn't just "different" from other Black people. My mother had warned me of this when I told her that during my first day of junior high, two or three of my teachers already knew who I was and smiled approvingly. I couldn't understand how they knew who I was, or why they didn't express their approval to other students. My mother replied matter-of-factly, "You're one of the few good Black students they've seen in the junior high." She added a word of warning, "And you be careful of them, too. They'll be the same ones that will talk about Black folks like dogs and tell you, 'Oh, we're not talking about you, Chantal, you're different.' You let them know that you're no different than any other Black person, you just work harder than most people, Black or white. Don't you let them make you into a 'token nigger.' You are where you are because you *deserve* it, not because they needed a Black face in the classroom." The next day I went to school with a new sense of dignity and resolve. I looked around my classroom and recognized that in four of my six classes I was the only Black person and in the other two I was the only Black female. I realized at that point that my next three years would be tough. Not because I hadn't been in this situation before, but because for some reason junior high seemed more hostile to me. The feeling makes me think of a phrase in a gospel song: "It's an uphill journey ya gotta keep climbin' all de time."

My mother's prophesy came true. White students and teachers treated other Black students who did fit their stereotypes ruthlessly—by name-calling, jokes, and more severe punishments than for whites committing the same offense. Many of my Black friends suffered from the looks and comments of whites in our school, who told me that I was "different" and therefore didn't treat me that way. I won the presidencies of both student council and national honor society and earned various athletic and academic awards. However, this charade of acceptance and harmony put on by many of my white classmates did not change their thinking about all African Americans. I was still "different," and "not like those other Black people."

Throughout high school I had to prove myself again and again. I put more pressure on myself than even my parents did. My mother gave me only one guideline and one condition, "Always do the best that you can and know that you'll always have to be twice as good and work twice as hard as any white person to get the same amount as them." I still follow this golden rule. My mother's death, which occurred when I was in eighth grade, caused me to push myself as a testament to her memory, as well as to make my father proud of me. I have always thought that God had a plan for my life since He prepared me for my mother's death that night the ambulance took her away. These factors gave me the motivation to succeed, through high school and to the present day. Unfortunately, even in the leadership positions that I earned in high school, my ethnicity still held a negative connotation. During the selection process for some positions, I heard rumors that "she only got it because she's black." Such statements disappointed me because I thought that, especially in these two organizations, I had overcome such stupidity. I really thought that I had made an impact that transcended race. Unfortunately, what I found out reaffirmed my parents' adage that no matter how much money, power, or friends you have, or how hard you try, white people never get around the fact that you're Black and that before they get to know you, they'll see your Black face and already have opinions, usually bad, about you. My schoolmates' comments and attitudes undermined all that I thought I had done to change white peoples' ideas of Black folks and to make the way easier for other Blacks.

I received support from my church family in dealing with a white world that refused to accept me for what I was: an intelligent, motivated, hard-working Black girl. Members of my church always encouraged my efforts, pushed me to do more, and told me they were proud of me. I was one of the few young people in our congregation who had succeeded in organizations outside the Black community, which made me even more "special." Older people in my church thought it was great for me to be able to relate to white people, that it would be necessary to succeed in the "real world." My personal relationship with God became the most important factor in my success and in the preservation of my sanity and self-esteem. This relationship mandated that I be faithful, patient, relentless, humble, caring, honest, and tough. Much of my character was shaped according to what I thought my responsibilities were as a faithful Christian.

My experiences in high school were similar to those I would have in college. I began to learn about the inner workings of the complex system of elimination and oppression against my people that originated hundreds of years ago. At times, my very spirit felt attacked by the traditions and networks that many of the students at my college had and which placed me one step behind them in the beginning of our college careers. *Daughters of the Dust*, a movie by an African American woman, reminded me of the privilege and heritage of many white students, as compared to mine. The movie showed how ex-slaves survived and passed African traditions and survival skills from slavery on to their descendants. More interesting, though, is that the movie centered on the lives of females and their relations with each other, and to men.

I called my father to talk to him about the movie. I told him:

> In many ways, it made me angry and sad. The movie told stories from slavery and it made slavery so alive in my mind. The writer, an African American woman, traced her family to the Gullah people who were taken to an island off of the coasts of South Carolina and Georgia. I was angry because I will never know the African country of my family, my ancestors. It makes me angry that even after all that those women and men endured, we as Black people aren't fully accepted in a society we helped build into the industrial power it is today. My friend Joanna has relatives in Poland, my friend Christina in Puerto Rico. I don't have any of that, and I'll never find it either. I don't know anything about my real culture, or history.

I stopped talking. Tears ran down my face. I panted lightly. My hands squeezed my pillow. The calm, though slightly worried voice on the other side said:

> Chantal, calm down. Like I've said before, we and the American Indians are the only true Americans. White folks made us into true Americans. They stripped us of everything we had: language, clothing, relatives, religion, tradition. But they will never and have never taken away our pride and our will to survive. We have created our own culture: our own dance, religion, music, language, clothing. Yes, we are of African descent, but we can't trace it. If we go back to Africa today, we wouldn't know where to start. Africans would call us foreigners because we don't know our tribal affiliation. Many of us don't know anything about Africa, because that's the way white America wanted it.

"I know," I said, "but I feel so rootless, so unattached to any specific country. I know I don't fit into USA, baseball and hot dogs, and the Grand Ol' Flag."

My father replied:

> You're right. Your culture is part of the family traditions that we practice: baking cookies and cakes with Grandma in December, barbecuing with the family on Labor Day, cooking and eating certain foods: greens, water bread, hamhocks, dirty rice, pig's feet, chitlins, blackeyed peas, sweet potato pie. It's being involved in the Black church every Sunday. It's listening to Black music and learning our dances. It's listening to what your grandmother has to say about her life and how life was for Black folks in her day. That's the Black American culture we know and we must save. Be proud of it, because it's made by us, for us, and it's all we got.

I vowed then to learn more about my history and culture, and to continue the tradition of perpetuating my own culture apart from mainstream American culture.

I realized how much some of my classes at college changed the way I viewed the world. Few of my courses at college were riveting, but I must admit that the majority of them exposed me to new perspectives that I have found quite fascinating. The few exceptional courses I have had in my college career have changed the way I view my life and society in terms of gender, education, and class. One of the most eye-opening courses I experienced was an African and African American studies course, which increased my awareness of some African cultures which made me more sensitive to, and more protective of, my African American heritage. Through this class, I learned about parts of the African culture that American slavery prevented me and millions of others of the African diaspora from retaining, thus affirming my need to protect what few cultural roots African Americans have in the United States.

Another cultural difference I recognized in contemporary African American society is our social behavior. We love to laugh, talk loudly, and joke. Many African societies do the same. Conversely, Western European societies find such behavior rude and barbaric when done at "inappropriate" times. In performances, African performers and spectators interact to make the performance successful and enjoyable. Spectators talk to the performers and clap, sing, and dance with dancers or instrumentalists. Similarly, African Americans shout "Amen" in traditional Black churches, sing spontaneously, talk to the movie or TV screen and to actors on stage—all actions that European Americans usually frown upon. This course opened my eyes to many aspects of African American culture that I had known existed, but could not see any reasons for. I realized that I should not try to change these aspects of my culture because the majority considered them inappropriate, but that I should retain them in order to keep my African American heritage alive.

My sophomore fall, I took a course on contemporary issues in education. I remember one particular week when the other students in my discussion disgusted me with their naiveté about inner-city schools. Being one of only two people in the group who had attended a city school, or had first-hand knowledge of city schools, I naturally spoke up in class. One of my classmates, whose comments drew a few nods of agreement from others in the class, said that inner-city schools needed parents who cared about their children's education, school boards who weren't just in education for status, and better enforcement of drug and weapons possession. I answered, "No, what we need is for someone to go to the suburbs and say, 'Look, you must help to: (a) redistribute the money for education across property tax districts more evenly; (b) invest in renovating and repairing these old schools; (c) buy books for these children; (d) pay teachers higher salaries with more benefits; and (e) invest in making schools safer places. Otherwise these same children whom you are trying so hard to keep away from your suburbanite kids will grow up with little education, which will lead to few or no job opportunities. They will come to your neighborhoods to rob and sell drugs. Do you want preventative medicine? Give kids a chance to do well by themselves. You can invest in them now, for schools, or later, for prisons." I spoke with a great sense of urgency voice and raised my hands at the end as if to say, "What's your decision?"

One woman in the class commented that my position would scare more people than it would get to help. I disagreed, saying, "No, I don't think so. If that community is close enough to the school district in trouble, then they will respond in some way. You see, people in the U.S. don't respond unless it affects them directly. As long as the poor minority kids are miles away in the inner city, it is considered their problem. People say, 'We (upper-middle-class whites) can't help it if the local government is corrupt and the teachers don't care. They should have a higher value on education.' But the minute those poor kids start bothering the suburbanites, *then* it's a *problem* and *something must be done about it.* It's a sad situation, but true." One young man asked me if I wanted to work in an inner-city school, to risk my safety and sanity there. I replied that I would if that's what I had to do to help students who did not have teachers or parents or school boards who cared. I would have to take some risks. Then I rhetorically asked the group, "Why are we in the business if not to help kids?"

I recognized that even in this education course, many of the students either did not want to become teachers, or may have fancied the idea but only wanted to teach in the elite private schools that many of them had attended. Putting themselves on the line was out. Giving too much time and energy was out. Risking a nice, well-paid "real" job for the sake of some unknown children out. The course made me see the inadequacies of my own primary and secondary education and it also made me see the dire need for teachers who are bright, creative, and, most importantly, who love to teach. I was convinced that I was one of those teachers and that the children back in my hometown, especially the children of color, needed someone like me.

I realized also, through another exceptional course, that girls and women of color in particular really needed caring support. I learned that women cannot be viewed as one monolithic group who have similarities just because of their gender. The professor of this class challenged my ideas regarding women, particularly how different classes of women have shaped feminist thought. She taught me that the feminist movement is not just a fight by women but also that men must play a part in it as well. The course taught me that history cannot be analyzed without examining issues of race, class, and gender and that studies which ignore these aspects miss a whole set of factors pertinent to whatever the subject may be. I have come to accept and advocate this position when dealing with issues specific to women, as well as other issues.

These classes forced me to think of all these issues daily. I knew that my view of the world was changing when a statement by a speaker at a conference I attended revived all of the analytical skills that I learned in my best classes at college. The speaker, an African American male, said that the Black feminist movement was destructive to the African American struggle for equality and self-improvement. He said that because the Black feminist movement is based on the white feminist movement, it is centered in the Eurocentric idea of individualism. In his opinion, Black feminists were against the family and were most interested in themselves. I thought to myself, "In many cases, without us, the Black family could not have survived!" He continued with the "fact" that the issues facing Black women were nothing compared to those faced by Black men (incarceration, murder, drug usage, etc.). I tried to argue with him, but I had no knowledge of Black feminism, so I floundered in my words.

I knew something about his statements was not right, but I didn't know what. His comments led me to the study of Black feminism in the United States. I visited the African American women "expert" on our campus. I told her my story, and she gave me a list of twenty or thirty books on Black feminism, its beginnings, its criticisms of white feminism, etc. This reading finally gave me the words, thoughts, and theories I needed to explain and discuss all of the issues especially relevant to women that I had been unable to discuss because of ignorance. My vision of the world has since become even more analytical. Knowledge truly is power.

I read throughout the summer of my sophomore year while I worked at a summer camp. The readings on Black feminist literature and theory helped me to understand the complexity of the fight for "women's equality." I found that Black women have, throughout our history in the United States, fought for fair treatment for themselves and other African Americans. I learned that, in many cases, Black women viewed white women as oppressors as well and that white women's ambivalence about and frequent perpetuation of racism within the lives of women of different races separated women of color from "mainstream white feminism" thus the usage of the term womanists has increased recently. I realized that only through discussion and arguments within the women's movement could a more comprehensive agenda be formulated that would include many women previously excluded from the feminist movement, which will hopefully strengthen the movement as a whole.

All of these discoveries (I call them discoveries because I know that these feelings and ideas existed within me, but that I could not recognize them due to my ignorance of the theory and terminology needed to express them) heightened my awareness of my femaleness and of all the positive and negative situations that this femaleness placed me in. I scrutinized men's and women's comments about women more carefully, trying to assess their ideas about women from these comments. I became aware of how the media portrays women and how women view themselves in American society. I see how these issues affect the way people view me as a woman. Now I am trying to deal with this heightened awareness of myself and the difficulties of being a double minority—African American and female.

This heightened awareness of my femaleness caused me to reflect on the few relationships I have had with men in my twenty years. In high school I felt that I didn't have time or "didn't want to be bothered" with a boyfriend; I was too busy with all my activities. However, I had two very close male friends with whom I spoke about everything. One cared for me deeply, but I put him off because I wasn't ready for a big commitment, and we didn't see each other often because he lived fifteen to twenty minutes away. I became attracted to the other young man, but he didn't want a public relationship; he wanted a private, sexual one. I refused to be someone's "mistress," so I had to say no. Also, this type of situation would go against my feelings at that time against premarital sex. Turing him down was very difficult (my mind said no, while my body said yes), but I wouldn't have been able to live with myself had I compromised.

Other boys in high school seemed too immature and unmotivated. They had no idea of what they wanted in life—they just wanted to have fun. Not having a boyfriend did not bother me; it was not a priority. However, once I arrived at college, I thought I could find a mature, ambitious young man. Unfortunately, I guess I was "too something," and I didn't get any offers. I had a conversation with Hezekiah, a Black male friend, during our first year of college. He told me that Black men did not want women to be "complaining, correcting, and checkin' them all the time. Black men want peace in a relationship. Guys hate rejection. Black women at this college dis' us so quickly that we are sick and tired of being rejected." I could not understand. When guys don't ask women out, is that not a form of rejection to the women? I know many of my female friends on campus thought so. We often do not feel acceptable to men because no men respond to us. He told me that my confidence and independence scared some men off. If that was true, then I would just have to deal with not having a man. That was my attitude throughout my college years; I decided I would have to wait until graduate school.

My double minority status as an African American woman caused people in my community to expect me to do certain things to prove my ability and to take advantage of opportunities that I could not have had a generation ago. When I explained in my senior year of high school that I wanted to become a high school teacher, people, men and women, Black and white, could not believe it. When I then returned home for a teaching internship my sophomore year at college, these same people seemed surprised that I still wanted to pursue a teaching career.

Many people felt that "I was too good to teach," or that "I could do so much better than just teach." I didn't dare tell them what I really felt, that if we, "the best and the brightest," did not help educate their children, then to whom are we leaving our children's learning? To people who do not care about either our children or their education, people who are just picking up a check and enjoying their summers off? How are we to inspire our children, especially minority children, to strive for excellence when they cannot find one teacher of color in their school, let alone teachers worth admiring? Our children need role models, and pushing good college students away from teaching as a career will not put role models in our schools. I took these attitudes into my internship at a university laboratory school and decided to get the most out of this opportunity. At one time I doubted my desire to teach. I began to believe all the negative things my friends, family, and other teachers told me about the profession. Throughout my senior year of high school I wrestled with the question of whether or not I wanted to teach. I tried to convince people that through teaching I could help Black children and thus the Black community. Several older people said that I could do that through engineering, the sciences (particularly medicine), or law. I continued to hear comments such as, "Why are you going to an elite college if you're only going to teach? You can go to a state school to become a teacher!", "It doesn't really matter what school you go to if all you're going to do is teach."

One evening, during my senior year of high school, when I began to doubt my own choice of teaching as a profession, I asked my dad about my plans. There was a time when my father felt the same way about my career plans as the people at church and my high school teachers. He and I had some arguments about the same issues the other people brought up, but he finally began to understand when he knew that I was serious and adamant about what I wanted to do. I told him that I was sick and tired of people questioning my life. Every time I told people what I planned to do, they told me I could do so much better than to teach. I was sick of having to defend my decisions. I didn't know what to tell them. Why couldn't people be more understanding of what I wanted do? My father told me:

> There will always be people who will doubt you and try to turn you away from what you want to do. They don't understand that you want to give to your community, because they don't give to theirs. They are too concerned with material possessions, so they want you to become something that will make you money. Many of them are jealous that you have the chance to go to such a fine college when they didn't, or their children didn't, and now they want you to do something *better* with that chance since you have it. People don't value their education, so they don't see the need for you to go to college to learn, not just to prepare yourself for a job, but to attend school for the sake of learning something. And because they don't value education, they don't see the need for well-educated teachers in the classroom. Any ol' dumb teacher will do. Don't worry

> about them, Chantal. You do what you want to do, and what I am able to do for you, I will. You see, most of those people would not go into debt for their kids' college education. They want to wear wing-tipped shoes, fart through silk, and drive Cadillacs and BMW's. Your mother and I made a promise that when our children were ready for college, we would do whatever was necessary to send them there. So you can go to your college, because I will make the sacrifice.

I hugged him with tears in my eyes. I thanked God for a father so caring and understanding.

Later, as I tried to decide which high school to select for my internship, I struggled with the idea of whom I wanted to teach. A conversation with one of my college friends caused me to question my choice of schools. I had decided to teach at the lab school of a prominent university in the Midwest, where the students were predominantly white and relatively affluent. Was I "selling out" so that I could have the experience in an affluent private school that would not help Black students? One of my goals was to help minority students through my teaching, and now I was taking a position at a predominantly white institution. Why? Was I being selfish? I talked to one of my former high school teachers, Ms. Powell, one of only three African American members of the faculty at my school. I visited her every college break to talk to her about what was happening to me in school and to ask her advice on many of the decisions I made in my life. I told her I was unsure about my decision to the lab school. She told me:

> Chantal, take this opportunity to do what you *want* to do. Once you enter the work force, you probably won't have that choice. Your talent will not be wasted no matter where you teach. Students of all colors need to see a bright, talented African American female teacher. You will help your community if there is only one student of color in your class because your enthusiasm will spread to the students. You will give them a perspective on the subject that other teachers cannot. Don't you let others sway you from your decision. You are making the right choice.

I thought about what Ms. Powell had to say and I realized that she too had to deal with that question. She is in a predominantly white, public high school with few minority faculty. She has been there for many years and still enjoys it. I know that many students of color, especially African American students, have looked to her for advice and friendship. If she had not been there, many students would have been lost. Looking at her choice to stay and teach made me realize that minority teachers are needed everywhere and that my going to a predominantly white school would not mean that I am short-changing my people at all. In fact, the few minority students in my high school needed the Ms. Powells much more than students in a majority setting. I could not abandon the few for the sake of the many.

I chose my teaching internship for many reasons. I knew that the majority of the students that attended the university's lab school wanted to learn and took their education seriously. I visited the school and received a warm reception from the administration and faculty. Teachers, administrators, students, and parents wanted one thing: the best education for the students. All of the branches worked together toward that end.

In 1 of the 3 days I led the classroom toward the end of the internship, we discussed whether or not the novel *The Dragon's Village* (1980), a work about a Chinese woman who fought in the Chinese revolution of the 1950s and who helped in the Communist reforms following the defeat of Mao Tse-Tung, could be considered a "woman's book." The students grappled with the question, and I used much of the feminist writings I had just begun reading to bring into the discussion issues involving women. I told them that girls have typically been required to read books written, for the most part, by and about men and that they did not have the option of not reading a book because they did not enjoy the issues it addressed. None of the boys in my class thought of that. I tried to make them think differently about applying labels to people and objects without analyzing why we apply those labels. I hope that I changed a few attitudes that day.

I learned that many of my students didn't think beyond their own communities or experiences. Although the school promotes respect for diversity, many of the students do not try to learn about the different cultures found within school. And although many teachers say they integrate minority groups in their classroom curriculum, the teachers' ignorance often hinders them from being able to present material relevant to a particular gender, class, or ethnic group to the class. I heard one English teacher say that "the classics" in literature are more important than others because once students understand the classics they will be able to read anything on their own. I suggested to her that without presentation of "the others" in class, the students will not be as likely to read them on their own. The U.S. educational system needs to include the people who may have been left out of history, literature, or science for whatever reason. If it does not, we will lose many students to disillusion, boredom, and disappointment because they will feel that only certain people (in this country, Anglo-Saxon males) do anything of importance in the world. That is not true and we should not teach our children that.

I wanted to uncover these issues for many of my students and I think I did so many times during the term. This feeling affirmed my choice of the lab school for my internship, because my experience taught me that I not only want to influence minority children (African American children in particular) but also that European American children also need to know these things, and without teachers to expose them to such ideas, they may never consider them.

As I look at myself now in light of my own life story, I see myself as an African American woman who has grown through hardships and triumphs to gain a better understanding of herself and her role as an African American feminist in American society. I am coming to understand and to accept many different viewpoints within the African American community and within American society. What is important, however, is that not only can I acknowledge different viewpoints, but now I can also argue against them and defend my own views. I am able to stand up and fight to change the problems within this society. I am beginning to understand how to simplify and combat the complex network of discrimination. I always knew I wanted to help the African American community, but now I have reasons and goals for my work: to combat the continued ignorance, segregation, and prejudice that prevents equal opportunity and peace from existing in this country. I see my goals as trying to change the way people view themselves, each other, and the world, so that we all can work to end the system of oppression and discrimination that American society was founded upon. I know that the eradication of this system will mean a transformation of our society. I also know that there are others who are working toward the same goals, so I am reassured that change will come.

Through the educational system, I can give students the opportunity to think about their lives and the inequities of American society and instill in them a sense of social responsibility toward humanity, expanding their knowledge so that they too can fight with words and encouraging them to be transformers of society. Right now I am grappling with how far I want to take my own formal education. I know that whatever my educational level is, I must teach high school. Then maybe I can save a few students that would otherwise be lost, as well as push a few who may not have motivation.

No matter where my education or career takes me in my life, I know that I will work for my communities—African American, female, working class, Christian, and global. I owe this work to my mother, my father, my God, and myself. Although my life has not been much of a struggle when compared to those African Americans who have lived in a different place or another time, the difficulties of growing up African American and female remain. Our mothers bear us into a hostile world that they know cares little about our existence. Our mothers whisper, shout, signal, and symbolize what we as women of our race must do: *fight, survive, grow, excel*! Throughout our childhood they guide and teach us how to adapt and adopt in order to accomplish. Their prayers ask God to bless, punish, and protect us. Our lives are full of tears, laughter, anger, fear, joy, and despair. But throughout our lives we have hope—hope that will take us through all the hardships that our mothers warned us of toward a place where African American women and others who have unnecessarily suffered lifelong trouble can live in peace and harmony, with freedom of choice. My mother instilled in me all of these characteristics and much more. Her life and her death have marked me forever. Moreover, my father—not the stereotypical irresponsible Black father—has refined my attitudes and challenged my assumptions. He serves as a model of what, in my opinion, I am looking for in a man with whom I would want to share my life. He has never claimed to be perfect, but his sacrifice, love, understanding, and endurance have affected the way I view men and society. I also cannot overstate how much the church has influenced my life. My relationship with my

God, my spirituality, and my church family implanted in me a certain joy—a joy about life that enables me to survive the hardest times. They love and comfort, support and lift me when I need it.

These people and communities, in addition to my peers, have helped me to reach the twentieth year of my life with many sad stories, but many happy ones, too. Unfortunately, many of my race, gender, and class do not have this kind of support. Parents who physically, mentally, and emotionally abuse young African American girls, and institutions and peers who prevent and limit girls from progressing, hurt not only the African American community but our entire society. Much of the intelligence, creativity, and talent of young African Americans have been lost to stereotypes, assumptions, greed, ignorance, fear, and hate. Until more people realize this, more will be lost. We have a responsibility to save those who have been lost, to end the system that attempts to push others to the margin of our society. In my own small way, I intend to fulfill my responsibility.

(A follow-up life story by Candice appears in Part IV of this anthology.)

## Reference

*The Dragon's Village : An Autobiographical Novel of Revolutionary China.* Penguin Books, Inc, 1980.

# 10 A Work in Progress

*Anise Vance*

The small fictions I play with are often more plausible than my true history. When I am asked "Where are you from," the conversation that ensues can last hours. I am poked and prodded as if I am a physical specimen of twentieth-century globalization. Sometimes, it is just easier to say that I am from Santa Fe.

My father is African American, born and bred in Hartford, Connecticut. He has the thick American accent of a Yankee broadcaster and speaks carefully, precisely, and authoritatively. He dons suits and ties now, but a college photo shows him sporting an Afro, a dashiki, and the wide smile of someone having a good deal of fun. He still wears the large square glasses popular in the 1970s, which somehow suited him, with his graying moustache and bald head. He is deeply intelligent, incredibly hardworking, wonderfully wise, and a devoted father.

Born in Iran, my mother left her home country in her early twenties to study in Boston. She describes her youthful self as a fiery liberal who defied conservative Persian norms and lived life to the fullest. By all accounts, my mom was a heartbreaker; when I was in my teens, I caught snippets of a conversation between her and an old friend about love letters some hapless suitor had penned for her when they were in college. Her voice has the elegant lilt of a poet and traces of Farsi cadences. Watching her work a room is unnerving; she wins people's affections like the Romans conquered the West. At my mother's core resides a certain toughness—a trait common among the women in my family—fortified by intelligence and understanding. Wrap that in a whole lot of love, empathy, and creativity, and *voilà*, you have my mom.

My mother never planned on living in the United States permanently. My dad's marriage proposal was vague at best: "Would you mind delaying going overseas for a few years?" After a couple of days, when he finally asked her directly to marry him, she replied that she thought she had already said yes. And so it was that the confusion surrounding my family began well before I was born.

My parents' first stop after college was Abidjan, Cote D'Ivoire, where they arrived with my older sister, an excitable and beautiful baby. Three years later my family was treated to a special delight: I was born, cross-eyed, yellow with jaundice, and troublingly sleepy. I remember nothing of my time in Cote

DOI: 10.4324/9781003376255-13

D'Ivoire; we moved when I was one year old to Nairobi, Kenya, where we would spend the next seven years. It was in Kenya that I learned to read, ride a bike, and play sports. We had three dogs—Nero, Meshki, and Heidi—and a basketball hoop. I loved school, loved my friends, and loved coming home to run around with the dogs. I would often beg my sister, whom I worshipped, for the tiniest scrap of affection. Life was blissful and I knew who I was: a Kenyan.

I was eight when the carpet was pulled out from under me and we moved to Botswana. There I attended British schools that demanded military-like discipline. I was heartbroken at leaving Nairobi. I missed our dogs, my sister was going through a moody puberty, and the upheaval in general left me grumpy. I did find comfort in the friendship of two fellow Iranians. We would play cops and robbers, shouting "*Khomeini Omahd*" (Khomeini has come) at the top of our lungs, and attended Farsi classes on the weekends. We idolized the older Persian boys, with their slick facial hair and off-color jokes, and nurtured crushes on the pretty Iranian girls. I still described myself as Kenyan, but others called me American and "colored," a term often used in southern Africa to describe people with brown skin. I accepted both identities nonchalantly because they mattered little to me. In my mind, I was somewhere between Kenyan and Iranian.

Three years after so abruptly moving to Kenya, my family once again picked up and shipped out. Cairo, Egypt, was to be our last stop in Africa and the city where I would complete middle and high school. On the Cairene streets I discovered that, to many Egyptians, I looked like one of them. Among the first and most necessary words I learned were "*Mish aref Arabe*" (I don't understand Arabic). At the international school I attended, I was considered American because I spoke no Arabic, had my father's thick Yankee accent, and was unacquainted with Egyptian culture. I was, however, also completely unfamiliar with mainstream American norms. I was an outsider to both the Egyptians and the Americans who attended my school. My closest friends shared my outsider status: we were the Black kids.

## This Thing Called Blackness

In middle school, my best friend was a dark-skinned Egyptian American who readily identified as black. God, how we "Black kids" loved race. I remember the nights we spent pretending to be stand-up comedians, using "negro" and "nigger" as punchlines. Like most boys our age, we obsessed over sports and girls while awakening to music and fashion. Predictably, we wore baggy clothing, tried out various neck chains, and drooled over all-white sneakers. Our musical tastes evolved from Nelly's party hip-hop to the socially conscious work of Mos Def and Talib Kweli (a.k.a. Black Star). Without truly understanding the meaning of the rhymes, I memorized verse after verse:

> I find it distressin'
> there's never no in-between
> We either niggaz or kings

We either bitches or queens
The deadly ritual seems immersed in the perverse

As we moved from mimicking shallow stereotypes to the very beginnings of comprehension, the word "nigger" held a place of particular import. It was something we only uttered around each other and with specific intent. We felt that using it made us part of a world where we weren't held at arm's length. We were brothers, and there were legions of us.

"Nigger" became our special code word. It took me years to use it in front of a white person, and I clearly remember the first time I did so:

PAUL (WHO WAS BLACK): No, man, this is the nigger couch.
DAVID (WHO WAS WHITE): Huh?
ME: Yah man, nigger couch.

As the word stumbled out of my mouth, it felt heavy, bloated, and out of place. It was the first and last time I would say the word "nigger" in the presence of a white person, and also the last time I would use it in front of Paul.

Paul arrived in tenth grade. A military kid from Hattiesburg, Mississippi, Paul and his brother, Dejuan, quickly became my closest friends. Paul was razor-smart and viciously determined. His stern attitude made him both feared and admired. Dejuan, on the other hand, was a jokester who could charm water from a rock. He was rarely seen without a grin and never without a girl. And yes, my two best friends were black. The three of us happened to be the only Black Americans in our class that year.

I felt at home with them, despite our enormous differences. My American family hailed from the North, as Paul and Dejuan would often remind me, while theirs was rooted in the South. They were staunch Christians while I was born into a Baha'i family. Both their parents were black; I was mixed. But in the dog-eat-dog world that is high school, you need people you can trust. We never felt the need to find an army of folk like us and, for me, our friendship was liberating: I no longer needed to rely on Black stereotypes—or to use the word that I thought came with it—to belong and to bond. Race may have been the original reason for our friendship, but it was not what kept us friends. We simply liked, believed in, and trusted each other.

When we graduated from high school, Paul and Dejuan enrolled in the Naval Academy, while I was lucky enough to go to Dartmouth College in New Hampshire. Culture shock does not even begin to describe my first impressions of that school. It was a freakishly foreign land to me. Unlike the countries of my upbringing, white folk were everywhere at Dartmouth, fraternities and sororities were the major social centers, and no one seemed to know the first thing about hummus or *shwarma*. I was not alone in my feelings of alienation—in that supposed wonderland of privilege, a lot of young people got lost.

Let us be frank: college is a circus. Groups of friends are shaped and reshaped constantly, people fall in and out of love in a heartbeat, and everyone freaks out when—boom—four years are quickly up and we discover that we still know next to nothing about ourselves or the world. I am still trying to work out what happened at college.

For starters, I dove into the Black community through various campus organizations. I served on our Black student union's executive board and on the Inter-Community Council. I was an advocate for issues affecting the Black community and helped found a group for men of color on campus. I wrote my thesis on segregated Black populations and spent a good deal of my time railing about inequality. Issues of race were, clearly, at the forefront of my mind. Yet despite the public face I showed on campus, it was in the most private sphere that I took another step forward in understanding my mixed identity.

During my junior year, I took a course on interracial intimacy. During a discussion on the relevance of mixed-race interactions to racial progress, one young woman remarked, "The key question is who is in your bed." She was making a simple point: intimacy, which is not synonymous with sex, is the final test of prejudice. Many students in the class shifted uncomfortably. I was involved with Black and non-black women during college. My two most serious relationships were with a white woman, Mary, and a Native American woman, Annette. Mary once repeated a joke that included the word "nigger." We both froze for a second and then moved forward as if nothing had happened. Loud thoughts screamed inside my skull: is she allowed to say that? Should I say something? What does it mean if I do or don't say something? Is it okay for me to tell that joke, but not for her?

I remember thinking, "Am I a race traitor?"

## Persia and Me: A Long-Distance Love Affair

I have never been to Iran, and I speak Farsi only on the rare occasions when I am around other speakers. Yet ask me for a list of Persian accomplishments and I will reel off facts from the *Achaemenid* dynasty through modern-day Iran. I store this information in some mental cabinet, where it is readily accessible and itching to come out. I am proud of being Persian.

However, if you ask me what Teheran is like at rush hour, or where poets find sanctuary in Shiraz, or what colors can be seen when dusk settles over Abadan's desert terrain, I cannot tell you. I do not know the names of the streets in any Iranian city, which flowers grow in Iran's parks, or the difference between kebab stalls for tourists and those for locals. I have no intimate knowledge of Iranian politics; what I know, I get from the BBC, CNN, and Al-Jazeera, just like other Westerners. We Iranians do not have a secret handshake or sly wink to let each other know what's up. I am woefully ignorant of my mother's culture.

That said, when I hear Farsi, I feel like I am home. It is the language I spoke before I learned English. My grandmother and I still speak it together. Its rhythm makes me comfortable, and its melody reminds me of a place to which I am—if only from a long, long distance—connected. My connection to Iran, and my "Iranian-ness," comes only from my family and their memories. As they get older, they embellish some moments and downplay others, reworking history into a narrative worth telling. Over time, their stories have become mine; my Iranian identity is a whirlpool of fact, myth, and imagination.

## Shaken *and* Stirred

I hate it when people refer to me as half-black or half-Iranian. I am not half of anything: I am fully Black and fully Iranian. Moreover, my identity cannot be reduced to mere fractions. It's complicated but also simple: I am mixed, and there is no personal distress in my being so. Others, however, seem to be confused about my identity.

When grocery shopping with my maternal grandmother as a child, people would stare at us and wonder why a Black kid was speaking a strange language with an elderly immigrant woman. When shopping with my mom, people would congratulate and admire her for adopting a poor colored child. Today, when I go shopping by myself, I occasionally catch people shooting me nervous glances, perhaps thinking I am a thief or hoodlum or even a terrorist. It appears that I am still somewhat out of place.

"Black American" is a term already fraught with difficulties. For centuries, being Black in America was the antithesis of the white American Dream. Being Black continues to be associated with aggressiveness, criminality, stupidity, and undesirability. Despite great advances in civil rights, a host of Black superstars, and a Black president, there is still an outsider status that comes with being Black in America.

Being Iranian American does not lessen my personal outsider status. The popular imagination in the West portrays the United States as the vanguard and protector of liberty and democracy, a stalwart ally of the Iranian people, and a beacon of hope in a dark, twisted world. Iranians, so the story goes, have responded to U.S. benevolence with prickly foreign policy, continual criticism, and an unrelenting sense of superiority. The sad reality is that American meddling helped spur (but did not cause) two Iranian revolutions that put the wrong people in power. Put simply, Iranians and Americans have a longstanding beef, and Iranian Americans desperately straddle the fence between their two cultures.

I have often joked with friends that I am America's worst nightmare, as I am both Black and Middle Eastern. There is a sad truth in the joke—Blacks and Middle Easterners are certainly stereotyped and often portrayed as elements to be feared by much of American society—but also a liberating reality. I never wanted to be the guy who held a corporate job so he could buy the white picket fence, move in with the girl-next-door, and have 2.5 kids. Growing up, I instinctively knew that that dream was for people who did not look like me and I did not care. I was left free to explore ways of being that were not scripted on sitcoms and glorified in TV ads. I was not resentful precisely because I did not see my world as "us" versus "them." Instead I saw multiple cultural practices in my home every day; I saw them clash and create new norms; and I saw those norms turn into a culture in and of itself. I saw that nothing was stagnant or fixed or solitary. I saw that I had options.

I was eager to explore the identity choices I found laid before me. Scholars and analysts often talk of "negotiating" or "navigating" identity. Clothing, speech patterns, hairstyles, rebelliousness, athleticism, flirtatiousness—all are used to project identity. Everyone navigates identity, but when race is introduced into the mix, the stakes are raised.

At an early age, I learned how to twist my self-presentation to provoke specific responses from those around me. I was eager to figure out what identity I could drape around my shoulders most naturally. It was not the most fun or ho-hum moments that taught me which parts of myself to camouflage or accentuate—quite the opposite. Put bluntly, I hated being followed around by store security and watching suburbanites cross the street when they saw me approaching. I learned quickly how to use my particular social constructions to my advantage.

I used my mixed identity to convey both positive and negative racial images. For example, I love coffee shops, and grabbing a cup of "Joe" is a daily ritual. I choose what I wear each day based largely on how I want to be treated at the coffee shop. If I want to get in and out without any hassles, I wear a Black hoodie, basketball sneakers, and worn-out jeans. If I am open to conversing with retired older men sipping their lattes, I wear slacks, a thin sweater, and a trimmed beard. If I want to get some work done, I wear a t-shirt, my good jeans, and a pair of Converse kicks. Here is the fun bit: after wearing a sweater in order to befriend latte-sipping regulars, when I walk in the next day wearing track pants and a Yankees cap, they often do not recognize me.

During my freshman year of college, I made the mistake of thinking that all liberal arts schools were bastions of liberalism. I dove headlong into a political conversation with a fifty-something academic, assuming he was the sort of person who would appreciate different people's perspectives and backgrounds. However, he soon started railing about then-candidate Barack Obama and his racial "double bind." According to this gentleman, Obama had either to choose to be Black or to claim his mother's whiteness. He could not do both because … well, I'm still unclear about the "why" of it all. I clearly recall the last few moments of our conversation:

THE GENTLEMAN: I can tell that you're just going to dismiss what I'm saying because I'm an old white guy.

ME: No, I'm going to dismiss it because you just don't get it.

And he didn't. He could not wrap his head around how President Obama's narrative was possible. He was looking right at me, and he could not see a damn thing. I took it personally.

When it comes to issues of race and identity, I am just as confused as everybody else. I speak of social constructs, performances of race, and fluid identities as if they are terms I instinctively understand. The truth is, I spend an obscene amount of time trying to connect clichéd questions like "Where are you from?" and "What makes you who you are?" to abstract conceptions of race, ethnicity, and nationality. I feel immense discomfort sketching even the vaguest outline of myself, as I fear I will exaggerate one part at the expense of another. I fear that I have somehow invested in stereotypical identity narratives that strangle racial discourse, and that I will one day regret typecasting myself within such boundaries.

Most of all, I fear that someone, somewhere, will attempt to extract a morsel of wisdom from my experiences. I do not write this with any intention of being self-deprecating or to downplay the value of my testimony. There is nothing stronger than a voice declaring, "I am." It is just that my voice has not yet found its pitch. My questions about identity can be answered with academic theories and clever argumentation, but gut emotion and intellectual satisfaction are distant, distant cousins. In seeking resolution on my "true" identity, I have unstitched and re-sown pieces of myself more times than I care to count.

Ten years from now, I may fume while reading this account of my life experiences. I may want to take red ink to the page with the fury of a moody English professor. I may think that my twenty-three-year-old self's musings are childish or presumptuous… I don't know. The point is this: I am a work in progress.

(A follow-up life story by Anise appears in Part IV of this anthology.)

# Part IV

# Finding Liberty: Renewal, Reflection, and Regeneration

# 11 Quest For Peace

## Follow-Up

*Deirdre Harris*

In 1979, a perfect storm developed within my family. A lack of sufficient, race-affirming medical care, racism in law enforcement, and a lack of sensitivity to a veteran's post-traumatic stress syndrome led to my stepfather's senseless murder. Moreover, after a series of intimidating and threatening phone calls from police officers, my mother eventually settled out of court with the police for very little compensation, which guaranteed that we would live in poverty.

Upon graduating from college, I felt I could finally say goodbye to my father, who was murdered by the police. As mentioned in my previous essay, "Quest for Peace," the man I called my father was actually my stepfather, whom I had grown up with from the time I was three years old. What helped me recover from his murder was the awareness that my family and I were not victims, but survivors.

Victims are helpless people who have no hope. My family and I were victimized by the murder, but we were neither helpless nor hopeless. We were able to recover and move forward with our lives. Granted, the recovery was messy, painful, and frightening, and we formed various coping mechanisms to help us deal with the murder. I was in elementary school at the time and became an avid reader to help me escape. Then, as an adolescent and young adult, I became a workaholic. Some of my siblings became alcoholics, drug addicts, drug dealers, and fighters. But, we made it to adulthood, and most of us have transcended these coping mechanisms to lead much healthier lives. The change in my perception—that I am a survivor—has helped me tremendously in all areas of my life because it means that I get to take full responsibility for every decision that I make.

The Chinese character for "crisis" has another meaning: opportunity. In examining my adolescence, during which I appeared to experience crisis after crisis, I now see that those crises were really opportunities. I realize that every single situation or experience in my life—from the murder and other untimely deaths of loved ones to inexplicable peace, from sexual abuse to embracing my bisexual orientation without apology, and from a breakdown to a breakthrough—has enabled me to call forth from within that which serves my highest good. I no longer look outside myself for happiness or

DOI: 10.4324/9781003376255-15

serenity. I know that peace, abundance, and vitality are all inside of me. I've learned that placing faith in the visible, including people or institutions, is unwise and unproductive.

The freedom I have found comes from knowing that God has changed my life. I'm now stronger and more grounded in reality than ever before. I am a better person for understanding that it's not what happens to me that matters the most; it's how I choose to respond to what happens that makes me who I am: a resilient expression of God.

As an adolescent, I was afraid of my emotions, especially my anger and rage, so I distanced myself from my uncomfortable feelings. I thought that emotions could and should be controlled. As an adult, however, I have come to understand that I am not my emotions. This enables me not to take other people's racist, sexist, and biphobic/homophobic perceptions of me personally. I can see these societal ills for what they are—systemic discriminatory practices rooted in maintaining a social caste system.

I also came to realize that I needed to reconcile *all* of my childhood violence with the woman I knew I needed to become. This woman within me needed to emerge so I could embrace my own sense of empowerment and serenity. I have grown to believe that emotions can be transcended and released. As a child, I was looking outside of myself for protection, but now I know that no human being can protect anyone, not really.

There is nothing I would delete from my earlier chapter because it provides an accurate snapshot of how I perceived my adolescence. I now have a much deeper understanding of the years that I spent in college. In my earlier essay, I wrote that my college was not good for my self-esteem. I was mistaken. Now I know that I was very depressed from a traumatic childhood that was unresolved, and I brought all my baggage with me to college. I would have been depressed anywhere.

That said, I believe the rural colleges that recruit students like me, including the one I attended as an undergraduate, need to be more mindful of our needs. Once on campus in a rural setting, students no longer have access to the resources that are available in multicultural cities to address emotional, mental, or spiritual needs. These schools ought to offer twelve-step programs for students with family members or friends who abuse alcohol or drugs, such as Al-Anon and Adult Children of Alcoholics. Providing group therapy could help students deal with their pre-college issues, such as domestic violence, sexual abuse/assault, a family member's mental illness, and loss. And these schools should have support systems in place to address racism, sexism, and classism. I sought help to deal with all of these issues—after I graduated and left campus. Although I was considered intellectually gifted while growing up, I didn't have the vocabulary to discuss how I felt. I was so emotionally stunted that I had to learn to name my emotions. If there were resources available on campus to deal with these kinds of issues, including individual therapy, students could begin their healing processes much sooner than I did.

Initially, my mother resisted helping me face my stepfather's murder because she had not yet faced it herself. By facing his murder, I helped her to deal with it, too. When I moved home to Texas from my college on the east coast, she and I talked and went through newspaper clippings she had saved about the murder. Now I can ask her questions about my stepfather and, although she is still very emotional about it, we are able to talk about him. Fully grieving for my stepfather enabled me to let him go.

Because I now have a greater awareness of institutionalized racism, I can say with confidence that my blanket mistrust of doctors and law enforcement was not as unfounded as I once believed. And I can say with confidence that it was not simply one random doctor's misdiagnosis of my stepfather's mental illness that led to his subsequent murder.

Unfortunately, this happens all too often to Black people, as the number of Black children whose parents are murdered by police is on the rise. A fraction of society is beginning to see policing for what it is—the enforcement mechanism of white supremacy—due to the multiple videos on social media of police officers killing unarmed Black people and to primarily Black athletes' protests against police brutality. Small, active segments of society, such as Black Lives Matter (BLM) and White People for Black Lives, are well aware of how white supremacy impacts us all. However, much of society still fails to acknowledge that white supremacy exists, much less how it perpetuates systems of injustice and inequality, such as institutionalized oppression in housing, education, health care, and employment. Even the corporate media's increased use of the term "white supremacy" to refer to neo-Nazis buries the reality of institutionalized oppression. Until we address the cognitive dissonance that was born in the genocide of the indigenous Native American/First Nation people of this land, the enslavement of African peoples in the U.S. and throughout the world, and the white supremacist ideation that is underlying it all, we will not heal. The inherited sense of entitlement that people like the current forty-fifth president of the United States exhibit is the cause for most of our societal ills today. These ills need to be addressed so that we can move forward together to heal as a society, and away from the white supremacy upon which this country was founded.

I am sometimes amazed that I can be so happy living in Los Angeles. Ironically, it was the acquittal of the Los Angeles police officers who beat Rodney King that began my healing. I now know that ending up in the student infirmary during my senior year in college was not a breakdown but my breakthrough—the catalyst that helped me to face my childhood traumas.

I have taken responsibility for my own health and healing. A combination of western and alternative health practitioners ensures that I get my health needs met. Along with my western doctor and dentist, I see a chiropractor, an acupuncturist, a massage therapist, and a psychologist. I also have a spiritual practice, which consists of meditation, chanting, and prayer.

As an adolescent, I used sports to help me release a lot of my pent-up energy from unexpressed feelings. Then, in college, my therapist at the student infirmary got me to start writing poetry again. I no longer play sports, but I belong to a gym where I am involved in a variety of fitness and mental health practices, such as yoga, weight training, and swimming. I have continued to write, and a few of my essays and poems have been published. I am currently writing a memoir, which I hope will be of help to anyone who has been through even a fraction of what I have experienced. I am no longer as absent-minded or struggling to stay in the present moment, as writing helps me process my emotions and thoughts. It also grounds me and enables me to deal with stress by connecting me to my deepest self.

I am married to Penny, and we have been together for sixteen years. We met at our loctician's shop, where I was getting my dreadlocs groomed. We became friends and started hanging out together. At the time, I was a fairly new English teacher and she was a seasoned art teacher. She taught photography, ceramics, painting, drawing, art history, and studio art. Los Angeles is our home, but we are both southern women with similar backgrounds. She and I are the first in our immediate families to go to college, and we both love to teach. As children, we both lived with alcoholic family members and experienced violence in the forms of racism, domestic violence, and sexual abuse.

What makes our relationship work is our commitment to our higher selves, first and foremost. Our higher selves is the eternal part of ourselves that has never been harmed or hurt, our God selves. When we see each other as God sees us, we are able to approach each other from a place of love, rather than fearing we will not get the other person to meet our needs. We both recognize that, when we put our expectations on things and in people that we can see, those transitory entities hold power over us. However, when we place our time, attention, and trust in that which is invisible, we are steeped in that which is real and everlasting—which is our soul's journey.

Penny and I are committed first to our spiritual growth, then to our relationship, our families, and, finally, to our careers. We relax together and go away to silent meditation retreats. Penny, who is a professional comedian, has taught me how to have fun, whereas I used to be a workaholic who tried please everyone. I laugh with her every single day, and the healing power of laughter runs through our relationship.

After marriage equality became a federal law, Penny and I were married at last. The issues Penny has helped me work through have to do with sharing my innermost self with another human being and knowing that she will love me unconditionally. I share all of my thoughts with her, no matter what. It is so freeing and comforting, and she does the same with me. We often marvel at the beauty of being able to be a life witness for one another.

When I came out, shortly after graduating from college, my mother was horrified because she thought I would go to hell. She believes in a physical place where the devil lives. I told her that hell was where I was coming from, not a place outside of me. Now my mother absolutely loves Penny. They talk on the phone often and my mother comes to spend weeks with us at our home. The three of us are close—we even went on a two-week vacation together to Brazil. I'm glad I was able to challenge and change my mother's beliefs about the range of human sexual orientation. Would my mother still like to see me with a man? I don't know, and that is actually none of my business. What is my business is how she treats my spouse and me, and she is very loving and nurturing toward both of us. I think that she really wants to see me happy, and she sees how happy I am with Penny.

My mother and I have been working on our relationship, and it is going well. I am no longer enmeshed with her. I no longer hold back my spiritual beliefs when she asks for them. I have a totally honest relationship with her now because I am fully honest with myself. I live my life according to my beliefs, not hers.

I've been teaching English and literacy at the secondary level for twenty years. I love it. There are a lot of challenging days, such as when a third of my students are truant, or I see them handcuffed by the police who have a satellite office on our campus, or they get pregnant, or run away from home, or curse me out. The rewards, however, always outweigh those trying days, because I know that by learning to read, the students are taking control over their lives. I feel that being a part of their journey is a calling for me and that in deciding to become a teacher I made the best decision possible.

I tell my students about my impoverished childhood and how I found my way out by working hard in school. I stress how far education can take them when nothing and no one else can, and remind them that they can create opportunities if they prioritize school and stay focused. I want my students to consider going to college, even if their family is unable to help with tuition. I am no longer ashamed of my childhood poverty, and I don't want my students who have similar stories to be ashamed either.

In class, we discuss how the system is designed for those on top to stay there. I'm grateful for the food stamps and the free-lunch tickets that helped me to survive, but they are a temporary solution to a generational problem that stems from a lack of equity and equality, and a lack of opportunity. I also recognize that my parents, just like other working people, paid into this welfare system with the taxes taken from each paycheck. My family earned the right to tap into the fund when it became necessary after the murder.

I became estranged from my alcoholic biological father when I was three years old. At that age, six of my siblings and I saw him take a butcher knife to our mother's face and head. She had fifty-two stitches, he went to jail, and they got divorced. I rarely saw him when he got out of prison, and I didn't want to. As a child, I was afraid of him. As an adolescent, I was angry with him for abandoning us, his children, and for his ongoing violence against my mother that culminated in the stabbing. He taught me about intimate misogyny.

However, when I was twenty-three, I was in a horrible car wreck involving an eighteen-wheeler truck. After that I decided to get to know my father. Having dealt with the murder of my stepfather freed me up emotionally, so when the time came, I was able to reconcile with my biological father. Therapy helped me to sort through my emotions about the stabbing. My father even came to therapy sessions with me.

My relationship with him began with me going to his home for weekly visits, during which he mainly busied himself with things to do around his shotgun house. When I came out to him, he accepted my sexual orientation, saying, "You're my daughter and I love you." I eventually challenged him to explain why he stabbed my mother. I was angry and accusatory, and he was defensive. We didn't get much communicating done.

At one point he promised to fix my car because he was a mechanic, but he ended up stealing it for his son, a half-brother I didn't know. One would think this betrayal would have been a setback, but it proved to be the catalyst I needed to learn how to speak up for myself. I had the help of a Black women's support group, which enabled me to stand up to my father and get my car back. It also forced my father and me to truly communicate. The experience was scary, but liberating. My father was sober for about five years, during which time we were able to establish a relationship.

About twenty years ago, however, his son, my half-brother, died suddenly from a heart defect and my father started drinking again. Eleven years ago, after serving time for a felony DUI, he got out of jail. After that he was what some people would call homeless, because he slept in the back room of a used car dealership where he sometimes worked. He had a series of strokes in 2016, after which he moved in with one of my older brothers and his family.

When I am upset I remain respectful, but I don't sugarcoat my feelings. I am no longer a people pleaser. I've learned to be more in touch with the expectations and goals that I have for myself, and to value my own opinions more than others'. It no longer matters to me if people like me, because I like myself. Most important, I get to enjoy my lovely marriage to Penny, our incredibly creative home, and the joy and laughter, challenges and solutions that each day brings. I know that I am blessed beyond measure.

# 12 Finding Blackness

## Follow-Up

*Samiir Bolsten*

Growing up, or "being a grown up," has been an interesting departure from my childhood. A very important part of figuring out who I am has been observing what things about me stayed the same, even after my circumstances changed drastically. Although my socioeconomic status and the racial demographics of my surroundings changed, one thing not only stayed the same but became even truer—which is that creative expression remains a fundamental key to my happiness and the nourishment of my soul. Because of the turmoil of my past, I have an undying desire to explore and explain who I am to both myself and the outside world.

One of the significant influences in my adult life is that, after a childhood and adolescence filled with what seemed like not enough blackness, I now live in Atlanta, Georgia, a major city that is majority black. I've also had the privilege of working primarily with and for Black people. I realized the significance of this privilege only in the past year, after working as an account supervisor in an agency that has 90 percent white employees.

Interacting with white people in professional settings has been revealing. I've noticed that many of them seem unfamiliar with interacting with Black people; in fact, it sometimes feels as if they're barely listening when I speak. They get a glazed look, as if they're trying to decipher what kind of interaction they're having: "Was that a joke he just told?" "Is he trying to contribute something to the conversation?" "Is he opening up to me?" Admittedly, I can be awkward and a bit slow, so their perceived confusion may be warranted. Or perhaps I'm the one who is confused. I really don't know.

In the first seven years of my career, working for black-owned businesses and living in a majority Black metropolitan area allowed me to explore different parts of myself with a far greater comfort level. I also learned more about various aspects of the Black experience. Because I'm Black but not African American, people from time to time would say things like, "But you're not black." And while that still bothers me, it no longer makes me question myself or my self-worth. As I was finishing up my previous essay, I had only recently reached this level of self-understanding. In the years since it has become ingrained in my being. I've become much better at understanding the nuances and differences in race and class.

DOI: 10.4324/9781003376255-16

One of the main things I've realized is that the world is never, ever (ever, ever) going to let me forget that I'm a Black man—it's the vehicle in which I move through the world. I can change the way people react to me by deciding how to speak, dress, express myself, and physically maneuver, but all those reactions are secondary. They come only after a person has identified me as a Black man. That's where the interaction starts; that's where the observer has their first physiological response to what/who is in front of them. Of course, this is something that few people admit openly and comfortably, which is part of why discussions about race often feel unproductive and dishonest.

The truth for most people is that we react first to the way a person looks (shocker!). It's part of how we become attracted to others and, on a more sinister note, it's how we develop feelings of being threatened by others. Admitting this fact when it comes to race can be tough for people because it may force them to admit that they exist somewhere on a bigoted spectrum. This applies to me as well. For example, I wrote in my previous chapter that I chose my friends at Dartmouth based on experience. While it was certainly true that I had good friends of all races, most of my friends were Black and I was involved primarily in the Black community. I'm not sure why I didn't feel that was my reality when I wrote my last chapter.

The media images programmed into the minds of many from a young age is that Black people are threatening: they are criminals, aggressors, hypersexualized, lower class, predatory, and carry weapons. Many people see those images and, being able to discern that they do not represent all Black people, can consciously classify them as false, but I believe the images nevertheless take a toll on Black people and white people alike. White people aren't the only group whose perceptions are likely warped by the destructive imagery of Black people often presented on television, and I've seen Black people harbor the same fear of "those kind of Black people" while also subconsciously afraid of being associated with those negative traits.

In myself, I've realized that these images created a deep-seated need for white validation, starting at an early age. Most children search for validation and acceptance from their peer groups and surroundings, and since my skin color was the most noticeable thing about me, I perceived that my path to peer group acceptance and social status was to be accepted in spite of being black. At this point in my life it's not so much a desire as a skill that I possess, one that sickens me a bit at times, such as when I meet someone and notice how their demeanor toward me changes as I spout bits of info to meet the "safe/acceptable Black person" threshold in their mind: I'm from Sweden, I went to Dartmouth, I work at such-and-such. Sure, I'll speak some Swedish for you! Anything to distance myself from how vile you subconsciously think African Americans are! I'm thankful to have this skill, as it has certainly helped me gain access to opportunities, relationships, and spaces that otherwise may have been off limits. It's what some angry white people like to refer to as "Black privilege"—special consideration given to a Black person who has successfully skirted many of the negative traits we associate with blackness.

Still, this privilege doesn't remove what it means to maneuver the world in a Black body. I can do things to shape a person's secondary and tertiary reactions to me, but ultimately one of the first things anyone will perceive about me is that I am a Black person. Speaking from experience, the implications of this is enough to drive many actions that affect my reality. Case in point—a couple of years back, a friend/co-worker and I were on a work-related road trip, having convinced the CEO to let us attend a festival to capture social media content for the agency blog. As we drove through Mississippi in the middle of the day, a state trooper pulled off from the side of the interstate after we passed and trailed us. We were driving with the flow of the light traffic at about three or four miles above the speed limit, and we couldn't have been going faster than 65 mph by the time the trooper's car caught up with us. Were we really about to be pulled over when every other car on the road was zooming past us?

After a minute or two of trailing us, the trooper turned on his lights and pulled us over. We would soon find out that he pulled us over because he "noticed us getting kind of close to the white lines" and "wanted to make sure everyone is okay." So, we essentially were pulled over for *almost* failing to maintain our lane. This pointless traffic stop escalated into extensive questioning about who we were, where we were going, our criminal history, whether we had guns, drugs, or grenades in the car, and finally a full search of the car. They checked the glove compartment, under the seats, opened the hood and looked in the engine, opened the bottom of the trunk and checked the spare tire, checked under the car, and dug through all of our bags, all while we waited on the side of the road. Finally they let us go, after a fruitless and incredibly intrusive hour of shenanigans. It would be tough for anyone to convince me that we weren't pulled over for being black. The police probably assumed we were transporting an illegal shipment of weapons or drugs across state lines in a rental car.

I think of this interaction from time to time, especially in the last couple of years, as police mistreatment of Black individuals has become a mainstream topic of discussion. I thought about the choices I made in terms of how I interacted with the officer—I was cordial, cooperative, even subservient—and how those choices may have been what kept me out of harm's way in this encounter. I also sometimes ask, what if? What if, after a lifetime of having dealt with blatant and subtle forms of the same racism that now had me standing on the side of the road while a white guy with a buzzcut dug through my underwear, I was just plain tired of proving that I'm "safe"? What if, on that day, I had grown so tired of having to validate my humanity that I leaned more on what I believed was right than on what I knew would keep me safe from harm? I think of how that situation could have gone awry, had I not already been so traumatized by racism that I clamored for white acceptance and cowered in the face of white authority. It's upsetting to know that I should probably consider my life at risk if I ever become so fed up with having to kneel down that I dare ask for humane treatment.

There are myriad factors present in how people are treated and how they experience the world. My life experience as a Black man has taught me that a very central one is skin color. The real question has gone from "Am I black?" to "What kind of Black man am I?" For example, I realize that there is a great difference between Black culture in California and southern Black culture, the latter being much more deeply entrenched in religion. Furthermore, because Black affluence is widespread in Atlanta, I have been able to see an entirely new part of the Black diaspora. I knew it existed but had never seen it up close, nor did I realize how disconnected from it I was. I had interacted with affluent Black and African American people at Dartmouth, but I'd never seen entire Black communities and neighborhoods that were affluent, had not spent extended time in their homes, joined them on family vacations, or observed their parenting styles.

I was less than a year out of college as I was getting to know Nikita, a Black woman my age who had recently graduated from Columbia. She lived in a suburb about an hour outside of Atlanta, and I distinctly remember my first time driving out to see her. I drove up to a gate bearing the same numbers printed on my MapQuest directions, but I double checked to make sure I was at the right place. This wasn't a house—it was an estate. I called her cellphone to confirm the location and she gave me the callbox number. The gate swung open and I drove up a winding hill, past a pond and a tennis court, and arrived at what could only be described as a mansion.

This woman and I never got serious, but I ended up getting to know her and her family rather well. I spent enough time with them to realize just how different it could be to come from a stable and affluent household. Her father was African American and her mother Jamaican American. Both were Ivy League-educated doctors who had worked hard to be able to give Nikita and her three younger siblings the ideal upbringing. While spending time with them I was constantly in awe at the thought of having an upbringing in which the words "I love you" fly freely from all directions (we don't do much of that talk in my family), having your own room is a given, learning to play an instrument is mandatory, and scholastic excellence is expected. After Nikita graduated from Columbia, her younger sister graduated from Harvard, then her younger brother from Dartmouth; the youngest is currently following in Nikita's footsteps and attending Columbia.

There was no real racial divide between us, but the class and culture divide at times felt massive. Even though I was technically "on her level" as an Ivy League graduate with a good job and career potential, I didn't come from money or great stability, and that affected our relationship a lot. I don't think it's big news to anyone that this is how the world works, but I was blown away by seeing it in action in the "real world"—not just with Nikita's family but all around me in the young professionals who were years ahead of me in terms of navigating the grownup world, sometimes through their own understanding but usually with hands-on help from their parents. Renting an apartment, purchasing and owning a vehicle, professional decorum, everything dealing with health insurance and taxes—I had to navigate all of these new milestones on my own.

Thinking back, it was of course often noticeable even in college. There were students whose parents visited campus multiple times every year, who received help moving in and out of their dorm rooms, constantly received care packages in the mail, had a car and cellphone paid for, and always seemed to go on a leisure trip during breaks. I've gotten to know myself well enough to understand that I'm simply a scatterbrained person, but I can't help but wonder how my behavioral patterns and ability to be on top of stuff might have evolved differently if such structure was ingrained in me it an earlier age.

I think of this quite often now. When you observe someone at a certain moment in life, what part of their grander story are you seeing? How is the person being shaped by the realities of their present? What kind of nurturing is shaping their nature? What gaps are being formed? On the flipside, being a person who has learned to appear relatively normal to the outside world also makes me ask myself what part of the grander story I am not seeing when observing someone else at a particular moment in their life? I've become more understanding of and empathetic to the fact that everyone has unique challenges. The people whose lives I envied as a child or those who seem to have it all together on the surface likely have had different issues that took an emotional toll on them.

When I reflect on my own case, I think about the many times I was made to feel or was explicitly told that I wasn't good enough. I think of how much we lacked structure and money in our home. I think of being forced to deal with adult emotions as a child and how navigating those emotions may have shaped my ability to deal with adult life. I have never been able to escape the feeling that I am somehow broken, and while I believe part of it is nurture, I've found it's also in my nature. At age twenty-four, I was taken in an involuntary psychiatric hold and hospitalized. I was diagnosed with psychosis, bipolar disorder, and ADHD. Identifying some of the underlying chemical imbalances that may contribute to my history of self-destructive behavior has been liberating in a sense, as I've been able to manage the emotional aspects of what's "off" about me much more effectively.

The key takeaway after my hospitalization, years of self-work, reflection, and searching is that I cannot function properly as a human unless I share my story and continue to explore the self through creativity. Within a month of being released from the hospital I decided that music and art simply had to be a larger part of my life, and I invested in my own music equipment. Beyond needing white validation because rapping is deemed "cool" and beyond wanting pats on the back because I'm doing something I'm good at, what's most important to me is creating works of art that bare my soul. Race, class, trauma, and mental health have all played a part in how I choose to express myself, but the core of what drives me as a human is self-expression.

# 13 Living, Learning, and Teaching Life Lessons in Middle Class Blackness

## Follow-Up to "Gotta Keep Climbin All De Time"

*Candice Jimerson-Johnson*

Writing as a college student in 1994, I thought I was ready for life. How wrong I was! My faith has provided me with the saving grace I have needed much of my adult life, but I certainly could not have prepared for what lie ahead. Yes, parts of me seen in my original story are still visible; however, I have developed new appendages, new understandings, new characteristics. Race and gender remain a central force in my life, always bringing me back to the frustrations and the joys of being an African American woman. As an adult, I am learning that one's socioeconomic status can literally deny or grant one the chance to partake in the rich possibilities U.S. life has to offer. Unfortunately, having a family of my own has made me cynical in many ways, but it has also helped me comprehend the daily struggle much of the world faces and made me thankful for what I have. My relationship with Christ has literally kept me sane when circumstances have threatened to tear me apart.

I graduated from college cum laude, a distinction I had not expected to earn. I was awarded several awards for campus leadership, including one from the Afro-American Society. Others saw me as a leader, but you could have fooled me. I truly felt I was just doing what anyone would do to fight against the injustices I saw and experienced and to make the campus a better place for everyone. Ironically, my working life would in time show me that this point of view is not ordinary. Most people would rather be blind to inequity so that they can continue living lives of comfort without guilt.

After graduation, I could not take one more minute on my college campus. However, lacking the financial resources to support myself for a semester while I completed my student teacher practicum, I decided not to complete my teacher-training program. I had to eat my words about wanting to go into the public schools to "really make a difference" and went to work instead as a faculty intern at Culver Academies, a private boarding school in Indiana. You may well ask, why rural Indiana?! After all, I hadn't liked the predominantly white, rural, rich college I went to. But I had good reasons: because I had worked at Culver during my college summers, I felt relatively comfortable there, and I also could get free room and board. Furthermore, they claimed they would work on my teaching skills and, as usual, I wanted a challenge. Well, I got it! I was the only intern of color and one of only three faculty

DOI: 10.4324/9781003376255-17

members of color—and the only woman of color in both groups. Students of color immediately flocked to me seeking discussion, advice, and friendship. This was the start of my fight for underrepresented students in independent schools. Working with the other faculty members of color, these students and I planned programs for the campus and held "rap sessions" exclusively for students of color to air their concerns. I advocated for students with faculty members, trying to get these adults to see how difficult it was for someone with a different childhood to adjust to a place like Culver. Some of the white folks got it, others did not. Although I worked like a dog, I actually loved my year there. However, I had to leave if I expected to have any type of social or spiritual life. Having lived four years at Dartmouth, I felt like I had spent enough time in the social desert.

For my first full-time job, I jumped feet first (more like head first into an empty pool) into a lower-level administrative position at a private school in Cincinnati, Ohio. Remember, I was just starting my teaching career and had to learn as I went how to administrate. In addition to teaching history, I was director of diversity—a position no one, including me, understood and even fewer people realized had been created. Fortunately, I was doing what I loved—working with "minority" students and fighting for fair treatment and better understanding of all people by fostering an equitable school environment. These two motivators energized me to work well beyond what I was actually trained to do. Making up much of the job as I went along and attending many conferences and workshops, I discovered two interesting aspects of liberal, white, upper-class America: first, they have great intentions, and second, they think that those intentions are enough to make the problems of racism and classism go away.

Many of the independent schools I visited tried to project the feeling that all their students were equal, that teachers cared about every single child no matter their background, and that because they were this elite institution, all students would be prepared for greatness just by association. These assumptions, however, flew in the face of reality. In my last twelve years of dealing with independent schools, I spoke to dozens of faculty of color who said that instead of truly understanding the variety of students in the classroom and adjusting their teaching styles accordingly, teachers treated everyone the same in the name of "equity." This meant that teachers treated everyone like white, upper-class Christians. Unfortunately, many baby-boomer teachers have taken Martin Luther King Jr.'s statement about people being judged not by the color of their skin but by the content of their character to the extreme. This prevailing color blindness promotes not inclusion, but exclusion. Parts of who people really are being excluded in an effort to make the majority—that is, those in power—feel comfortable. I often had to tell my white colleagues, "If you say you don't see me as Black when you see me, then you don't really see me! Blackness *is* who I *am*. Do not ignore who I am!" On some days this conversation really sickened me. Thirteen years after graduating from college, I was still having the same conversations!

As an African American woman, this often put me in a dilemma. Wanting to do the right thing was indeed half the battle; however, the second half was actually *changing* what I was doing. This created many tension filled conversations and uncomfortable interactions, as I was always the one speaking against the establishment, answering questions about various ethnic groups or students who did not have money, or helping schools deal with girls who were not achieving to their potential. Being the gadfly, as one principal called me, often placed me in an awkward position:

> "No, Mr. Smith, it is *not* appropriate to ask the one African American student in your English class how he feels 'as a Black person' about hearing the word 'nigger' in *Huckleberry Finn.*"
>
> "Tati does not have the money for the warm outfit she needs for lacrosse, but she was too embarrassed to tell you. Did the team think that everyone could afford to pay $200 for a uniform?"
>
> "Please do not pressure the Jewish students to do homework during the High Holidays. I know that you do work around Christmas, but their practices are not the same."

I usually felt that if I did not speak up, then no one would. The staff was well intentioned but clueless—they represented aversive racism at its best. Ironically, God knew that my professional life was preparing me to deal with racism and with events in my personal life that I could not have imagined.

I married Nelson Johnson, a divorced man nine years my senior who had four children—something I had always said I would never do—and thus instantly became the mother of the three boys and one girl, although only the boys lived with us. Step parenting is a *very* hard thing to do, but God saw me through many a frustrating situation. At times marriage and parenting almost snatched away my bubbly spirit, my love of life, and even my sanity. However, once again, my relationship with Christ redeemed me from certain destruction. My faith has been tested to its outer limits: I have been through the fire and not been consumed, have been through the flood and not drowned! However, I have learned many harsh life lessons in the process.

My husband had had emergency heart surgery six months before we got married. Not realizing it at the time, our marriage was withering before it had a chance to grow. The first two years were not bad, although his recovery was slow and difficult. I jumped right in with my giving personality and my "fix-it" attitude. He returned to work and we seemed to be living a relatively normal life. However, his health got the best of him and he could no longer drive a truck. Financially we plummeted, arguments increased, and my husband sank into depression. Thinking that a move out of Cincinnati and a more lucrative job for me would help us all, we packed up for Massachusetts and begin our stint living on a boarding school campus. Thus began my personal course in racism and classism in the United States.

Being married to an African American man and raising African American boys, I truly learned what it means to be a Black man in the U.S. You might wonder how I missed that lesson, having spent my adolescence with my father and my younger brother. My father did not talk about his experiences with racism much, except those from his childhood, which I viewed as ancient history, and I went to college before my brother became a teenager, the age at which the system's enmity toward Black men begins to rear its ugly head. Living in Cincinnati, my husband knew firsthand the relationship Black men had with the police, the neighborhoods, and the situations to avoid. He talked to our sons about those things, but I do not think they could comprehend it because they had not experienced it. In the summer of 2001, when the fifteenth Black man was killed by Cincinnati police officers in six years and widespread violence erupted in Black neighborhoods, including ours, I told Nelson that we needed to move so we could raise our sons in a safer environment. "Cincinnati is not a healthy place for African American boys," I said. So we both started looking for jobs.

I landed one first, and when we visited the campus in a suburban Massachusetts town, the boys were awed. There were huge fields to play in, woods, a lake, a fitness center, and all you could eat at the dining hall. What more was there to ask for? Considering the fact that we could live and eat for free, I thought the same. Nelson looked forward to an opportunity to use the degree he had earned to change careers.

The people on campus were super friendly, lending us a truck to move bikes and bringing us food until we got our cooking utensils from the moving truck. Once we ventured off campus, however, we found cold stares and few smiles. New England is not an easy place for newcomers, and my sons asked, "Why don't people smile up here?" Since they were to attend a strong suburban public school system, I thought their having success at school would perhaps help ease the transition. Unfortunately, once they got comfortable, there was trouble. With very few students of color and even fewer African American students, my sons were disoriented. When we lived in Cincinnati they could go home at the end of the day to play with African American kids. Now there seemed to be none anywhere, and that caused them a lot of frustration. As a defense mechanism, my oldest son, at the time fourteen years old, leaned toward being like the majority white kids, my middle son, then thirteen years old, became what I call "super black," and my youngest son, eleven years old at that time, tried to walk the line between. My husband also felt quite lost; a relative introvert, he had a hard time making friends. I was too busy to know if I was adjusting or not. I prayed.

All of my sons were athletic, so once school started, we connected them with sports teams. They earned respect in their sports and began making friends. However, when the competition got rough, the word "nigger" was never too far from opponents'—and sometimes teammates'—lips. Lesson number one: no matter how old this word gets, the sting it causes when spat out of the angry lips of a white person hurts every time. My sons had to learn to deal with the word much more in New England than they had living in a city a stone's throw from slave territory. As the boys gained height and weight, the coaches loved them. But the teachers feared them. I got several phone calls saying that the boys were "aggressive," "intimidating," and that they scared teachers when they got angry. The way my sons were being described made me think that either no other male students got angry or they were all smaller than my sons. Of course that was not the case. I truly believe that the teachers' stereotypes of angry, violent Black men caused them to view my sons as dangerous. Lesson number two: it is assumed that when African American men get angry, they will automatically get violent.

All along I had shared with my sons the life lessons I had learned—of having to be twice as good as any white person to get the same job or same recognition; of understanding that whites will be scrutinizing you in stores, on the job, etc.; of doing the right thing and doing your best in everything you do; of honoring the sacrifices made by earlier generations to give you the rights you have today; of recognizing that life is not fair. Nevertheless, it is so difficult to have your children believe that there is justice in the world when they are treated differently just because of how they look. For example, one winter day, some students were having a snowball fight after school in the parking lot. According to one teacher, one of the students threw a snowball at her car as she drove by. She reported it to the vice principal, who questioned some of the boys, one of whom was my middle son. He came home that day fuming:

> "Ma, do you know what those white people did to me today?"
> "What?"
> "They said I threw a snowball at a teacher's car."
> "Why did they think that?"
> "Because the teacher said it was a Black kid who did it."
> "Really."
> "They called in me and my boys and asked us about it."
> "Did they find out who did it?"
> "No. White people get on my nerves. I hate that school."
> "Now don't say that. I'll call tomorrow and talk with Ms. Smith."
> "Ma, they only called in the *black* kids."
> "I'll talk with her."

I was outraged, though I did not let my son see it at the time. Early the next day, I called the vice principal and asked why my son had been called into the office. I acknowledged that he was indeed among the group of boys in the parking lot, but said my issue was that my son was under the impression that only the African American and Latino boys were called in because the teacher had described the boy in question as "having brown skin and wearing a hood." I asked the vice principal whether she would have called in every blond boy if that had been the description given (almost certainly not!). I informed her that I did diversity work at my school and recognized what the school was doing as racial profiling. She assured me that they had called in several other boys as well, but unfortunately, the damage had been done to my son's psyche. Lesson number three: Even when you are innocent, as a Black man you are presumed guilty.

Another challenge to my family's self-concept was in the area of socio-economic status. When we lived in Cincinnati, my sons attended the private school where I taught, but they went home to a working-class neighborhood where they played with children who were living the same lifestyle we were. That changed when we moved to the campus of Brooks School. My sons no longer had a neighborhood to come home to where people looked and lived like them. When you work and live on a campus where some of the students' families have more money than you will ever make in your lifetime, and when your children go to a school where their peers, even as public school kids, have all the material manifestations of having money—cars, cell phones, iPods, etc.—it is difficult to help them develop a sense of self-worth that is not based on what they have. Unfortunately, my sons associated wealth with happiness, and they began to talk about how much better life would be if we were wealthy. Granted, we lived on a shoestring budget because my husband had not worked for years, but I thought that having a close, loving family should be enough. Nonetheless, my sons struggled with this philosophy.

A loving family would have been enough for me, if my family members had lived longer. My small family had dwindled quickly: My mother died suddenly when I was thirteen. My uncle died when I was in college. My grandmother ended up in a care facility with Alzheimer's. My father died two years after I moved to Massachusetts, and his death devastated me. My best friend and role model was gone overnight, just like my mother. Although my father was on dialysis, his diagnosis of kidney disease was new, and we thought he had many years of life remaining. But it was not to be. One night, after not feeling well, my father went to bed early. Later that evening he called out to my brother, who held my dad in his arms until the ambulance arrived. That night my father's spirit went home to glory. Once again, so much was cut off from me: the possibility of creating more great memories with him; the opportunity for him to share additional wisdom; the unconditional love that only a parent gives; the blessing of my children having a grandparent—gone in a heartbeat. I was angry with God. My father's death tested the foundations of the faith that had brought me through so much. Once again, prayer sustained me. I began to believe, like Job, that "though he slay me, yet I will trust him." I still do not understand the reasons for my father's death so early (age fifty-nine), but I have come to a point of blind faith. God knows all and he knows what is best for me. Some might call the view unrealistic or naïve, but I call it the strength of my life.

Trying to raise my sons with a healthy self-concept, a tolerance for people who are different (particularly white people), and with strong Christian values, and at the same time being married to a man who had deteriorated emotionally, strengthened my belief to a level I had never known or imagined possible. I thought that my time in college had prepared me spiritually for the obstacles of the adult world because I had had to study, pray, and worship alone—I could not rely on a pastor or even Christian friends (few of whom had Christian beliefs as strong as mine) for support. Little did I know how much and how often life would challenge the very foundations of my faith. Prayer became a cornerstone of my daily routine, and over time the ways I prayed changed. I discovered the strength of praise and worship—I cried, sang, danced, and shouted my way through life. Death of my father. My husband's emotional breakdown. Financial disaster. Raising children I did not birth. That which did not kill me made me stronger. My life continues to exemplify the fact that only by the grace of God have I made it this far.

# 14 Forever Home

## Follow-Up to "A Work in Progress"

*Anise Vance*

At nine months old, my son Joon's cheeks look like they are stuffed with marshmallows.[1] When he is cold, they brighten to a pinkish red. His hair has just begun curling at his ears. At the back of his head, two cowlicks live side by side. If you squint, or use a smidgen of imagination, you might think they form the sign for infinity.

Joon furrows his eyebrows in a way that makes me think I'm looking into a tiny mirror. He explores the world by putting anything and everything in his mouth. He is entirely uninterested in crawling; he prefers to jump with his legs splayed apart and squeals while taking his own parent-aided steps. His impressive vocalizations include a guttural thing somewhere between a yell and the growl of a wild bear. He mutters "cha-cha-cha" under his breath when he is concentrating on something. Every week or so he experiments with a new sound, using it indiscriminately until he figures out just where it fits in his growing communications toolbox.

Joon is scared of dogs, vacuum cleaners, and food processors. He loves singing with his mother, eating almost anything put in front of him, and snoozing with his feet firmly dug into the nearest abdomen. One of his favorite games—and the first he ever played with me—is to roll onto his stomach while I am out of the room. When I re-enter, peals of laughter greet me. Maybe he thinks he is playing a trick on me, or maybe he thinks the roll causes me to come back. Either way, I walk in and out of the room as long as he keeps laughing.

When Joon sees his mother, his eyes light up. Never have I seen someone so in love. My wife often puts him on her knees and sings "Yankee Doodle" while bouncing him up and down. The expression on his face says he was wholly unprepared for such excitement.

At nap time and at night, Joon falls asleep with a light green bunny. My wife, a fluent Spanish speaker, calls it his *conejito*. He inspects it briefly before grabbing its ear in one hand and running his fingers over it with the other. It is soft and comforting and relaxes him in a way few things do. As drowsiness overcomes him, Joon will offer its ear to his mother or me, an act of sweet generosity hard to believe someone so young can offer. He is happiest when both his mother and I are close by, a fact I cherish.

DOI: 10.4324/9781003376255-18

Before I speak of any created identity, any racial or ethnic or national construct, I want you to meet my son as exactly what he, and every nine-month old baby, is: a child of astonishing beauty and potential.

My wife's pregnancy coincided with her first year of graduate school. Every morning, she would steel herself against the nausea and exhaustion and forgetfulness her pregnancy caused. I would fix breakfast and pack her lunch before dropping her off at Vance Street, next to the University of North Carolina's Gillings School of Public Health. I took Vance Street and Vance Hall at UNC as positive signs for our family's future in North Carolina (our last name is Vance).

After that routine start to our day, the rest of our morning, afternoons, and evenings were mad scrambles. My wife was pushing through a difficult pregnancy while trying to establish friendships with her new classmates and engage in challenging coursework. Meanwhile, I was taking on more responsibility both at work and at home because my wife was over-taxed and bone tired.

It was an exciting and stressful time that had a curious side effect: for the first time in my life, I didn't think much about race. I thought about fatherhood and birth and my wife's health and grocery lists. When I wasn't thinking about those things, I was thinking about the New York Football Giants. In the rare moments I did consider the world in terms of groups, I would distinguish between people with and without kids, people with life experience beyond college and people without it, people who like to play games with my wife and me on Friday nights and people who preferred to go someplace they called "out."

Racial, ethnic, and national identities were, and are, farther back in my consciousness than at any previous point in my life. I don't know if that is good or bad. Nevertheless, I have no doubt that my wife, my son, and I will, in the coming decades, devote much thought and energy to navigating my son's background. Joon's grandparents are African American, Persian, Jamaican, and white. The identities invoked in these straightforward descriptions are anything but straightforward. African American makes a claim to Black racial identity and American national identity; Persian is a national and ethnic term that also carries racial undertones; despite Jamaicans' vastly different treatment of race, Jamaican is a national identity that conjures up a particular racial image in the American imagination; and white is a category so vague, so indebted to what it is *not* that it can sometimes feel devoid of any meaning beyond the privilege associated with whiteness.

More complicated than any single identity is the particular combination of identities my wife and I have given our son. While norms and laws around interracial relationships have greatly progressed in the last half-century, African American and white identities are still often constructed in opposition to each other. American and Persian are not exactly on friendly terms, either, and the Jamaicans I have met, while not antagonistic to any American group, are rarely inclined to embrace an American racial identity as their own. These are only a few of the tensions that will compete for Joon's attention and push him to claim, disavow, champion, or neglect parts of his lineage.

Between changing diapers and cooking meals and working at my day job, I have spent little time reflecting on how my son's mixedness might affect his sense of self. As a robust academic literature, an enormous body of creative work, and vigorous public debates attest, it is extraordinarily difficult to evaluate the importance of a group identity. That group identities vary over time, geography, and context complicates the picture to an almost unimaginable degree. So, please forgive the simplistic analysis that follows; my parent brain is not fully prepared to handle the thousands of nuances the concept of identity invokes.

At their roots, I think group identities carry stories that address basic questions of human belonging: who we are, who we came from, and where we are going. These stories give us historical footing, a place where we can stand and navigate our futures. They orient us. Two sets of stories embodied in one person, like my own Persian and African American identities, seem reasonably negotiable. They bend when needed and shift when appropriate, they melt away in one moment only to solidify in the next.

But four stories? That's a lot of mixing. How will Joon adapt to narratives that put him in historical contexts that are continents apart and point him north, south, east, and west? How will he know which way to walk? If he holds a compass, will its needle settle in one direction at the expense of the others? Will it spin in circles? Or maybe it will break, like an instrument that can no longer keep pace with reality. I think a key piece of Joon's identity will be disorientation, including about the world's rules on race.

Thank God.

I hope my sentiments convey my hope that race can be reimagined, that our constructs must and will change with time, as they have in the past. However, this is easier to write than to live. Personal experience with sirens and flashing lights tells me that human beings are fickler than pens.

I get stopped by the police at least once every six months. My wife and I moved to North Carolina almost three years ago, and geography has made no difference in the frequency with which I am pulled over. Boston, D.C., Chapel Hill—it doesn't matter. About a year ago, I was driving with a couple of fourteen-year-old Black boys whom my wife and I mentor. As we passed their middle school, I noticed police lights flashing behind me and heard a siren. I pulled over and glanced at the two youth. They were frozen in self-consciously relaxed poses. In my side mirror, I watched the officer approach. It was ten on a Saturday morning, and I was driving no faster than the person in front of me. Except for the occasional passing car, there was nobody else around.

The officer walked with a bit too much sway in his body. My gut tightened and I remember thinking, "Please God, don't let whatever is about to happen happen in front of these boys." I rolled down my window well before the officer got to the car. I held my license and registration in my left hand and placed my right hand on the steering wheel, clearly visible. When the officer arrived, I introduced myself and the youth, using my best Ivy League accent. (When I told my sister this story, she quipped, "Your regular accent is an Ivy

League accent." Still, when speaking to law enforcement I speak in a higher pitch and enunciate more than is normal.)

The officer, curious as to my relationship with the teenagers, asked what we were doing. His tone was strangely defensive, as if I had offended him simply by driving on the weekend. I told him that my wife and I mentor a youth group and that we meet with them at our home every Saturday morning to improve their literacy and promote character development.

The officer's shoulders relaxed and he nodded his head while listening to me. When he spoke again, his tone was still authoritative but the defensiveness was gone. He told the youth to keep going to the group and to follow whatever advice I give them. They nodded and said, "Yes, sir." The officer said he pulled me over for speeding and would let me off with a warning this time. I thanked him and reached out to shake his hand, a gesture which, judging by his facial expression, both surprised and pleased him. I made sure to remember his name and made a mental note to visit the police department. I thought, maybe this is an opportunity to build a relationship with the officer, and the local police force in general, based on this short, problematic, but somehow still hopeful interaction.

When we drove away, the young men and I agreed that I had not been driving faster than anyone else on that road. However, I made sure to note that the interaction, not the cause of that interaction, went as well as it could have. I wanted them to know that, while they could not avoid law enforcement, they could sometimes manage that unwanted attention and keep damage to a minimum.

Our conversation on the topic was shorter than one might suppose, just a few minutes. Frankly, I'm exhausted by dealing the police, and we didn't need to remind ourselves that the same basic scenario—a Black person confronted by the cops—has had the worst possible outcome over and over and over again. That happens to Black men, Black women, Black children, Black people who have mental challenges, Black people in their own neighborhoods, Black people visiting other neighborhoods, famous Black people, poor Black people, college-educated Black people, working-class Black people.

Once upon a time, I felt overwhelming outrage at being pulled over when I believed, with cause, that my race was a factor. Now I hardly feel outrage at all. Perhaps this is a product of getting older or of a conscious shift in my mentality: I now spend more time searching for the people, practices, and processes that might enable us to transform social relationships than I do critiquing the state of society. Perhaps I don't feel outrage anymore because I have become cynical and simply expect terrible things to happen. The growing number of people who feel as I do is a sad indication of our era's deplorable social and economic conditions. Or perhaps my immense privilege protects me more than many. I have a loving family, a house, a car, a nest egg, a college degree, two graduate degrees, a job. Because I am free of the unrelenting stress that characterizes the daily lives of so many people in our deeply unequal country, I feel the stickiness of America's racial web far less than most people of color.

Yet despite my privilege, my shift in perspective, and my theorizing about my son's identity, a lingering inevitability haunts my history with law enforcement: I know that eventually Joon will be pulled over or taken aside or somehow challenged by a police officer. This will probably happen multiple times throughout his life. Despite his mixed heritage, Joon is Black and he looks like me. That fact alone will put him in harm's way. That said, my son and I are far from the first members of our family to be targets of discrimination. I am keenly aware that Joon and I experience far less oppression than my known ancestors on my father's side. The history of our last name testifies to that truth.

The legend surrounding the Vance name goes like this: my great-great-grandfather was a seven-foot-tall former slave who lived with a Jewish woman in a cabin in the woods in some southeastern state. I used to fantasize that he had broken free of his slave masters and, out of fear, they did not dare attempt to enslave him again. The legend, however, has a less hopeful and more realistic end: some white people burned his cabin to the ground, with him in it.

My great-great-grandfather's name was Hudson Vance. My sister, who has spent countless hours investigating our family history, uncovered his name about two years ago. He was married to a Black woman named Elmira but lived with a white woman named Harriet Horn in the mountains of western North Carolina. The exact timing is vague, but we do know this was in the late 1800s, and census records suggest that Hudson and Harriet had seven children together. Perhaps I am easily overcome by wishful thinking, but I happily believe that Hudson Vance and Harriet Horn broke the law and countless racial taboos, risking their very lives in a romance that lasted decades because they loved one another in a way that hate and ignorance and blind tradition could not prevent. I wonder if my great-great-grandparents would be pleased at the mixedness their family line has since produced.

My sister discovered that Hudson Vance was the son of Richard and Aggy Vance. Richard and Aggy were owned by the family of Zebulon Vance, a two-time governor of North Carolina, U.S. Senator, and Confederate Army colonel. He was one of the most famous people in North Carolina in the mid-1800s, and one of the most popular. Schools, towns, and a county are named in his honor, and Vance Hall at the University of North Carolina-Chapel Hill is named for Zebulon, as is the street where I dropped off my wife every day for a year. A portrait of Zebulon hangs in the UNC building in which I am currently pursuing my doctorate.

When my sister first unraveled our family history, I was excited and eager to share the news with whoever came my way. "Isn't it incredible?" I would ask. "Somehow we landed in the same state my ancestors are from!" Of the thousands of places my family and I could have settled, we wound up in a place where the echoes of my history, a past greatly defined by race, are written on street signs and engraved on building plaques. And yet, truth be told, my sister and father, who live near D.C., feel more closely tied to our history than I do. My father, for example, has related feeling a stronger sense of connection to his ancestors. They are now more than bits and pieces of a legend. They are real people who led very real lives.

My reaction, on the other hand, is more of indignation at the past than a connection with it. For months I felt angry when I drove down Vance Street or passed Vance Hall. I still feel embers of outrage when I think about the injustices inflicted on my ancestors that continue to this day. A man who laid claim to my family and literally fought to keep them in bondage has his name in places of honor across the state. Where are Richard and Aggy's monuments? Where is the building named for Harriet Horn? Where is Hudson Street? How do we mark their pains and their joys in our public landscape? How can we pay tribute to their full humanity, which North Carolina's Vance family denied? What am I to do with the Vance name?

I idolized my parents and my sister while growing up. I didn't exactly think of them as my heroes, but that's what they were. As I've gotten older, my family relationships have gone through a natural progression. I distanced myself for a time, searching for independence. I was also critical of them, thinking I had far more answers than I actually did. In my twenties, when I finally became what could generously be considered an adult, I really began to learn about my family.

By any modern standard, they are all tremendously accomplished people. That, however, is far from important to me. Warped definitions of success that place an undue emphasis on status or notoriety or wealth have rendered our society's standards of accomplishment almost meaningless. What I value most about my family is that they are driven by a desire to serve humanity. Their lives are a testament to dedication, patience, and sacrifice. Those virtues have given the name Vance a far different meaning than in generations past.

***

About six months after Joon was born, a 7.3-magnitude earthquake struck the Iran-Iraq border. I remember watching the news and grappling with the scale of the devastation. Hundreds died, thousands were injured. What stuck with me was the story of a baby, less than a year old, found crying under the rubble twenty-four hours after the earthquake. I don't know if the child's parents survived.

I stopped following the news for a while after that. My heart, freshly full of love for Joon, panicked when I thought about the child found alive in the earthquake and all those not found. Of course I could not truly empathize with the people affected by the disaster, or with the many more people harmed by the litany of catastrophes the world experiences yearly. But the tragedies that surround us, and especially the suffering of children and families, have taken on a new intimacy for me.

For all of humanity's tremendous diversity, the joys of parenthood feel universal: Smelling the top of your child's head, a scent somewhere between sweet milk and soap. Helping him learn to walk, his stride that of a cowboy who needs to stretch. Watching as he discovers his favorite foods, the juice of a mandarin dripping down his chin. While the smells and the strides and the foods may change, parents' hearts are blanketed in a love for their children that knits tighter and tighter with each day.

Some tragedies that affect families are largely unavoidable, like natural disasters, but many others are human-made. I am not naive. I know there are a million and one reasons why people oppress each other and the complex combination of motives at play. I get it. I grew up experiencing it. I studied it. I wrote two theses on it. I work to fight it. You can talk to me about methods to dehumanize, about ideologies of superiority, about fear-based neurological pathways, about group survival. I've heard the stories and read the histories and listened to as much analysis as I can bear. And yet, "they" love the sound of their kid's laughter just as we do. There is more truth in that fact alone than there has been or will be in all of the reasons all people ever have come up with to treat one another as anything less than their own.

We used to have a children's book that included the phrase "sing you home." It was a sweet story narrated by a couple telling their young child how much they had wanted him, how much they loved him, and how he made their home complete. I misplaced the book months ago, but one of its central ideas has stayed with me: the couple tells the child that he is their "forever home." I thought about the concept for a while, wondering if perhaps the reverse holds more truth, at least for me.

Joon has nestled into a singular space in my identity. Whether or not he knows it, I will be a forever home for him. In fact, that space in who I am, Joon's home, has steadily annexed most of my other identities. It's not that race and class and gender and nationality don't matter anymore. It's just that they have now become parts of the house that belongs to my son.

And so, when I do focus on racial or ethnic identity, the motive and purpose of those thoughts must be love. Joon deserves as much. The questions I ask now are quite different from those I asked before: How do we nurture genuine friendships between families of vastly different heritage? How can we learn from each other's ways of parenting, of seeing, of living? How do we encourage our communities and institutions to move beyond simple openness to embrace diversity and rely on its strength? Most essentially, how do we practice the kind of love worthy of our children?

## Note

1 Please note that I refer to my son as Joon throughout this chapter. My wife and I still haven't figured out exactly what privacy should mean for a baby, so we have chosen to keep his name confidential. Joon is a term of affection in Farsi, similar to "dear" or "sweetie" in English.

# Index